MASTERS OF MYSTERY AND DETECTIVE FICTION

THE
MAGILL
BIBLIOGRAPHIES

Other Magill Bibliographies:

The American Presidents—Norman S. Cohen
Black American Women Novelists—Craig Werner
Classical Greek and Roman Drama—Robert J. Forman
Contemporary Latin American Fiction—Keith H. Brower
Nineteenth Century American Poetry—Philip K. Jason
Restoration Drama—Thomas J. Taylor
Twentieth Century European Short Story—Charles E. May
The Victorian Novel—Laurence W. Mazzeno
Women's Issues—Laura Stempel Mumford

MASTERS OF MYSTERY AND DETECTIVE FICTION

An Annotated Bibliography

J. RANDOLPH COX

Reference and Government Documents Librarian
Saint Olaf College

SALEM PRESS

Pasadena, California   Englewood Cliffs, New Jersey

Library of Congress Cataloging-in-Publication Data

Cox, J. Randolph.
  Masters of mystery and detective fiction / J. Randolph
  Cox.
      p.   cm. — (Magill bibliographies)
    ISBN 0-89356-652-7
    1. Detective   and   mystery   stories—Bio
  bibliography.   2. Authors—Biography.   I. Title.
  II. Series.
Z5917.D5C69   1989
[PN3448.D4]
016.8093'0872   89-10987
                                                 CIP

To Allen J. Hubin, founding editor of *The Armchair Detective*, Walter Albert, bibliographer, Steve Stilwell, bookman, and Charles Shibuk, astute critic, without whose inspiration and guidance this bibliography might never have been completed. And to Robert E. Briney, gentleman scholar, who will read it through from cover to cover and then tell me (politely) what I might have done differently.

CONTENTS

CONTENTS

CONTENTS

EDITORIAL STAFF

MASTERS OF MYSTERY AND DETECTIVE FICTION

INTRODUCTION

For more than a century, the mystery and detective story has been among the most popular forms of fiction in the bookstores and libraries of the nation. The principal reason for this popularity is human curiosity. People read mystery and detective stories because they are eager to learn what will happen next—and to match wits against those of the master detective. The increasing demand for more stories that reveal the secrets of murderers, thieves, and confidence agents is enough to support an industry of writers.

The modern detective story traces its origins to the short stories of ratiocination written by Edgar Allan Poe. To be sure, there are earlier examples of a sort of protodetection in fiction, since no writer creates entirely out of thin air. Voltaire describes the results of the deductions of Zadig in his 1749 novella *Zadig: Or, The Book of Fate*; Alexandre Dumas and Auguste Maquet sent musketeer d'Artagnan down the sleuth's trail in *The Vicomte de Bragelonne* in 1848-1850; and Daniel demonstrated his deductive ability in the Apocryphal books of the Bible. These, however, consist of incidents within a larger narrative, or they contain a purpose other than determining the perpetrator of a crime. The true father of the detective story is Poe, and most of the conventions and traditions associated with the modern detective story can be found in Poe's "The Murders in the Rue Morgue," "The Mystery of Marie Rogêt," and "The Purloined Letter," written between 1841 and 1844.

All elements are present: the eccentric and omniscient detective, the story narrated by his less astute comrade, the police who see everything but observe little, the staged ruse to force the perpetrator's hand, the clues placed so that the reader should be able to follow the detective's reasoning (but he does not), the surprise solution, the explanation, at some length, in which the reader is shown how simple it was to determine the solution. If the pattern calls to mind a Sherlock Holmes story, the reason is that Sir Arthur Conan Doyle, too, was influenced by Poe.

Historians of the detective story outline its development by references to "firsts": the first English detective novel, the first woman detective, the first scientific detective, the first use of fingerprints in fiction, the first use of an unbreakable alibi, and the like. Each first, firmly established, becomes the subject of a challenge by a later critic eager to explain the hitherto unsuspected existence of an even earlier example of the category.

It is interesting to realize how soon all these conventions became clichés. All that is required is to consult the early literature on writing techniques or some early example of the mystery genre itself to find examples. Carolyn Wells's *The Technique of the Mystery Story* (1913) contains a chapter on outworn motifs, while Wilkie Collins' Sergeant Cuff is described in *The Moonstone* (1868) as not looking anything like the popular conception of a detective. Since there was no real "detective police force" prior to 1829, when Robert Peel established the Metropolitan Police in

London, how quickly society must have produced a recognizable stereotype in the intervening four decades.

In viewing the development of the detective story, one naturally focuses on the authors who have made significant contributions in their own right or whose works have influenced the work of later mystery writers. With his creation of Sherlock Holmes in 1887, Arthur Conan Doyle vastly affected the course of mystery and detective fiction. It is difficult to imagine the direction that the genre might have taken had it not been for the creator of Sherlock Holmes. No other author, with the possible exception of G. K. Chesterton, influenced the detective story of the early twentieth century as did Doyle. He accomplished this primarily through his memorable characterization: His refinement of the character of Holmes created a figure recognizable even to people who have never read his stories.

Additional major innovations in the development of the genre are open to individual interpretation, but certainly the introduction of the naturalistic school by E. C. Bentley and the creation of the hard-boiled American story by Dashiell Hammett and Raymond Chandler should be noted. The refined, classic tradition based on the concept of fair play established in the 1920's was shortly followed by the realistic hard-boiled style developed in the pages of *Black Mask* and other pulp magazines. Additional writers whose work expanded the limits and possibilities of the genre in distinctive ways are, among others, Dorothy L. Sayers, Margery Allingham, Ellery Queen, Ruth Rendell, Cornell Woolrich, and Robert Barnard.

Readers respond to the detective and mystery story in different ways, bringing to their reading their individual experiences. Perhaps most are not as interested in who the author is as in what else that author has written. Many readers are able to recite the details of the plot of any story they have read yet are unable to recall the author's name or the title of the book; such readers may inadvertently begin to read a book they have read before. Some readers are comfortable only with a formula, and always the same formula, while others seek the challenge of new ideas. Still others want to read as many stories by the same writer as possible and are interested in the influences on that writer and in the influences that the writer may have had on others. They treat detective and mystery fiction no differently from any other form of literature in terms of being a valid subject for study. It is for these readers, or for those who would like to read more about the authors and the stories, that this book is intended.

Biographical and critical studies of the detective story have developed slowly from reviews of individual novels to surveys of the work of a single writer, to a consideration of a specific category within mystery fiction and its representative writers. The most common approach has been the brief biographical sketch of an individual writer followed by a checklist or bibliography (with or without explanatory notes) of the works of that writer. If the writer has received a significant amount of critical attention, there may be a selective bibliography of secondary sources or a list of the reviews of each novel in the bibliography. If the author is a significant figure in the genre, the biographical section may be expanded and accompanied by a critical survey of the works or a study that focuses on a perceived theme in the works of the author. Some writers (Dashiell Hammett, for example) have attracted a considerable body of critical response to their works; others have been the focus of less scrutiny.

Even from the outset of the criticism of detective fiction, there have been critics who looked at other, broader topics related to the field. Topics addressed are, for example, a consideration of why detective stories are popular, an examination of writers who represent a particular school or subgenre within the genre—regional writers, hard-boiled writers, the classic British school—a study of the treatment of the protagonist-detective not as a character in a work of fiction but as a real person (as has been the case with Sherlock Holmes). As more and more scholars have been attracted to a study of the field, approaches to the subject have become more varied.

Magill's Bibliography on Masters of Mystery and Detective Fiction is intended for the person who needs some basic information about the mystery genre and its representative authors. Selective rather than exhaustive, it should be considered an introduction to the subject. The bibliography includes entries on seventy-four writers who can be considered representative of the best, most popular, or most influential writers of mystery or detective fiction. The parameters of inclusion were fairly rigid. With few exceptions, writers of espionage were excluded. Some writers had to be excluded simply because there was very little written about them. Their books may be popular, but they have not yet attracted significant critical attention. Other notable writers were excluded because their work in mystery or detective fiction is secondary to their other contributions to literature.

The sources for the entries on each author vary. The principal sources are books about the writer, or books of essays about several mystery writers, or general works about detective or mystery fiction. Citations of periodicals have been included when there is little, if any, information in book form. These have been limited to the specialist journals, *The Armchair Detective* and *Clues: A Journal of Mystery and Detection*, or the more popular periodicals that consistently publish book reviews and articles on detective fiction. Consideration in all cases has been accessibility to the reader.

Included have been those items that seem to provide a significant amount of information and should be available in most high school, university, and public libraries. Some very brief articles have been included if they contribute some unique understanding of the subject. Reviews of individual detective novels are traditionally very brief. These sources have been cited only if the review or the reviewer has some significance. An example would be some of the reviews of Ross Macdonald's novels.

The author sections are arranged alphabetically, with sections devoted to biography and commentary. The arrangement within categories is alphabetical by author of the book, chapter, or article. Some writers have not been the subject of a formal biography. For example, so little is known of Josephine Tey's life that no one has attempted to write even a chapter on her. Short biographical entries have been included for such writers. In addition, the category of biography has been expanded to include articles by writers on their theories and techniques of writing. It may be possible to read between the lines of such articles to gain insight into the life and character of the authors in question.

Full publication information is given for each entry, with citations for current or recent editions when the original is either out of print or difficult to find. Wherever possible, the citations are to the American editions, although a British edition may exist and the book may have been published originally in Great Britain. Works that have been published under more than one title (including novels and short stories) are generally referred to by the American title. Dates following titles refer to the original publication of the book.

Each entry has been annotated to describe the type of information found in the source, not to present an abstract or summary of the information itself. Each annotation should serve as a guide to research rather than as a substitute for the original source. The number of entries for each writer varies, though not always in proportion to his or her significance or popularity. Some authors have been the subject of many articles and books while others have been virtually ignored. Where there has been a wealth of material, only the best books and articles on that writer have been included. Nearly half of the books on Agatha Christie are annotated bibliographies of her works or dictionaries of her characters. Nearly all of the biographies of Arthur Conan Doyle recite similar facts about his life, but provide different pictures of the man while trying to say something new about Sherlock Holmes.

Apart from the standard indexes to periodical literature there are many works on literature in general and detective fiction in particular that were useful in compiling this bibliography.

General Studies

Albert, Walter, ed. *Detective and Mystery Fiction: An International Bibliography of Secondary Sources*. Madison, Ind.: Brownstone Books, 1985.
    The most comprehensive source in the field. Includes bibliographies, diction-aries, encyclopedias, checklists, general reference works, books and articles on dime novels, juvenile series and pulps, and works on individual authors. Includes an index of titles and names. Supplements appear in issues of *The Armchair Detective* after 1987.

Barzun, Jacques, and Wendell Hertig Taylor. *A Catalogue of Crime*. New York: Harper & Row, 1971.
    An idiosyncratic selected and annotated bibliography and guide to the litera-ture of mystery, detection, and related genres. Includes sections on Charles

Dickens' *The Mystery of Edwin Drood* (1870), as well as on Sherlock Holmes, ghost stories, and true crime. Contains an author, title, and subject index.

Breen, Jon L. *What About Murder? A Guide to Books About Mystery and Detective Fiction*. Metuchen, N.J.: Scarecrow Press, 1981.
A selective, annotated bibliography of about 250 books. Includes histories, reference books, works on individual authors, and coffee-table books. Contains an author, title, and subject index.

Current Biography Yearbook. New York: H. W. Wilson, 1940-
A standard source of information. Particularly useful for articles on writers who have achieved a newsworthy status among those who are not regular mystery readers. Agatha Christie, Mickey Spillane, Elmore Leonard, and John le Carré are among those profiled here.

Hoch, Edward D., ed. *The Year's Best Mystery and Suspense Stories*. New York: E. P. Dutton and Walker, 1976-
These annual volumes, published before 1982 as *The Best Detective Stories of the Year*, often contain notes about the authors included in each collection. A regular feature since 1963 has been the "Yearbook of the Detective Story." The volumes have had several editors in the past: David C. Cooke, 1946-1960; Brett Halliday, 1961-1962; Anthony Boucher, 1963-1968; and Allen J. Hubin, 1970-1975.

Hubin, Allen J., ed. *Crime Fiction, 1749-1980: A Comprehensive Bibliography*. New York: Garland, 1984.
The best, most complete source for the works of fiction that comprise the corpus of crime fiction. The *1981-1985 Supplement to Crime Fiction, 1749-1980* (New York: Garland, 1988) should also be consulted. Provides indexes of titles, series characters, settings, and movie adaptations.

Kunitz, Stanley J., and Howard Haycraft, eds. *Twentieth Century Authors: A Biographical Dictionary of Modern Literature*. New York: H. W. Wilson, 1942.
A standard reference work available in many libraries. Also recommended are: *Twentieth Century Authors: First Supplement* (1955) and John Wakeman's *World Authors, 1950-1970* (New York: H. W. Wilson, 1975) and its supplement, *World Authors, 1970-1975* (1980).

Magill, Frank N., ed. *Critical Survey of Mystery and Detective Fiction*. 4 vols. Pasadena, Calif.: Salem Press, 1988.
Surveys of the life and literary career of nearly three hundred authors of mystery and detective fiction arranged in alphabetical order from Edward S. Aarons to Israel Zangwill. Authors date from the mid-eighteenth century to the

late 1980's. Each entry includes a list of principal series characters, an assessment of the author's contribution to the genre, a brief biographical sketch, and an analysis of the author's work. Includes checklists of each author's work with selected references to secondary sources about the author. Individual entries are signed by the contributors. Index and glossary.

Reilly, John M., ed. *Twentieth Century Crime and Mystery Writers*. New York: St. Martin's, 1980, 2d rev. ed. 1985.

More than six hundred writers of crime fiction are covered. Entries include a biographical outline, lists of works, selected secondary sources, an autobiographical statement, and a signed critical article. Bibliographies are not entirely reliable.

Steinbrunner, Chris, and Otto Penzler, eds. *Encyclopedia of Mystery and Detection*. New York: McGraw-Hill, 1976.

The first comprehensive reference book on the mystery and detective genre. Entries are arranged alphabetically under the names of authors and major detective characters, with checklists of books and films about those detectives. Well supplied with cross-references. Illustrated.

MARGERY ALLINGHAM

Biography

Allingham, Margery. "Party of One." *Holiday* 34 (September, 1963): 11-15. (Also published as "Mystery Writer in the Box." In *The Mysterious Mr. Campion: An Allingham Omnibus*. London: Chatto & Windus, 1963.)

An autobiographical account of Allingham's early days as a writer and the development of her detective, Albert Campion. Discusses the patterns and conventions of the mystery story, where they have remained rigid and where they have changed. Compares the necessary elements in the genre to the four sides of a box.

Allingham, Margery. Preface to *Mr. Campion's Lady: An Allingham Omnibus*. London: Chatto & Windus, 1965.

Discusses the problems caused by allowing Albert Campion and Amanda Fitton to marry. Allingham distinguishes between what the author calls her "left hand writing" and "right hand writing" and explains much of how she learned her craft. The maturation of Campion is traced from *Sweet Danger* (1933) to *Traitor's Purse* (1941).

Allingham, Margery, and Carl G. Hodges. "Dialogue." In *Mystery Writer's Handbook*, by the Mystery Writers of America. Rev. ed. Cincinnati, Ohio: Writer's Digest, 1976.

Discusses the importance of the art of dialogue to the mystery or detective story in allowing the author to reveal character in a small space. Allingham believes that the rhythm of speech is important but that no character should speak without having a reason for doing so.

Breit, Harvey. "Miss Allingham Speaks." *The New York Times Book Review* 54 (March 20, 1949): 23.

The British take their thrillers seriously, so any acclaim Allingham has received is due, she believes, to this factor alone. She finds no difference between the thriller and the mainstream novel, one writer choosing to use a thriller shape as another writer might write a sonnet. Her goal is to write simply and clearly, like Robert Louis Stevenson.

Carter, Philip Youngman. Foreword to *Mr. Campion's Clowns: An Allingham Omnibus*, by Margery Allingham. London: Chatto & Windus, 1967. (Also published as "Preface: A Profile of Margery Allingham." In *The Allingham Case-Book*. New York: William Morrow, 1969.)

A biographical sketch focusing on Allingham's early years; her father, Herbert

Allingham, a prolific contributor to penny periodicals; psychic experiences influencing *Blackerchief Dick: A Tale of Mersea Island* (1923); the impetus behind her nonmysteries, *The Oaken Heart* (1941) and *Dance of the Years* (1943); and her marriage to P. Youngman Carter. A conscious craftsperson, Allingham was openhearted to her critics and a gentle woman with her own personal brand of Christianity.

Mann, Jessica. "Margery Allingham." In *Deadlier Than the Male: Why Are So Many English Women So Good at Murder?* New York: Macmillan, 1981.
A biographical and critical essay. Trained as a writer by her father, Allingham understood even the technical details associated with typescripts and copyrights. She was a true professional, although she never found writing easy. Mann discusses her early books as novels of event, her later ones as novels of character. Believes that her most completely realized character is police detective Charles Luke. The popularity of the murder mystery was a sign of an instinct for order and form and not due to a love of violence.

Martin, Richard. *Ink in Her Blood: The Life and Crime Fiction of Margery Allingham*. Ann Arbor, Mich.: UMI Research Press, 1988.
The first full-length biography of Margery Allingham, whom Martin considers more "responsible for the development of the contemporary sophisticated mystery story" than either Agatha Christie or Dorothy L. Sayers. Presents a general overview of Allingham's work with a summary of her theories about the mystery story, followed by chapters of biography alternating with critical discussions of the major novels. Does not discuss the early work, the novellas and short fiction, or the novels that do not feature Albert Campion or Philip Youngman Carter's continuation of the series. Extensive bibliography, Allingham family genealogy, indexes. Nearly twenty photographs.

"Obituary: Margery Allingham." *The New York Times*, July 1, 1966: 35.
In her early years as a writer, Allingham produced a new novel every year; later, she spent three or four years on each one, rewriting each paragraph if necessary, but some readers found these later works heavy-handed. Cites Phyllis McGinley's praise for *The Tiger in the Smoke* (1952) as a demonstration that Allingham had the talent for graceful, perceptive prose and was able to make all of her characters human beings.

"Obituary: Margery Allingham." *The Times* (London), July 1, 1966: 16.
Suggests that Allingham's strength as a writer was that she could adapt to the needs of more sophisticated readers after World War II. Notes how her narrative force has been compared to that of Robert Louis Stevenson and suggests that her writing skill and her detective, Albert Campion, developed and reached maturity together.

Commentary

Allen, L. David. "The Fashion in Shrouds." In his *Detective in Fiction*. Lincoln, Nebr.: Cliffs Notes, 1978.
A detailed plot synopsis in ten paragraphs, followed by a character sketch of Albert Campion and his methods as a detective. Allen discusses the significance of this novel's focus on an elite social group in which the murders provide an opportunity to study the relationships between the characters— which in turn, become the basis for the solution to the mystery. Discusses Allingham's use of love as an important, but secondary, theme and the low-key humor in the story.

Anderson, Isaac. "New Mystery Stories." *The New York Times Book Review* 39 (April 15, 1934): 18.
A review of *Death of a Ghost* (1934). The problem for Albert Campion is not discovering the identity of the murderer but finding the necessary evidence for a conviction. Anderson finds the settings (the artistic world of London) perfect and the characters interesting for their own sake, with Belle Lafcadio, widow of the man whose will causes the series of tragedies, especially delightful.

Boucher, Anthony. "Criminals at Large." *The New York Times Book Review* 70 (July 18, 1965): 28.
A review of *The Mind Readers*, which concerns telepathy as a serious means of communication between military leaders and which is more plausible than one might believe. Boucher suggests that the traditional conventions of the thriller, even with Albert Campion present, tend to overshadow the telepathy theme so that it is lost in the process.

Cox, J. Randolph. "Miss Allingham's Knight: The Saga of Albert Campion." *The Armchair Detective* 15, no. 1 (1982): 86-91.
Allingham intentionally projected the image of the knight-errant onto her gentleman detective Albert Campion. Cox traces the evolution of the series from adventure stories through formal detective fiction to those stories in which Campion is an observer and wanderer in search of other people's troubles, living by his own code of honor. Particular emphasis on *Dancers in Mourning* (1937).

"Detective Stories." *The Times Literary Supplement*, July 9, 1938: 467.
A review of *The Fashion in Shrouds* (1938), which is recommended as a well-planned and well-written novel. Finds the characters interesting, especially the actress Georgia Wells and Campion's factotum, Magersfontein Lugg, with the greatest amount of danger in the book provided by the love interest for Campion, which does not succeed.

"Detective Stories: Loss of Memory." *The Times Literary Supplement*, March 1, 1941: 105.
A review of *Traitor's Purse* (1941), an unusual mystery in which the detective's resources are limited by a case of amnesia. Suggests that if this is a spoof then it fails, for the sense of the writer's having her tongue in her cheek destroys the necessary belief in Campion's condition as an amnesiac. Finds it a disappointment after the success of *Black Plumes* (1940).

"Detective Stories and Thrillers." *The Times Literary Supplement*, July 3, 1937: 496.
A review of *Dancers in Mourning* (1937) as a detective story in which atmosphere is crucial to making the solution seem the only logical one. Considers that Allingham's "naturally vivid descriptive style" is heightened by her use of the theater as background and the presentation of Campion with the problem of not letting his emotions stand in the way of finding the truth.

Duffy, Martha. "Exit Mr. Campion." *Time* 97 (February 1, 1971): 79.
Duffy considers Allingham to have succeeded as a mystery writer by virtue of her clear, serviceable prose. Campion was agreeable, intriguing, and eccentric, but not a caricature. Discusses the author's life in London and on the edge of the Essex salt marshes, where she avoided interviews and lectures but enjoyed life. (A review of *Mr. Campion's Quarry*, 1971; by Philip Youngman Carter, the final Campion novel.)

"Fiction." *The Times Literary Supplement*, September 6, 1923: 590.
A review of *Blackerchief Dick: A Tale of Mersea Island* (1923) which can stand on its own merits without the help of William McFee's introduction, which discusses Allingham's having received the plot by supernatural means. Explains that the title character is a Spaniard who resembles Captain Hook too closely. Suggests that, while the story is fun, it needs a happier ending.

"Fiction: On the Run." *The Times Literary Supplement*, August 1, 1952: 497.
A largely negative review of *The Tiger in the Smoke* (1952), in which Allingham has failed in her purpose of writing a superior thriller peopled by characters with real motivation by trying too hard. Considers the story of the homicidal excommando Jack Havoc is above the average although the narrative lacks a central focus and her regulars (Albert Campion, Magersfontein Lugg and Charlie Luke) play subsidiary roles.

Gaskill, Rex W. "Margery Allingham." In *And Then There Were Nine . . . More Women of Mystery*, edited by Jane S. Bakerman. Bowling Green, Ohio: Bowling Green University Popular Press, 1985.
Gaskill suggests that social class as an issue is developed more extensively by Allingham than any other mystery writer. By this she fulfilled the purpose of

the novel—to hold up the beliefs of a culture and a time to scrutiny. Gaskill believes that she was a master of descriptive prose with the ability to create believable and interesting characters. Includes a chronological checklist of her detective fiction.

Haycraft, Howard. "England: 1930- (The Moderns)." In his *Murder for Pleasure: The Life and Times of the Detective Story*. New York: D. Appleton-Century, 1941.
Allingham began writing at the age of seven and published her first novel at sixteen. Haycraft assesses her work, in which superior characterization and narration are combined with penetrating comment on the contemporary social scene, so that, had any of her more recent novels not been labeled detective fiction, they might have passed for mainstream fiction.

Huey, Talbott W. "Mr. Campion and the Survival of the Great Detective." *Clues: A Journal of Detection* 3 (Spring/Summer, 1982): 90-104.
The "death" of the Great Detective in fiction is premature reporting, according to Huey. By building Albert Campion on paradox and contradiction, Margery Allingham made his adaptation in a changing world plausible and inevitable. Huey proposes that Campion's special qualities as a character include dealing reassuringly and responsibly with both upper and lower classes and that one compelling reason for reading the stories is the appearance of recurring characters such as the members of Campion's family.

McGinley, Phyllis. "A Report on Criminals at Large." *The New York Times Book Review* 57 (September 7, 1952): 26.
A review of *The Tiger in the Smoke* (1952), the work of a writer willing to take pains with such basic elements as plot and character. McGinley finds it not a detective story but suspense in the Buchan tradition. Discusses the style of the novel and its unsentimental treatment of the killer.

"Other New Novels: Detective Stories." *The Times Literary Supplement*, November 30, 1940: 605.
A review of *Black Plumes* (1940), which may fail to be mystifying but which succeeds in its sense of atmosphere and character. Finds crude attempts to inject suspense where none exists but notes that the well-read devotee of detective fiction will not be fooled by this ruse. Describes it as an outstanding example of a detective novel which has charm without being a puzzle. (Not a Campion story.)

Panek, LeRoy L. "Margery Allingham." In *Watteau's Shepherds: The Detective Novel in Britain, 1914-1940*. Bowling Green, Ohio: Bowling Green University Popular Press, 1979.

Allingham's first Albert Campion story, *The Crime at Black Dudley* (1929), is a combination of spoof, detective story, and thriller, elements which recur throughout her work. Panek places Campion in the hero tradition that includes Robin Hood and A. J. Raffles, the changes in his character being the result of Allingham's inclination to experiment in her writing. Includes a selective checklist of the novels.

Pike, B. A. *Campion's Career: A Study of the Novels of Margery Allingham.* Bowling Green, Ohio: Bowling Green University Popular Press, 1987.
Pike discusses the way Allingham came to her profession from a family of writers, consciously in charge of her craft with a consistent philosophy regarding the mystery. Her fictional world is cozy, eccentric, sentimental, and permanent, and her detective, Albert Campion, deserves his popularity. Pike, in a close, sequential reading of the series, examines Allingham's developing technique in great detail. Includes an extensive checklist of all Allingham's work.

Routley, Erik. "Quartet of Muses: Second Pair." In his *The Puritan Pleasures of the Detective Story.* London: Victor Gollancz, 1972.
In Routley's opinion, Margery Allingham brought the detective story to its greatest maturity by recognizing that the proper form of passion is a passion against evil. She created Albert Campion as a reaction against the superdetective and made it possible for him to survive in a changing world. Routley discusses *The Tiger in the Smoke* (1952) and the character of Charles Luke.

Symons, Julian. *Bloody Murder: From the Detective Story to the Crime Novel, a History.* Rev. ed. New York: Viking Press, 1985.
Beginning with *Death of a Ghost* (1934), Margery Allingham's talent for portraying society with gentle irony became apparent, according to Symons. Compares Campion's characteristics to those of Philo Vance and suggests that he began as a near-parody of Bertie Wooster but matured into a serious figure by the time of *Coroner's Pidgin* (1945). Symons explains how Allingham broke with convention in her masterpiece, *The Tiger in the Smoke* (1952), a thriller about a manhunt.

Watson, Colin. *Snobbery with Violence: Crime Stories and Their Audience.* London: Eyre & Spottiswoode, 1971.
It took ten years (1929-1939) for Albert Campion to shed the image of the "silly ass," once popular in British fiction, and become a cerebral and dignified detective. Watson demonstrates the manner in which Campion's creator developed her own attitudes toward fiction writing and used names from the social scene to which she had committed her detective as points for satire.

Welty, Eudora. "Victorian Half-Breed." *The New York Times Book Review* 48 (October 31, 1943): 6, 12.

A review of *The Galantrys* (1943), in which Allingham attempts to express her vision of English society, past and future, but fails. Welty considers the narrative style too remote for the reader to care about James Galantry; the events move too swiftly for there to be much pleasure in watching his reactions. (Not a detective story.)

[Winn, Dilys.] "Margery Allingham and 'That Silly Ass.'" In *Murderess Ink*, edited by Dilys Winn. New York: Workman Publishing, 1979.
Winn claims that Albert Campion was insufferable as an upper-class clown in the early novels but that his later, serious, and sophisticated characterization was based in part on Margery Allingham's husband, the artist Philip (Pip) Youngman Carter. Discusses how Carter encouraged Allingham to keep writing even when she grew tired of her creation. Includes photographs of Allingham as a child and as an adult.

Woods, Katherine. "An English Village Sees It Through." *The New York Times Book Review* 46 (September 21, 1941): 8.
A review of *The Oaken Heart* (1941), in which Allingham depicts the heart of England with her portrait of democratic life in a small country town. Woods considers the novel direct and moving because of its timeliness during World War II. Summarizes the plot, in which the citizens of Auburn awaken from complacency to discover that their strength is in being so representative of all of England.

ERIC AMBLER

Biography

Ambler, Eric. *Here Lies: An Autobiography*. London: Weidenfeld & Nicolson, 1985.
Covers Ambler's life from his childhood in South London, the son of theatrical
parents, through his early career as an engineer in a cable factory, his desire to
be a playwright, his work as copywriter for an advertising agency, and his
decision to write thrillers because he did not think that he had the skill to be as
ingenious as John Dickson Carr. Ambler discusses his life through World War
II to the publication of *Judgment on Deltchev* (1951).

——————. "The Novelist and Films." In *Crime in Good Company*. Compiled by Michael Gilbert. London: Constable, 1959.
Writing for films is a complex discipline which differs from that required to
write books. Ambler finds that the nature of the critic inside the writer is
important to his work. The absolute control that the writer of prose possesses
is challenged by his encounter with the filmmaker, because the line of communication between writer and audience differs in each form. Based on Ambler's own experiences as a screenwriter.

——————. "Voyages—and Shipwrecks." In *Whodunit? A Guide to Crime,
Suspense, and Spy Fiction*, edited by H. R. F. Keating. New York: Van
Nostrand Reinhold, 1982.
Writing is a combination of false starts and much reflection without knowing
what the book will look like ahead of time. For Ambler, the complexities of
the plot are a product of frequent and careful rewriting. The first draft is
written by hand; subsequent ones are typed, with three fingers, on an electric
typewriter. By not planning ahead, Ambler finds that each day's work becomes
a time of anticipation and distractions are more easily avoided. Ideas come
from everywhere and anywhere.

"Correspondence: The Ambler Case." *The Reporter* 30 (February 13, 1964): 6-10.
A letter to the editor from Ambler, refuting the earlier claim made in an article
for *The Reporter* (October 24, 1963) that he was involved in a correspondence
school for writers as a "hired hand" for the industry. At issue is whether he
had attended the Eighth Annual Pacific Coast Writers' Conference.

Hopkins, Joel. "An Interview with Eric Ambler." *Journal of Popular Culture* 9
(Fall, 1975): 285-293.
In Ambler's work, the primary theme is loss of innocence, with the Middle
East and Eastern Europe as proper settings in which his characters can be

presented. Ambler portrays women as he sees them in real life, strong and mature. His characters seem prone to suicide, because they are faced with intolerable situations. To Ambler, research is not as important as observation and experience.

Kalb, Bernard. "The Author." *The Saturday Review* 36 (July 18, 1953): 11.
A varied background (engineer, vaudeville actor, press agent, and writer of advertising copy) may not seem traditional for a writer of intrigue. Ambler notes the time of change for his genre as the 1940's and suggests that the novelist may replace the entertainer in the thriller.

Mitgang, Herbert. "The Thrilling Eric Ambler." *The New York Times Book Review* 86 (September 13, 1981): 3.
Interviewed on the occasion of the publication of *The Care of Time* (1981), Ambler suggests that thrillers reveal more of the way people think and governments behave than do conventional novels. Unlike contemporary serious novels, Ambler's work is relevant in a social context. Mitgang suggests that Ambler's liberal political views have always been in support of political and social justice, and the thriller form allows him an opportunity to speak his mind.

Oram, Malcolm. "Eric Ambler." *Publishers Weekly* 206 (September 9, 1974): 6-7.
An interview. In the best tradition of his own thrillers, Ambler set out deliberately to change the genre of spy fiction. His scientific training as an engineer helped him add the touches of realism to his work that impressed the experts. Explains that he regards fictional violence as phony and avoids it when possible. Writing slowly, rewriting constantly, he has been known to abandon a book entirely if he becomes dissatisfied with it.

Commentary

Ambrosetti, Ronald. "The World of Eric Ambler: From Detective to Spy." In *Dimensions of Detective Fiction*, edited by Larry N. Landrum, Pat Browne, and Ray B. Browne. Bowling Green, Ohio: Bowling Green University Popular Press, 1976.
Ambrosetti believes that Ambler never wrote pure spy novels but presented a story of foreign intrigue within the detective-novel form. By making his protagonists amateurs, he increased the ability of his readers to identify with them. Compares him to John Buchan, who also emphasized how thin a protection civilization offers. Discusses the way Ambler's philosophy appears to have moved from a search for logic in history to an acceptance of history at face value.

Bayley, John. "Soberly Thrilling." *The Times Literary Supplement,* August 2, 1985: 839-840.

The reader of thrillers pays more attention to characters than to plot or the artifice of the genre which creates its plausibility. Bayley thinks that Ambler avoids fantasy and self-projection so the reader does not need to be reminded of the difference between truth and fiction. His best work succeeds by its combination of sobriety, discretion, and accuracy. (Reviews *Here Lies*, 1986; with reissues of *The Levanter*, 1972; and *Doctor Frigo*, 1974.)

Boucher, Anthony. "The Witness in the Bikini." *The New York Times Book Review* 69 (October 18, 1964): 4, 39.

Reviews *A Kind of Anger* (1964), a thriller of high quality—ironic, witty, ingenious, understated, and filled with suspense. The story of journalist Piet Maas is told with a facility that combines satiric comedy with tension. Boucher comments on Ambler's shift from espionage to stories of "international male-faction" with praise for his contribution to the literate thriller.

Broyard, Anatole. "Books of the Times." *The New York Times*, September 11, 1981, sec. C: 25.

A review of *The Care of Time* (1981), demonstrating Ambler's ability to stay ahead of the competition in the field of suspense writing. The most exciting parts of the book may lie in the conversation between characters; Broyard believes that Ambler belongs to a generation that enjoys good conversation. The theme of the novel concerns how international diplomacy has become a kind of terrorism.

Buckley, Priscilla L. "Of Banana Republics and Habsburgs." *National Review* 26 (December 20, 1974): 1475.

Reviews *Doctor Frigo* (1974), in which Ambler has lost none of his powers of intrigue. It is a tale of mystery and adventure combined with a zany love story. Buckley demonstrates how the story is told with an eye for description, a detached attitude, and a precision of detail, so that the atmosphere never dominates the plot but renders the incredible completely plausible.

Buckley, Tom. "About New York: From Ambler to Istanbul." *The New York Times*, April 28, 1975: 34.

Buckley notes that Eric Ambler's spy stories have an implicit ideology and that his heroes always seem somewhat leftist. On the occasion of accepting the Grand Master Award from the Mystery Writers of America, Ambler reflects on the incompetence of real intelligence agents in comparison to the fictional ones. The columnist concludes with a fantasy in which Ambler entices him to try a drugged cigarette.

Cain, James M. "Color of the East." *The New York Times Book Review* 65 (March 6, 1960): 38.

Reviews *Passage of Arms* (1959), a novel that begins with Ambler's typical skill at setting a scene, letting the details take control of the reader, but in which the story becomes overwhelmed by those same details. Cain finds that Ambler's protagonist is not only a quiet American but also a dull one to whom a love interest should have been introduced. Notes that he gives an excellent portrait of Southeast Asia.

Clemons, Walter. "Years of Writing Dangerously." *Newsweek* 108 (August 11, 1986): 56.

Review of *Here Lies* (1986), which takes the reader back to the youthful years when Eric Ambler transformed the spy story as completely as Dashiell Hammett did the detective story. Clemons believes that Ambler wrote so convincingly of places he had never seen because he had an ear for the music of the dialogue of his characters.

Day Lewis, C. "With a Flair for Creating Alarm." *The New York Times Book Review* 58 (July 26, 1953): 5.

John Buchan elevated the chase to a ritual in the thriller, and the writers who followed him were heavily influenced by his lead. Day Lewis believes that Ambler became a master of tension by giving a new twist to this old formula. For Ambler, surface appearance often masked some foundation in nightmare. Discusses *The Schirmer Inheritance* (1953), where expertise and verisimilitude replace suspense, but not enough to dispel the required illusion.

Eames, Hugh. "Eric Ambler." In *Sleuths, Inc.: Studies of Problem Solvers.* Philadelphia: J. B. Lippincott, 1978.

Eames finds that it is not Ambler's characters, but the social setting in his novels that is remarkable. By examining the themes of the thriller, Ambler either adapted them or completely reversed them. Basically a leftist in politics, he was the first thriller writer to attack capitalism. Contains sketchy biographical details but devotes much attention to *A Coffin for Dimitrios* (1939), his masterpiece, and three novels from his later period, *The Intercom Conspiracy* (1969), *The Levanter* (1972) and *Doctor Frigo* (1974).

Gorner, Peter. "Thriller Master Still Intrigues." *St. Paul Sunday Pioneer Press*, November 8, 1981, Accent section: 6.

Gorner interviews Eric Ambler, whose gritty novels changed the tone of the espionage genre, but who finds it difficult to continue to write something different in each book. Generally avoiding series heroes because he found them boring, Ambler intentionally set out to write literate spy stories. Among his trademarks is the ordinary person who survives being caught up in a web of intrigue.

Gross, John. "Books of the Times." *The New York Times*, July 29, 1986, sec. 3: 15.
Review of *Here Lies* (1986), a conventional but hardly commonplace autobiography. Gross believes that Ambler brings to his own story the same dry wit
and sense of character that enliven his novels. Cool in his appraisal of motive,
the greatest disappointment for Gross is Ambler's failure to be more precise
about why he became a writer and his cutting off of the account just after
World War II. Hopes for a sequel.

Hitchcock, Alfred. Introduction to *Intrigue: Four Great Spy Novels of Eric Ambler*.
New York: Alfred A. Knopf, 1943.
According to Hitchcock, Ambler's heroes are anything but heroic and are not
even wise or daring, they are simply pleasant, ordinary people with whom the
reader has instant identification, sharing the same emotions, including fear.
Hitchcock claims that the wise man in Ambler is not the traditional figure
from British intelligence but often an agent for the opposition. In short, he
explains why Ambler is credible.

Lambert, Gavin. "The Thin Protection: Eric Ambler." In his *The Dangerous Edge*.
London: Barrie & Jenkins, 1975.
Lambert discusses how, in novels written like intelligence reports in spare,
lucid prose, Ambler uses the passport as a metaphor of identity in a society
that appears to be preparing for death. Considers *A Mask for Dimitrios* (1939)
his best book and its multinarrative structure a brilliant achievement. Discusses several titles, specifically *Epitaph for a Spy* (1937), *Cause for Alarm*
(1938), *The Light of Day* (1962), and *Intercom Conspiracy*, as well as the
nonfiction reports in *The Ability to Kill* (1963).

Lourie, Richard. "Code Name Eric." *The New York Times Book Review* 91 (August
17, 1986): 14.
Review of *Here Lies* (1986), a book of both good and ill humor, which covers
the early years of Ambler's life with dogged chronology but divulges no
intimacies about what writing really meant to him. Lourie discusses the lack of
real precision in the story of a life which remains a mystery.

Merry, Bruce. *Anatomy of the Spy Thriller*. Montreal: McGill-Queen's University
Press, 1977.
Merry classes the Ambler protagonist as a confused amateur and idealist
drawn into a situation too complicated to comprehend and entering the espionage field because someone has a hold over him. He is the hunted man.
Discusses Ambler's making a character in *The Intercom Conspiracy* (1969)
both a scholar and a thriller writer, by which Ambler creates an impression of
the secret agent with skills the reader can comprehend and appreciate. Believes

that *Uncommon Danger* (1937) lacks accelerated storytelling and that the suspense does not build to a climax although the ending comes as a surprise.

Panek, LeRoy L. "Eric Ambler." In his *The Special Branch: The British Spy Novel, 1890-1980.* Bowling Green, Ohio: Bowling Green University Popular Press, 198.
Discusses Ambler's method of borrowing the stock characters of his predecessors in the spy novel and altering the attitudes of his readers toward those stereotypes. Suggests that Ambler gave the genre a new realism and changed forever the opinions of his readers toward capitalism, espionage, and political and economic reality. Discusses the air of "distanced analysis" in Ambler's work that makes him a superior exponent of the genre.

Redman, Ben Ray. "The Ansbacher Incarnate," *Saturday Review* 36 (July 18, 1953): 11-12.
In *The Schirmer Inheritance* (1953), Redman finds that Ambler appears to be following the style of Graham Greene by moving from entertainments into the world of serious fiction. Redman discusses the earlier work, which was more spontaneous and less leisurely, the melodramatic adventure tracing its lineage to the romances of chivalry through the picaresque novel. Believes that Ambler now needs to learn to integrate his literary conventions into his narratives.

Symons, Julian. *Bloody Murder: From the Detective Story to the Crime Novel, a History*. Rev. ed. New York: Viking Press, 1985.
Symons indicates that Ambler expressed a left-wing point of view in his earliest novels and thereby added color to the spy story. Symons considers Ambler's masterpiece from the early period to be *A Mask for Dimitrios* (1939). Traces differences in Ambler's attitudes from the years before the war to those he held afterward. His finest work, *Doctor Frigo* (1974), a political thriller narrated with skill and subtlety, justifies the detachment some critics find to be his greatest liability.

——————— . "Confidential Agents." *The Times Literary Supplement*, July 20, 1956: 434.
A review of *The Night-Comers* (1956; U.S. title: *State of Siege*) with comparisons to *Epitaph for a Spy* (1937), *A Mask for Dimitrios* (1939), *Journey into Fear* (1940), *Uncommon Danger* (1937), *Judgment on Deltchev* (1951) and *The Schirmer Inheritance* (1953). Symons notes that Ambler achieved his status in the spy story by recognizing that the political climate of the world had changed from the early days of the genre and by expressing a point of view about society. To Ambler, no agent is important as an individual, and both sides are menacing. Seemingly at a loss for an attitude after the war, he never repeated the success of *A Mask for Dimitrios*.

——————— . "Subtleties of Power." *The New York Times Book Review* 86 (September 13, 1981): 3.

In *The Care of Time* (1981), Eric Ambler has produced another thinking man's thriller, even if it is not among his better novels. Symons considers Ambler an old-fashioned writer, who carefully rations his action scenes. Discusses what Ambler learned from W. Somerset Maugham's *Ashenden: Or, The British Agent* (1928), how to avoid sentiment and present coolly realistic detail, adding to that his own brand of humor and an attention to technical detail.

Trevor, Elleston. Introduction to *A Coffin for Dimitrios*, by Eric Ambler. Del Mar, Calif.: Publisher's Inc., 1977.

The rogue is often the central figure in any Ambler novel and Ambler knows his rogues from having been something of the sort as a schoolboy. Trevor considers Dimitrios a man of his time as is Arthur Abdul Simpson (*The Light of Day*, 1962) and Frits Bühler Krom (*The Siege of the Villa Lipp*, 1977). Ambler beguiles with urbane ease, making the evil all the more real by his method.

"Two Yawns Later." *Newsweek* 57 (June 12, 1961): 63.

While covering the murder trial of Raymond Bernard Finch and Carole Tregoff in 1960 for *Life* magazine, Eric Ambler conceived the idea for the television series *Checkmate*. The concept of an agency devoted to preventing crime rather than stopping the criminal after the fact was sold to the Columbia Broadcasting System with Ambler as consultant but not as scriptwriter.

ROBERT BARNARD

Biography

Barnard, Robert. "Growing Up to Crime." In *Colloquium on Crime*, edited by Robin W. Winks. New York: Charles Scribner's Sons, 1986.

Planning a novel too carefully in advance tends to spoil the fun for Barnard, who finds a zest in improvising. He admits that nearly all of his characterizations are caricatures, the basis of the humorous novel, but that this makes it easier for him to present the surface of a suspect without revealing too much. Having spent so much of his life outside England has made Barnard view his native heath as a foreigner might.

Herbert, Rosemary. "Robert Barnard: An Interview with a Man Called Bob." *The Armchair Detective* 17 (Summer, 1984): 290-294.

Having recently left the academic world to devote his time to writing, Barnard talks about his childhood (no one is likely to remember him for his wit) and the liberating effect of Oxford. Other subjects covered include influences from other writers (Agatha Christie in particular), his lack of religious convictions, the sources for his grotesque characters, and the importance of entertainment to the detective story.

Ross, Jean W., and Brian Ryan. "Robert Barnard." In *Contemporary Authors*, edited by Linda Metzger and Deborah A. Straub, vol. 20. Detroit: Gale Research, 1987.

An interview conducted by telephone on October 25, 1985. Covers Barnard's targets for satire, his enjoyment of the writing process, the influences of Charles Dickens and Agatha Christie on his work, his use of research, his lack of advance planning, his writing schedule, the reasons for the popularity of *Death in a Cold Climate* (1980), and his experiences teaching in Australia and Norway.

White, William. "Robert Barnard: A First Bibliography and a Note." *The Armchair Detective* 17 (Summer, 1984): 295-299.

A brief, biographical account praising Barnard's depiction of time and place, as well as his precision in background description. Primary bibliography includes articles, book reviews, and his books published through *Little Victims* (1983). Secondary bibliography lists reviews of titles from the published version of his dissertation, *Imagery and Theme in the Novels of Dickens* (1974), through *The Case of the Missing Bronte* (1983).

Commentary

Auchincloss, Eve. "Nonfiction in Brief." *The New York Times Book Review* 85 (July 20, 1980): 14.

A review of *A Talent to Deceive: An Appreciation of Agatha Christie* (1980), an "elegantly perceptive appreciation of the author most read after the Bible and Shakespeare," Agatha Christie. Auchincloss finds Barnard's central thesis to be that the classic English detective story is a puzzle in fictional form and should not be analyzed as if it were a character study.

Barnard, Robert. "The English Detective Story." In *Whodunit? A Guide to Crime, Suspense, and Spy Fiction*, edited by H. R. F. Keating. New York: Van Nostrand Reinhold, 1982.

Like the comedy of manners and Restoration drama, the classic crime story is an ageless and artificial literary form created as an escape from "intolerable reality." Barnard believes that half the contemporary crime fiction published fits this category but that today it is more realistic and humorous, with greater psychological depth than the works of Agatha Christie, Margery Allingham, Ngaio Marsh, and Dorothy L. Sayers. Barnard's work fits this definition well.

_____ . "Murder—Cranford Style." *Books and Bookmen* 15 (June, 1970): 30-32.

Even by the 1920's the picture of village life in detective fiction was anachronistic, an image borrowed from Elizabeth Gaskell's *Cranford* (1853). In Barnard's view, nostalgia and an appeal to class were basic elements in the continued popularity of the classic detective story. Interesting as reflections of habits of thought, they retain a value for him as an index of the tenacity or attitudes and behavior found in popular fiction.

Callendar, Newgate. "Crime." *New York Times Book Review* 89 (March 25, 1984): 24.

Review of *School for Murder* (1983) as a novel written by a former teacher from the viewpoint of a teacher. Callendar finds the novel to be a slow-moving, orthodox mystery that engages the reader by its commentary on the goals of certain types of English schools. The setting, Burleigh, differs only slightly from Dotheboys Hall in Charles Dickens' *Nicholas Nickleby* (1838-1839). Finds Barnard's manner graceful and lethal.

_____ . "Loose Ends." *Newsweek* 98 (October 19, 1981): 103.

A review of *Death of a Perfect Mother* (1981), which Prescott believes breaks the implicit pact between reader and mystery that the former will be comforted by the resolution of the latter. An absolutely clueless mystery, Barnard's novel is really a comedy of working-class manners disguised as a detective story. Believes that the ending is disordered but that it works.

Herbert, Rosemary. "The Cozy Side of Murder." *Publishers Weekly* 228 (October 25, 1985): 20-32.
While Robert Barnard has used a variety of backgrounds in his novels, most have a basis in his personal interests or experiences. Writing *Out of the Blackout* (1985) was difficult because he was unable to use his characteristic humor. Barnard admits that in writing his own dust-jacket blurbs he has given some thought to a precise description of his work: acerbic, even abrasive. Interviewed at home outside Leeds.

Prescott, Peter S. "Fiction: Lovers and Killers." *Newsweek* 99 (March 22, 1982): 77.
A review of *Death by Sheer Torture* (1981), which Prescott believes offers wit and a sense of energy and style in place of a flawless puzzle. This elitist comedy features Peregrine Trethowan, a detective whose own relatives form a staple of the traditional crime novel, the eccentric aristocrats. Believes that it is likely to appeal to Anglophile readers in particular.

E. C. BENTLEY
(Edmund Clerihew Bentley)

Biography

Bentley, E. C. *The First Clerihews*. New York: Oxford University Press, 1982.
An interleaved facsimile of the notebook kept by E. C. Bentley in the 1890's
containing 132 "clerihews" or biographies in verse. Illustrated with sketches
by G. K. Chesterton. This edition includes accounts of Bentley's years at
St. Paul's School, his friendship with Chesterton, and a history of the clerihew
excerpted from Bentley's autobiography, *Those Days* (1940).

——————. *Those Days: An Autobiography*. London: Constable, 1940.
Bentley's story of his own life covers his schooldays at St. Paul's School and
Merton College, Oxford, his friendship with G. K. Chesterton, the history of
the "clerihew", the biographical verse he created in the 1890's, with extensive
commentary on the detective story as it existed prior to the Golden Age, the
creation of Philip Trent, and the writing of *Trent's Last Case* (1913).

Leitch, Thomas M. "E. C. Bentley." In *Dictionary of Literary Biography*, edited by
Bernard Benstock and Thomas F. Staley, vol. 70. Detroit: Gale Research, 1988.
A critical survey of Bentley's detective stories against a background of his own
life. Includes a comprehensive bibliography of Bentley's works and a selected
secondary bibliography. Illustrated. In Philip Trent, Bentley re-created the
detective as Everyman, in opposition to the superhuman Sherlock Holmes.
Scrupulously fair in *Trent's Last Case* (1913), Bentley's performance in *Trent's
Own Case* (1936) and *Trent Intervenes* (1938) is not so original or satisfying.
Leitch believes that Bentley's final novel, *Elephant's Work* (1950), a story of an
amnesia victim mistaken for an American gunman, "lacks conviction."

Stein, Aaron Marc. Introduction to *Trent's Last Case*, by E. C. Bentley. Del Mar,
Calif.: Publisher's Inc., 1977.
Stein believes that in creating Philip Trent, Bentley may have been presenting a
self-portrait. A biographical sketch of Bentley, who was at school with
G. K. Chesterton, where he invented a quatrain of nonsense verse known as
the "clerihew." Discusses Bentley's training as a lawyer and a journalist.
Notes that the work for which he is remembered was the product of his leisure
time.

Commentary

Bentley, E. C. "Meet Trent." In his *Trent's Last Case*. Del Mar, Calif.: Publisher's
Inc., 1977.

While not wishing to demean the virtue of the Sherlock Holmes stories in any way, Bentley believed that he needed to get as far away from that tradition as possible. Unlike Holmes, Philip Trent does not take himself seriously, and his attitude toward the police is that of a sportsman. Constructing the mystery was more difficult than Bentley had imagined and led to his choice of title as *Trent's Last Case* (1913).

Ewart, Gavin. Introduction to *The Complete Clerihews of E. Clerihew Bentley*. New York: Oxford University Press, 1983.
On the development of the "clerihew" from a schoolboy invention to the subject of a competition in *The Sunday Times*, 1981. The classical clerihew is free from malice, as was its inventor, E. C. Bentley. Cultivated and widely read, Bentley was a philistine in "matters of taste" according to his son, Nicholas. Comments on G. K. Chesterton's influence on the "social radicalism" found in *Trent's Last Case* (1913).

Haycraft, Howard. "England: 1918-1930 (The Golden Age)." In his *Murder for Pleasure: The Life and Times of the Detective Story*. New York: D. Appleton-Century, 1941.
While World War I marks a division between the old-style detective story and the modern form, the first example of the latter, *Trent's Last Case* (1913), appeared a full year before the beginning of the war. The success of the novel did not change its author's life in any degree according to Haycraft, who believes that Bentley symbolizes the finer side of the English character. Bentley often regretted his books of humor were not as well known as the stories of Trent.

_____ . " 'Trent's Last Case' Reopened." In *Trent's Last Case*, by E. C. Bentley. Del Mar, Calif.: Publisher's Inc., 1977.
Haycraft reassesses *Trent's Last Case* (1913), which is now recognized as a literary landmark and its author acknowledged as "the father of the contemporary detective novel," by noting how such a reputation came gradually. Haycraft refutes the legend that Bentley wrote it as the result of a wager with G. K. Chesterton. Discusses how its qualities withstand a rereading a half century after its publication.

Murch, A. E. "The Early Twentieth Century." In her *The Development of the Detective Novel*. New York: Philosophical Library, 1958. Reprint. Port Washington, N.Y.: Kennikat Press, 1968.
Trent's Last Case (1913) is rare among detective novels in that, once the solution is known, it can still be read with pleasure for its prose and its "sensitive study of character," since the truth discovered by Philip Trent is only part of the whole solution. Murch demonstrates how Bentley broke with the convention which Edgar Allan Poe had created.

Panek, LeRoy L. "E. C. Bentley." In *Watteau's Shepherds: The Detective Novel in Britain, 1914-1940.* Bowling Green, Ohio: Bowling Green University Popular Press, 1979.

Discusses *Trent's Last Case* (1913) in the context of its day and what it contributed to the structure of the evolving detective story. Comments on whether Bentley intended to play fair with the reader and allow the crime to be solved.

Redman, Ben Ray. Introduction to *Trent's Case Book*, by E. C. Bentley. New York: Alfred A. Knopf, 1953.

In three books about Philip Trent, Bentley produced a body of work enjoyable for its own sake but influential on the course taken by detective fiction in the twentieth century. A biographical sketch and appreciation of the liberal journalist who wrote his most famous book, *Trent's Last Case* (1913), in six months and sold it to an American publisher for a five-hundred-dollar advance against royalties.

Routley, Erik. "Coming of Age." In his *The Puritan Pleasures of the Detective Story*. London: Victor Gollancz, 1972.

Routley believes that Bentley reacted against his predecessors in detective fiction with grace. His contributions came at precisely the right time to establish a "true principle of originality." Discusses Bentley's contributions to the detective story in some detail and suggests the influence his detective, Philip Trent, had on a long line of gifted amateur sleuths.

Sayers, Dorothy L. Introduction to *Trent's Last Case*, by E. C. Bentley. New York: Harper & Row, 1978.

According to Sayers, the plot of *Trent's Last Case* (1913) is sound, logical, and fair, and the characters are real people. Even the murdered man, never seen alive, dominates the book by his personality. The theme is handled with a light touch. Anyone adapting it for radio will need to be careful, especially in casting the parts, or it will not succeed. (Text of an undated radio talk; there is no evidence that it was ever delivered.)

_____ . "The Omnibus of Crime." In *The Art of the Mystery Story*, edited by Howard Haycraft. New York: Simon & Schuster, 1947. Reprint. New York: Grosset & Dunlap, 1961.

In this introductory essay to her anthology of detective fiction, Sayers discusses the importance of viewpoint to the detective novelist with examples from *Trent's Last Case* (1913). The reader is shown what the detective sees but not what he surmises from it.

Shibuk, Charles. "Edmund Clerihew Bentley." In *Trent's Last Case*, by E. C. Bentley. Del Mar, Calif.: Publisher's Inc., 1977.

An annotated bibliography of Bentley's work, arranged chronologically. Of nineteen titles, only a handful are crime fiction: the three Trent books, an omnibus edition of the same, a thriller, two short stories (uncollected), a parody of Dorothy L. Sayers, three collections of "clerihews," and several anthologies. Notes are perceptive, evaluative, informative, and all too brief.

Symons, Julian. "The Rise of the Novel." In his *Bloody Murder: From the Detective Story to the Crime Novel, a History*. Rev. ed. New York: Viking Press, 1985.
E. C. Bentley's career as editorial writer on the *Daily Telegraph* with a talent for humorous writing indicates the fine line between the comic and the serious in the detective story. Symons discusses Bentley's achievement in *Trent's Last Case* (1913) and considers whether his reputation is altogether merited, since the later Trent stories show Bentley unable to adapt to the continually developing form.

Thomson, H. Douglas. "The Domestic Detective Story." In his *Masters of Mystery: A Study of the Detective Story*. London: Collins, 1931. Reprint. New York: Dover, 1978.
The supersleuth having become dated, Thomson believes that it was inevitable that someone would attempt a corrective to the format. Bentley violated the rules which prevailed in his day and created a classic. An analysis of the structure of the novel which integrates the formal detective story with a character study. Thomson suggests that *Trent's Last Case* (1913) has a solution that fools the detective as well as the reader.

ANTHONY BERKELEY
(Anthony Cox)

Biography

Shibuk, Charles. "The Literary Career of Mr. Anthony Berkeley Cox." *The Armchair Detective* 2 (April, 1969): 164-168, 170.

A brief biographical sketch of the writer whose "own private life [was] perhaps the most notable mystery of all" as preface to an annotated bibliography of Cox-Berkeley-Iles organized by author on the title page of the works cited. Perceptive comments with reference to contemporary reception of many titles.

Commentary

Berkeley, Anthony. "Concerning Roger Sheringham." In *The Poisoned Chocolates Case*, by Anthony Berkeley. Del Mar, Calif.: Publisher's Inc., 1979.

A somewhat tongue-in-cheek biographical sketch of Roger Sheringham who was born in 1891, the only child of a doctor and attended public school followed by a period at Merton College, Oxford (like E. C. Bentley). Sheringham served in World War I (recommended twice for the Distinguished Service Order, but never awarded it). Careers: schoolmaster, chicken farmer, and successful novelist, before becoming a criminal investigator. Chief interests in life: "criminology, human nature, and good beer." This description appears in Berkeley's *Dead Mrs. Stratton* (1933).

Carr, John Dickson. "A Tribute to Cox." In *The Poisoned Chocolates Case*, by Anthony Berkeley. Del Mar, Calif.: Publisher's Inc., 1979.

Having learned of the death of Anthony Berkeley Cox some fifteen months late, Carr offers an apology and a tribute to his old friend. Berkeley founded the Detection Club, possibly in 1928, but certainly by 1932, giving himself the title of First Freeman. Carr prefers Cox as Berkeley rather than as "Francis Iles" (his other pen name) and recommends *Trial and Error*, *The Poisoned Chocolates Case*, *The Piccadilly Murder*, *The Silk Stocking Murders*, *Dead Mrs. Stratton*, and *Top-Storey Murder*.

Haycraft, Howard. "England: 1918-1930 (The Golden Age)." In *Murder for Pleasure: The Life and Times of the Detective Story*. New York: D. Appleton-Century, 1941.

Haycraft discusses Berkeley as a literary descendant of E. C. Bentley, both schooled as humorous journalists; his founding of the Detection Club; and how he has remained reticent about his personal life. Discusses his achievements in the detective story, which include a fresh viewpoint, a lively wit, and an attempt at replacing the "puzzle of time, place, motive, and opportunity" with one of character. Comments on the influence of his work as "Francis Iles."

Moy, Paul R. "A Bibliography of the Works of Anthony Berkeley Cox (Francis Iles)." *The Armchair Detective* 14 (Summer, 1981): 236-238.
A comprehensive bibliography prefaced by brief note on Anthony Berkeley Cox's life. The son of a doctor, he took his pseudonym Francis Iles from his mother's maiden name. Includes all of his sketches in *Punch* (1922-1929) and British Broadcasting Corporation radio broadcasts; notes films and television serials based on *Before the Fact* (1932) and *Malice Aforethought: The Story of a Commonplace Crime* (1931). Additions and corrections appear in letters from Paul Moy in *The Armchair Detective* 14, no.4 (1981): 381 and 15, no. 2 (1982): 181.

Panek, LeRoy L. "Anthony Berkeley Cox." In his *Watteau's Shepherds: The Detective Novel in Britain, 1914-1940*. Bowling Green, Ohio: Bowling Green University Popular Press, 1979.
Panek finds that Berkeley's faults are obvious: identical plot patterns, unsympathetic characters, and an awkward and dull prose style through which his stories become passive. Discusses Berkeley's use of character and plot and how he balanced books written for fun (as Berkeley) with those intended to be serious (as Francis Iles). Each novel grew from ideas designed to react against standard detective-story plotting.

Routley, Erik. "And a Large Supporting Cast." In his *The Puritan Pleasures of the Detective Story*. London: Victor Gollancz, 1972.
Anthony Berkeley's detective stories seem peopled with characters from Noël Coward. His detectives (Roger Sheringham and Ambrose Chitterwick, for example) are amateurs on good terms with the police. Discusses how Berkeley's liberal attitudes allowed him to experiment with events leading up to the crime but not to trace the paths leading away. Notes that no one else ever managed to tell the same story twice (as he did in "The Avenging Chance" and *The Poisoned Chocolates Case*, 1929) and give each a different ending.

Sandoe, James. "A Checklist, with Some Notes of the Tales and Other Pieces by Anthony Berkeley, A. B. Cox, and Francis Iles." In *The Poisoned Chocolates Case*, by Anthony Berkeley. Del Mar, Calif.: Publisher's Inc., 1979.
A chronologically arranged list of twenty-six books with contributions by Berkeley and nine short stories, arranged alphabetically by title. Not all the nondetective works have been seen by the compiler. Most of the notes are extensive and evaluative. Liberal quotations from Berkeley's letters to Harold T. Gray of Brooklyn enliven the entries.

_____ . Foreword to *The Poisoned Chocolates Case*, by Anthony Berkeley. Del Mar, Calif.: Publisher's Inc., 1979.

Biographical details about Berkeley are scarce. Discusses his opinion of Alfred Hitchcock, who filmed *Before the Fact* (1932) in 1941 as *Suspicion*. Berkeley's charm was noted during a visit to Boulder, Colorado, in 1960. Sandoe notes Roger Sheringham's resemblance (in *The Poisoned Chocolates Case*, 1929) to G. K. Chesterton in his role as first president of the Detection Club.

Strickland, William Bradley. "Anthony Berkeley Cox." In *Twelve Englishmen of Mystery*, edited by Earl F. Bargainnier. Bowling Green, Ohio: Bowling Green University Popular Press, 1984.

Considers Berkeley's detective fiction to fall into two categories: the formal puzzle and the inverted detective story. Discusses his work as a bridge between the British Golden Age and the modern study of crime and criminology. Strickland notes that while Berkeley's use of psychology may appear dated, his characters unsympathetic, and his works unfocused, there are delights to make them worthwhile to any reader of mystery fiction.

Symons, Julian. *Bloody Murder: From the Detective Story to the Crime Novel, a History*. Rev. ed. New York: Viking Press, 1985.

Berkeley's zest and gaiety often became mere flippancy, but he contributed "one of the most stunning trick stories in the history of detective fiction" in *The Poisoned Chocolates Case* (1929) and all of his early novels remain lively and fresh. Symons believes that Berkeley's greatest contribution to the genre lies in the novels he wrote as "Francis Iles": *Malice Aforethought* (1931), *Before the Fact* (1932), and *As for the Woman* (1939), which were planned as serious novels with crime themes.

NICHOLAS BLAKE
(Cecil Day Lewis)

Biography

Blake, Nicholas. "The Detective Story—Why?" In *The Art of the Mystery Story*, edited by Howard Haycraft. New York: Simon & Schuster, 1947. Reprint. New York: Grosset & Dunlap, 1961.

The question in the title refers to the popularity of the genre. Blake answers it by discussing the juxtaposition of fantasy with reality that gives the genre an identity. Blake believes that the writer is thus allowed to put real characters into fantastic situations or unreal characters into realistic situations. The genre is on a higher literary level than ever but can still be read for sheer pleasure.

Day Lewis, Cecil. *The Buried Day*. New York: Harper & Brothers, 1960.

Apart from the financial circumstances which prompted Day Lewis to write *A Question of Proof* (1935), there is little about his detective fiction in this autobiography, but the author does convey a sense of the intellectual milieu behind the Nigel Strangeways books. Emphasis is on childhood and growing up and the account ends in 1940 with a postscript dated 1959 as a retrospect. Reticent about any intimate facts of his adult years.

Day-Lewis, Sean. *C. Day-Lewis: An English Literary Life*. London: Weidenfeld & Nicolson, 1980.

The biography of the writer who combined careers as poet and detective novelist, written by his son, Sean. According to his son, Day Lewis was a man of deeply conflicting emotions, who loved life and formed strong human attachments in spite of his melancholy temperament. His detective novels closely reflect his own experiences. He saw the genre as a substitute for religious ritual with detective and murderer representing the light and dark sides of human nature. Well illustrated; includes selected discography of Day Lewis reading his own verse.

Marder, Daniel. "C. Day Lewis." In *Dictionary of Literary Biography*, edited by Bernard Oldsey, vol. 15. Detroit: Gale Research, 1983.

Discusses Day Lewis' detective fiction as even more autobiographical than his serious fiction or his poetry. Ten novels are discussed with reference to incidents in the life of their author. Warning: the solutions to some of the mysteries are included in the discussion. Marder explains that as Nicholas Blake, Day Lewis used elements as intimate as his marital problems and extramarital affairs in his detective novels. *The Private Wound* (1968) deals with his adulterous affair with Billie Curral.

Commentary

Anderson, Isaac. "New Mystery Stories." *The New York Times Book Review* 46 (October 19, 1941): 26.
A review of *The Corpse in the Snowman* (1941), in which the title does not begin to reveal the mystery in this Nigel Strangeways novel. Anderson finds that the tragedy of Elizabeth Restorick, begun before the events of the novel, is more important to reader interest than the detective investigation. Anderson discusses the merits of the book as a novel and as a detective story.

Bargainnier, Earl F. "Nicholas Blake." In *Twelve Englishmen of Mystery*, edited by Earl F. Bargainnier. Bowling Green, Ohio: Bowling Green University Popular Press, 1984.
Blake's detective novels follow the general formulas and conventions of the genre for the years 1935 to 1968. Bargainnier explains how Blake used his own experiences, showed compassion for murderers, presented explicit themes, allowed children to appear as characters, and made his work less typical than others of the same period. Considers the lyrical quality of his detective novels to come from his skill as a poet.

Boucher, Anthony. "Criminals at Large." *The New York Times Book Review* 61 (August 12, 1956): 20.
A review of *A Tangled Web* (1956), in which Boucher believes that Blake replaces the formal detective puzzle with a "persuasive study in criminal character." Based on a true crime case of the early twentieth century. Boucher explains how the novel depicts fully realized characters in a story of great plausibility and told with irony and warmth.

_____ . "Criminals at Large." *The New York Times Book Review* 73 (April 7, 1968): 20.
A review of *The Private Wound* (1968), which Boucher considers the best work by Nicholas Blake in a dozen years. A "powerful story of murder and its aftermath" with a subplot centering on Irish politics. Blake's insights into Anglo-Irish and male-female relations "consistently illuminate" the story. Boucher explains that this is not a Nigel Strangeways novel; the narrator is an Anglo-Irish novelist.

Dyment, Clifford. *C. Day Lewis*. New York: Longmans, Green, 1955.
Primarily a discussion of Day Lewis as poet. Dyment considers him a poet of "our modern ambivalence," who has given more attention to this theme than any other modern poet. Day Lewis' unwillingness to withdraw poetry from everyday life makes him try to share it with others in varying forms. Dyment argues that Day Lewis' novels (including the detective novels) and his poetry

are unified: the former demonstrate the "same sensuous enjoyment of nature, narrative verse, and flair for descriptive precision" as the latter. Checklist of all works through 1954.

Hart-Davis, Rupert. "The Poetics of Detection." *The Spectator* 156 (March 13, 1936): 484.

A review of *Thou Shell of Death* (1936), which might appeal to Aristotle as it adheres to many of his principles: unity of plot, character, peripeteia, suffering, and discovery. Hart-Davis suggests that Nicholas Blake is a literary descendant of the other Blakes, William and Sexton. Having shown great promise in his first novel, Blake can now be considered in the front rank of detective novelists.

Haycraft, Howard. "England: 1930-   (The Moderns)." In his *Murder for Pleasure: The Life and Times of the Detective Story*. New York: D. Appleton-Century, 1941.

In Haycraft's opinion, Nicholas Blake combines thrills with literacy without being either condescending or pretentious. The detective element in his novels is "meticulous and soundly reasoned," abandoned only for something unique such as a "gripping internal study of murder" in *The Beast Must Die* (1938). Discusses *The Smiler with a Knife* (1939) in which Blake produced a thriller in the John Buchan tradition.

Parsons, Ian M. Introduction to *Poems of C. Day Lewis, 1925-1972*. London: Jonathan Cape, 1977.

A discussion primarily devoted to Day Lewis' poetry. Day Lewis had a catholic taste in poetry and experimented with a wide range of poetic styles: lyric, elegiac, narrative, and dramatic. Not all were successful, but he persisted in the attempts. Passionately interested in form and widely read, he was influenced most by writers such as Thomas Hardy, W. H. Auden, and Maurice Bowra. Totally committed to poetry, not even his detective fiction, written to provide himself with a living, prevented him from practicing his craft.

"Poet's Mystery." *Time* 32 (July 25, 1938): 55-56.

A review of *The Beast Must Die* (1938), the first detective novel by Nicholas Blake to appear with both his pseudonym and his real name on the dust jacket. Reviewer wonders whether Lewis did so because the plot involves a mystery writer who gets into trouble because of the pseudonym he uses. Considers the conclusion to be surprising as it depends upon the critical analysis of a piece of prose.

Riddel, Joseph N. *C. Day Lewis*. New York: Twayne, 1971.

Most of the criticism on Day Lewis concentrates on his relationship to W. H.

Auden or discusses him as a political or radical poet of the 1930's. Riddel presents the first book-length study of Day Lewis as poet and the mind which lies behind the work. Very little biography, no discussion of his fiction or the detective stories written as Nicholas Blake. Chronology and selected bibliography.

Routley, Erik. *The Puritan Pleasures of the Detective Story*. London: Victor Gollancz, 1972.
Routley believes that Blake was gifted, but a "somewhat unreliable writer," good with language, character, and specialized backgrounds. The novels are built around a situation with only "mild detective interest." A contemporary of Michael Innes, Blake is "less adventurous, less literary and precious," but his world is one of "intellectual gentility."

Stanford, Derek. *Stephen Spender, Louis MacNeice, Cecil Day Lewis: A Critical Essay*. Grand Rapids, Mich.: Wm B. Eerdmans, 1969.
No extensive references to Day Lewis' work in detective fiction as "Nicholas Blake." Stanford discusses his poetry as definitely lyrical. Throughout his work, there is a sense of writing within imagery imposed by W. H. Auden, writing verse of social commentary which in later years gives way to verse rooted in private experience. Stanford argues that this transition can be found in the detective fiction as well.

Symons, Julian. "The Golden Age: The Thirties." In his *Bloody Murder: From the Detective Story to the Crime Novel, a History*. New York: Viking Press, 1985.
Symons discusses Cecil Day Lewis, the only poet laureate who wrote detective fiction and introduced both a literary tone and a definite left-wing political attitude to the genre. Nigel Strangeways, based on W. H. Auden, was unique in being a real literary detective and not a figure who only quoted literature. Symons believes that as "Nicholas Blake," Day Lewis obviously enjoyed writing the books.

JOHN BUCHAN

Biography

Buchan, John. *Pilgrim's Way*. Boston: Houghton Mifflin, 1940.
Not a standard biography, this is what its author calls a collection of "active memories" about those people alive in the author's mind. Their essence replaces catalogs of physical detail and incident. Buchan explains that he does not deal in family intimacies. He wrote to please himself, and his books were never "standardized"; readers expecting another Richard Hannay story were often disappointed. Buchan waited until the entire story had formed itself in his mind and then wrote it fast, as excited as his readers to learn what would happen next.

Buchan, William. *John Buchan: A Memoir*. London: Buchan & Enright, 1982.
The second son of John Buchan presents what he calls "a handful of domestic recollections, reinforced by some history and designed to complement the public idea of my father which developed in his lifetime, and which the very legend of his successes has somewhat distorted." Well illustrated with photographs not generally available in other sources.

Smith, Janet Adam. *John Buchan: A Biography*. London: Rupert Hart-Davis, 1965.
Buchan's life was filled with such a multitude of interests that only an exhaustive study could hope to suggest their scope. Not given to introspection in public or in print, Buchan emerges as a knight of the old school, trying to keep pace with a rapidly changing world, a talented craftsman who achieved success because he worked hard, not because it was thrust upon him. The definitive biography. Well illustrated. Includes a checklist of Buchan's works and an index.

——————— . *John Buchan and His World*. New York: Charles Scribner's Sons, 1979.
A lavishly illustrated biography based on material discovered since Smith's earlier study, published in 1965. Includes a chronology of Buchan's life, a selected bibliography of secondary sources, and a checklist of his writings, arranged by year of publication. Invaluable source for photographs of Buchan, his family, friends, and colleagues and settings from his life and work; facsimile pages of manuscripts.

Turner, Arthur C. *Mr. Buchan, Writer*. London: SCM Press, 1949.
A biography with brief comments on Buchan's more prominent books. His many interests and activities contributed a freshness to his writing that it would

have lacked otherwise. Discusses the influences of his native Scotland and his religion on his writing, the clarity and aristocratic grace of his style, and his instinct for form, which allowed him to write quickly. A creative conservative, Buchan wrote his own political and social credo in his biographies.

Tweedsmuir, Susan. *John Buchan by His Wife and Friends*. London: Hodder & Stoughton, 1947.
A memoir and a collection of essays by some who knew Buchan personally; valuable for portraits of his personality. Not all contributions are given separate identities in the text or table of contents, but they are linked by Tweedsmuir's comments. Contributors include: Charles Dick, Roger Merriman, Violet Markham, Sir Roderick Jones, Lord Macmillan, Lord Baldwin, Walter Elliot, Catherine Carswell, A. L. Rowse, Janet Adam Smith, Leonard Brockington, Sir Shuldham Redfern, and Alastair Buchan.

Commentary

Brown, Barbara B. "John Buchan." In *Dictionary of Literary Biography*, edited by Thomas F. Staley, vol. 34. Detroit: Gale Research, 1985.
A biographical account with brief remarks on some of Buchan's novels, including *Huntingtower* (1922), *Castle Gay* (1929), and *The House of the Four Winds* (1935) considered to be lively but "marred somewhat by lack of unity of plot and of tone." Critical interpretations do not stress his contributions to spy fiction.

Cawelti, John. "The Joys of Buchaneering: John Buchan and the Heroic Spy Story." In *The Spy Story*, by John Cawelti and Brian A. Rosenberg. Chicago: University of Chicago Press, 1987.
Buchan may have written his spy stories in an attempt to create a contemporary fantasy with some of the power of John Bunyan's *The Pilgrim's Progress* (1678). Cawelti believes that the hurried journey was developed by Buchan as the basic plot of the spy story and discusses some of the reasons that his works survive while those of his contemporaries do not.

Cox, J. Randolph. "John Buchan." In *Dictionary of Literary Biography*, edited by Bernard Benstock and Thomas F. Staley, vol. 70. Detroit: Gale Research, 1988.
Brief but detailed notes on the thrillers, taken in the order of publication. While there is disagreement among critics about what it is that makes Buchan worth reading carefully, the characters or the plots, most agree there is more beneath the surface of his books. Discusses the basic theme that Buchan introduced to spy fiction: that evil and worldwide conspiracies can lie just beneath the surface veneer of so-called civilization.

_____ . "John Buchan: A Philosophy of High Adventure." In *The Thirty-nine Steps*, by John Buchan. Del Mar, Calif.: Publisher's Inc., 1978.
The incidents in Buchan's own life combined with his preferences in popular fiction; the influence of Robert Louis Stevenson and Sir Walter Scott explain his choice of character and incident in his own fiction. Cox discusses the manner in which high adventure became a rebellion against boredom for Buchan's heroes and a way to express the excitement of life for the author.

Daniell, David. *The Interpreter's House, a Critical Assessment of John Buchan*. London: Thomas Nelson, 1975.
The first full-length analysis of Buchan's work, nonfiction as well as fiction. Devotes more attention to the early and lesser known novels (*John Burnet of Barns*, 1898; and *A Lost Lady of Old Years*, 1899) than they may deserve and discusses few of the major biographies except *Sir Walter Scott* (1932). Perceptive assessment of the adventure and spy fiction.

_____ . Introduction to *The Best Short Stories of John Buchan*, edited by David Daniell. 2 vols. London: Michael Joseph, 1980, 1982.
Critical comments on Buchan as a writer of short fiction (only a fraction of which belongs in the category of "thriller"). Discusses how his stories fall into categories: special and powerful places, heroes who are wise and imaginative classic scholars, Scottish moorland settings to reveal the power of the irrational, and stories of flights to the north.

Gilbert, Michael. Introduction to *The Thirty-nine Steps*, by John Buchan. Del Mar, Calif.: Publisher's Inc., 1978.
Re-creates the way the events in Richard Hannay's adventure took shape in Buchan's mind. In Gilbert's view, the improbabilities in the plot of *The Thirty-nine Steps* (1915) did not seem to matter; they could be minimized by keeping the action moving, by writing "good, simple, and attractive English," and by Buchan's offhand references to people in power whom he really knew. Discusses Buchan's ability to keep his work fresh and believable.

Lambert, Gavin. "The Thin Protection: John Buchan." In his *The Dangerous Edge*. London: Barrie & Jenkins, 1975.
In spite of a nature polarized between the life of commerce and the life of a minister, Buchan grew up quietly self-assured. Lambert describes how, achieving success with ease, Buchan still felt an obligation to earn it, to put himself to the test physically. The characters in his stories did likewise. Discusses *Prester John* (1910), *The Thirty-nine Steps* (1915), *Greenmantle* (1916), *Mr. Standfast* (1919), *The Three Hostages* (1924), and *Sick Heart River* (1941).

Masters, Anthony. "John Buchan: The Romantic Spy." In *Literary Agents: The Novelist as Spy*. New York: Basil Blackwell, 1988.

Writing *The Thirty-nine Steps* (1915) and *Greenmantle* (1916) led to Buchan's being offered the post of director of propaganda by Prime Minister David Lloyd George, and the government made good use of Buchan's lively imagination. Masters admits that the amount of time Buchan really had for intelligence work can be only estimated, but makes the attempt to distinguish fact from fancy.

Panek, LeRoy L. "John Buchan." In *The Special Branch: The British Spy Novel, 1890-1980*. Bowling Green, Ohio: Bowling Green University Press, 1981.
Panek believes that one cannot understand the development of the spy novel without reading Buchan. Discusses how he took the form from Edgar Wallace, E. Phillips Oppenheim, and William Le Queux and made it spare and entertaining. He created "clear, individual characters" the reader could recognize. Describes the Buchan story as having two climaxes, one to explain the plot, another to explain the characters. Discusses the significance of pursuit and danger in Buchan's fictional world.

Swiggett, Howard. Introduction to *Mountain Meadow*, by John Buchan. Boston: Houghton Mifflin, 1941.
An account of the adventure novels that promise each reader the same chance for excitement that Buchan's heroes experienced. Swiggett finds analogies between Buchan's life and the exploits of his characters. Discusses the influence of Aubrey and Auberon Herbert, T. E. Lawrence, Basil Blackwood, Raymond Asquith, and Sir Edmund Ironside on Buchan's characters.

Usborne, Richard. "Edward Leithen." In his *Clubland Heroes*. London: Barrie & Jenkins, 1974.
A slightly tongue-in-cheek account of the life of Edward Leithen, hero of several of Buchan's novels and short stories. According to Usborne, Leithen, a gentle, perfect knight, has a life of solid success but never loses his modesty. A good shot with a rifle, an "artist as a fisherman." His inner life is not revealed until his final adventure in the north in *Mountain Meadow* (1941). Usborne speculates that while one can see the origins of several of Buchan's characters in people he knew, the original of Leithen must be Buchan himself.

_____ . "John Buchan." In his *Clubland Heroes*. London: Barrie & Jenkins, 1974.
Usborne notes that Buchan was a success at telling a story but not at delineating character. Discusses his idea of depicting character by describing Buchan's achievements. Describes how Buchan was skillful at giving the impression that he knew his background, even if he had never visited the country he described. Discusses Lewis Haystoun of *The Half-Hearted* (1900) as prototype for the heroes of the later books.

_____ . "Richard Hannay." In his *Clubland Heroes*. London: Barrie & Jenkins, 1974.

A biographical sketch of Richard Hannay, hero of several of Buchan's novels and short stories. In Usborne's view, Richard Hannay is the most modest of all Buchan's heroes. He has an ability to solve ciphers, possesses a considerable amount of luck, and has no more ambition than to serve someone greater than he.

_____ . "Sandy Arbuthnot and Others." In his *Clubland Heroes*. London: Barrie & Jenkins, 1974.

Usborne discusses the manner by which Buchan's characters often begin as interesting personalities but become "submerged" by success in later stories and offers Sandy Arbuthnot as a typical example. Blessed with strength and endurance, a fine horseman, a fabulous linguist, a good shot, with much of Lawrence of Arabia about him, Sandy seems to require excitement to keep him going. Usborne believes that with middle age, marriage, and success he loses his appeal. Discusses Archie Roylance, Peter Pienaar, and Dickson McCunn as well. A somewhat tongue-in-cheek account.

Winks, Robin W. "John Buchan: Stalking the Wilder Game." In *The Four Adventures of Richard Hannay*, by John Buchan. Boston: David R. Godine, 1988.

Some of Buchan's best writing and most sincere thought went into *The Thirty-nine Steps* (1915), *Greenmantle* (1916), *Mr. Standfast* (1919), and *The Three Hostages* (1924). Often he is not taken seriously as a writer because the writing seems so effortless. Winks effectively answers the charges of anti-Semitism, racism, and jingoism leveled at Buchan by noting the context in which the criticized passages appear. Includes bibliographic notes with references to libraries with holdings of Buchan papers.

JAMES M. CAIN

Biography

Cain, James M. Preface to his *The Butterfly*. New York: Alfred A. Knopf, 1947.
According to Cain, his idea for this novel came to him in 1922 and took him a long time to develop. He claims that he belongs to no particular school of writing, "hard-boiled or otherwise," as these are invented by critics with no connection to real writing. Admits to some similarities between himself and Ernest Hemingway in writing lean prose, though this was not intentional.

——————— . Preface to his *Three of a Kind*. New York: Alfred A. Knopf, 1944.
Cain finds that his greatest problem in writing is technique. The novels he tried to write never reached logical conclusions, but the short stories told in the vernacular of rural California were easy. From this he developed his famous style. As a storyteller Cain was influenced by screenwriter Vincent Lawrence, who introduced him to the concept of the "loverack," the situation in which lovers are tortured, and who provided him with the title for *The Postman Always Rings Twice* (1934).

Carr, John C. "An Interview with James M. Cain." *The Armchair Detective* 16 (1983): 4-21.
An interview conducted at Cain's home in 1973. Cain speaks of his newspaper days with H. L. Mencken and Walter Lippmann, how he would have written *Mildred Pierce* (1941) differently, that he had not read Dashiell Hammett and Raymond Chandler though he liked Chandler's screenplay for *Double Indemnity* (1944). Cain believes that it is not violence in a book that is harmful. Carr profiles eight individuals who played key roles in Cain's life. Bibliography of Cain's work.

Chastain, Thomas. "*PW* Interviews: James M. Cain." *Publishers Weekly* 206 (July 24, 1972): 40-42.
Interviewed at the age of eighty, Cain says that his real concern is not with the past but the future and with the book he is working on currently, *The Institute* (1976), for which he has already done four versions. Arthur Conan Doyle was a great influence on him and the theme of all his own work is the secret wish come true with "terrifying consequences." By writing in the first person in colloquial, informal language, Cain found that the writing itself never distracted the reader and the story came across more clearly.

Hoopes, Roy. *Cain*. New York: Holt, Rinehart and Winston, 1982.
An exhaustive, detailed biography of James M. Cain who is considered a

"writer's writer." Despite a career of writing seventeen books, many of them best-sellers, Cain claimed that he never had a sense of accomplishment. Discusses his work as an editorial writer and screenwriter, and the adaptation of his books into memorable films by other hands. Bibliography and extensive section of notes. Illustrated.

Commentary

Chastain, Thomas. Introduction to *Past All Dishonor*, by James M. Cain. New York: Arbor House, 1984.
Chastain believes that Cain's novels are controversial because his writing is intentionally disturbing. All the vintage ingredients are present in this novel in spite of its form as a story set on the Western frontier during the Civil War. The detail is authentic; the author is compassionate toward his characters; and his work is highly moral.

Frohock, W. M. "Two Strains of Sensibility." In *The Novel of Violence in America*. Dallas: Southern Methodist University Press, 1950, rev. ed. 1957.
Frohock claims that Cain never wrote anything "completely outside the category of trash," yet many intelligent, literate people read him. Discusses his achievement and tries to explain why *The Postman Always Rings Twice* (1934) made such an impression on people. Examines the essence of a Cain novel and how the material is handled in a fresh manner. Contrasts the "climate of sensibility" from which William Faulkner and Ernest Hemingway emerged to that surrounding *The Postman Always Rings Twice*.

Hoopes, Roy. "An Appreciation of James M. Cain." *The New Republic* 179 (July 22, 1978): 23-26.
Cain's biographer describes him as a prolific and versatile writer whose novels are remembered when his journalism, scripts, and short stories are forgotten. Discusses Cain as influenced by Ernest Hemingway in his style and dialogue. Suggests reasons that Cain should be remembered amid the contradictory critical response he has received and why he should not be classed as a detective novelist in the strict sense.

_____ . Introduction to *The Baby in the Icebox and Other Short Fiction*, by James M. Cain. New York: Holt, Rinehart and Winston, 1981. Reprint. New York: Penguin Books, 1984.
Discusses how Cain decided to be a writer while sitting on a bench in Lafayette Park, Washington, D.C., in 1914. Describes his early days as an English teacher and the influence on his literary style of people such as H. L. Mencken, Ring Lardner, and a bricklayer named Ike Newton.

Madden, David. *Cain's Craft*. Metuchen, N.J.: Scarecrow Press, 1985.
A reworking and updating of Madden's earlier essays and his Twayne book on
Cain in an attempt to show the author in six different perspectives: as a tough,
proletarian writer; as a professional writer of popular fiction, as a screenwriter
whose books were adapted to film; as a pure novelist; as an influence on
European fiction; and as a phenomenon of popular culture. Expanded and
updated bibliography.

—————————— . *James M. Cain*. New York: Twayne, 1970.
No extravagant claims for Cain's achievements are made in this brief overview
of Cain's life and work. Examines the work as both a phenomenon of American popular culture and as a valuable, but minor, contribution to literature.
Evaluates Cain's place among the tough-guy writers but discusses "special
sensibilities" that set him apart from them. A chronology, a selected primary
bibliography (short fiction, essays and articles are annotated), and a secondary
bibliography.

—————————— . "James M. Cain: Twenty-Minute Egg of the Hard-Boiled School."
Journal of Popular Culture 1 (Winter, 1967): 178-192.
According to Madden, it was the so-called tough-guy novel that provided "an
impersonal vision of American civilization during the Depression" and made
way for the minor classics of American literature produced during the late
1920's and 1930's Madden considers *The Postman Always Rings Twice* (1934)
"the quintessence of the tough guy novels." Surveys Cain's novels from *The
Postman Always Rings Twice* to *The Magician's Wife* (1965).

—————————— . "James M. Cain and the Tough Guy Novelists of the 30s." In *The
Thirties: Fiction, Poetry, Drama*, edited by Warren French. Deland, Fla.: Ever-
ett Edwards, 1967.
Considers Cain's first novel, *The Postman Always Rings Twice* (1934), his best,
approached only by *The Butterfly* (1947). Explains that in viewing Amerian
history as a panorama of violence, Cain provided insights into "the American
dream turned nightmare." Melodrama, disaster, tough optimism, humor, wit,
and lyricism have their place in his writing. Notes Cain's reputation as a tough-
guy writer in Europe.

—————————— . "Morris' *Cannibals*, Cain's *Serenade*: The Dynamics of Style and
Technique." *Journal of Popular Culture* 8 (Summer, 1974): 59-70.
Madden describes his use of Cain's fiction to introduce college sophomores to literary techniques by presenting them in "crude but sharp relief." The same
aesthetic concepts can be used to discuss formula fiction and nonformula stories.
To understand the nature of all fiction is to learn to distinguish and even to
discriminate among the variety of fiction available in a media-centered society.

Oates, Joyce Carol. "Man Under Sentence of Death: The Novels of James M. Cain." In *Tough Guy Writers of the Thirties*, edited by David Madden. Carbondale: Southern Illinois University Press, 1968.

A largely negative survey of Cain's work. Oates believes that Cain does not write literature, so any discussion of his work must concentrate on his relationship to his audience. Finds that what characterizes his novels as crime or suspense is the recurrence of murders of people beyond the "emotional radius" of the killers. Cain is a craftsman and *The Postman Always Rings Twice* (1934) is an example of his best craft. Faithful to the mythology of America, Cain writes of its "ideals and hatreds."

Root, Robert L., Jr. "Hard-Boiled Tragedy: James M. Cain's Classical Design." *Clues: A Journal of Detection* 5 (Fall/Winter, 1984): 48-57.

Root finds that it is limiting to compare Cain to detective writers such as Dashiell Hammett and Raymond Chandler or novelists such as Ernest Hemingway and Horace McCoy. Undercurrents in his great works, especially *The Postman Always Rings Twice* (1934), indicate that a more appropriate comparison is with classical themes. Discusses the classical themes found in *The Postman Always Rings Twice*, *Double Indemnity* (1936), and *The Butterfly* (1947).

Starr, Kevin. "It's Chinatown: James M. Cain." *The New Republic* 173 (July 26, 1975): 31-32.

Considers Cain's view of human events "brutal, elemental, and intrinsically pessimistic." Compares the vision of evil in Southern California captured by Roman Polanski in his film *Chinatown* (1974) to that found in Cain's "fables of lust, murder and money." Discusses *The Postman Always Rings Twice* (1934) as "one of the finest moments of Depression literature." Considers his message and style.

Wilson, Edmund. "The Boys in the Backroom: James M. Cain." In his *Classics and Commercials: A Literary Chronicle of the Forties*. New York: Farrar, Straus & Giroux, 1950.

Compares Cain to Ernest Hemingway and Dashiell Hammett. Capable of extraordinary exploits, yet doomed to fail, Cain's heroes are different in that they carry the reasons for their destruction within themselves. Based on a reading of Cain's first two novels. Wilson believes that there is enough of the poet in him for the reader to be optimistic about his future work.

Wolfe, Tom. Introduction to *Cain x 3*, by James M. Cain. New York: Alfred A. Knopf, 1969.

A rereading of Cain reveals how complex his technique of writing fast-paced, hard-boiled fiction really was. Details are never used gratuitously, merely for shock effect. Wolfe believes that while Cain's novels may concern murder and violence, he does not dwell on the experience. He puts the reader inside the psyches of his characters and makes him care about them, even about the losers. Momentum is achieved with a minimum of detail.

JOHN DICKSON CARR

Biography

Briney, Robert E. "The Books of John Dickson Carr/Carter Dickson: A Checklist." In *The Crooked Hinge*, by John Dickson Carr. Del Mar, Calif.: Publisher's Inc., 1976.
A list with some notes, mostly of a bibliographical nature, of Carr's more than seventy titles. Arranged according to byline, then by series, then in order of publication. Complete contents of short-story collections are indicated. Title changes between British and American editions or paperback publications noted. Omits *To Wake the Dead* (Carr, 1938).

——————. "Introduction: The Art of the Magician." In *The Crooked Hinge*, by John Dickson Carr. Del Mar, Calif.: Publisher's Inc., 1976.
Biographical details on both Carr and his detective, Dr. Gideon Fell. Apparent that Carr had a clear idea of what he wanted to do with the detective novel from the beginning of his career. Details were added later— "the historical reconstructions; the broad, sometimes farcical humor; the expert deployment of bizarre incident and eerie atmosphere; the occasional touch of outright fantasy." Everything is "set forth with all the illusionist's skill at deception."

Carr, John Dickson. "The Grandest Game in the World." In *The Door to Doom and Other Detections*. New York: Harper & Row, 1980.
A spirited and totally committed defense of the classic detective novel which plays fair with the reader, combined with a witty, but scornful, denunciation of the hard-boiled school. Carr includes a brief historical survey of the genre and four basic rules: The detective shall not be the murderer, the identity of the murderer shall be a secret until the end, the crime shall be the work of only one person, and the crime shall be clean-cut.

——————. "The Locked Room Lecture." In *The Art of the Mystery Story*, edited by Howard haycraft. New York: Simon & Schuster, 1947. Reprint. New York: Grosset & Dunlap, 1961.
This chapter from Carr's 1935 novel *The Three Coffins* stands as his statement of the problems presented by committing murder in a locked room. Dr. Gideon Fell analyzes the techniques of practitioners of the form, including those of S. S. Van Dine and Ellery Queen. He speaks of "personal tastes and preferences" and not rules and (of course) speaks for his creator.

Greene, Douglas G. "A Bibliography of the Works of John Dickson Carr." In *The Door to Doom and Other Detections*, by John Dickson Carr. New York: Harper & Row, 1980.

An extensive, annotated bibliography arranged according to format and byline. Short fiction includes uncollected stories from *The Haverfordian*, *Dime Mystery*, *Horror Stories*, and *Detective Tales*, as well as an early version of *It Walks by Night* (1930). Radio scripts, stage plays, and adaptations made from his works for radio, television, and motion pictures are noted.

Mitgang, Herbert. "John Dickson Carr Is Dead at 70: A Master of the Mystery Novel." *The New York Times*, March 1, 1977, sec. M: 32.
An obituary. Mitgang explains that Carr considered writing detective fiction an objective craft; he was concerned with putting "everything in their right places," not with a morbid nature or with solving chess and mathematics problems. Master of the locked-room mystery, a "pioneer" in consistently using attractive women as characters, Carr was a meticulous researcher and often visited the scenes of the crimes for his historical mysteries.

Taylor, Robert Lewis. "Two Authors in an Attic." Parts 1/2 *The New Yorker* 27 (September 8/15, 1951): 39-48, 36-49.
A profile of Carr, written with tongue in cheek. Taylor describes Carr as a precocious child who authored a newspaper column on prizefighting while in his teens. Determined to be a mystery writer, Carr spent two years in Paris writing novels he later destroyed as unworthy. A survey of his literary career, his working habits, and the seventeen years he and his family lived in England. Taylor attributes Carr's appeal in part to his "Halloween mind" and his sense of humor.

Commentary

Boucher, Anthony. Introduction to *The Blind Barber*, by John Dickson Carr. New York: Collier, 1962.
Boucher considers the comic element to be more often present in the books Carr wrote as "Carter Dickson" about Sir Henry Merrivale, but on occasion it may be found in the Dr. Fell stories. Notes that unlike the tragedy in which comedy comes as a relief, *The Blind Barber* (1934) is a farce in which the murder comes as an intrusion.

_____ . Introduction to *Hag's Nook*, by John Dickson Carr. New York: Collier, 1962.
It is Boucher's belief that the Golden Age of the detective novel was the 1930's, when John Dickson Carr was writing four books each year, demonstrating how much fun could be had with the traditional form. The influences on the young author appear to have been G. K. Chesterton, P. G. Wodehouse, and M. R. James. In *Hag's Nook* (1933), the first Dr. Fell story, the reader learns who the murderer is before he knows how or why the murder was committed.

Dettman, Bruce. "The Most Dangerous Man in Europe." *The Armchair Detective* 2 (July, 1969): 253-254.

A profile of Carr's first detective character, Henri Bencolin, with brief discussion of the five novels in which he appears. Having attended college in the United States, Bencolin became a spy for France in World War I, later turning to criminology. The foremost police official in Europe, Bencolin is "*juge d'instruction*, adviser to the courts and director of the Paris police." Only *It Walks By Night* (1930) and *Corpse in the Waxworks* (1932) are locked-room mysteries.

Dueren, Fred. "Henri Bencolin." *The Armchair Detective* 8 (February, 1975): 98, 123.

Jeff Marle, the young author-narrator of four of Henri Bencolin's five recorded cases is the reader's only source of information about the French detective in Carr's first novels. From these sources, Dueren puts together a portrait of the Mephistophelean police agent from their first adventure in 1927 (*It Walks By Night*, 1930) to the last recorded case after Bencolin's retirement (*The Four False Weapons, Being the Return of Bencolin*, 1937). Marle is not the observer-Watson in that case, and the picture of Bencolin differs from the earlier one.

Greene, Douglas G. "Adolf Hitler and John Dickson Carr's Least-Known Locked Room." *The Armchair Detective* 14 (1981): 195-296.

Greene discusses how Carr wrote mystery and historical dramas for the British Broadcasting Corporation during World War II to "relieve the horrors of war by presenting cozier and, with the solutions at the end of each play, more manageable horrors." In addition to adventure and detective stories for radio, Carr wrote propaganda plays, many of them unreadable in the late 1980's. In "Army of Shadows" (March 8, 1944), he invented a newspaper article about Adolf Hitler's disappearance from a locked room.

───────────── . "Introduction—John Dickson Carr: The Man Who Created Miracles." In *The Door to Doom and Other Detections*, by John Dickson Carr. New York: Harper & Row, 1980.

Almost all Carr's novels are formal detective stories in which he combined the terrifying suspense of Edgar Allan Poe with the humor of P. G. Wodehouse. Greene surveys Carr's literary career in the context of his life and the developing detective story. Believes that it was in his historical detective novels that he expressed his attitudes toward the world.

───────────── . "John Dickson Carr, Alias Roger Fairbairn, and the Historical Novel." *The Armchair Detective* 11 (1978): 339-341.

Within the traditional form of the detective novel, Carr has employed numerous innovations: primarily experiments with interesting characters and with combining other forms of literature with the detective novel. Discusses *Devil Kinsmere*, published in 1934, under the pseudonym "Roger Fairbairn," as Carr's first example of the detective novel with a historical setting. Describes its unfavorable reception and how Carr rewrote it thirty years later as *Most Secret* (1964).

_____ . "Introduction: John Dickson Carr and the Radio Mystery." In *The Dead Sleep Lightly*, by John Dickson Carr. Garden City, N.Y.: Doubleday, 1983.
The golden ages of the detective novel and radio drama coincided in the late 1930's and the early 1940's with John Dickson Carr's participating in both. Greene presents an account of Carr's work with the British Broadcasting Corporation in London, with Columbia Broadcasting System in New York, and his very brief experience as a screenwriter for Great Britain's Korda studios. Collects nine plays from more than seventy-five that survive.

_____ . "John Dickson Carr on British Radio." *The Armchair Detective* 12 (Winter, 1979): 69-71.
A chronologically arranged list of Carr's radio plays for the British Broadcasting Corporation from 1939 to 1955. Stories which were later broadcast on the American programs for the Columbia Broadcasting System, *Suspense* and *Cabin B-13*, are noted as are his scripts for the BBC's *Appointment with Fear*. Includes adaptations of two Carr novels for radio. Corrects the suggestion that Carr adapted Arthur Conan Doyle's *The Lost World* in 1944 or *The Adventures of Sherlock Holmes* in 1954 using the name "John Keir Cross."

Haycraft, Howard. "England: 1930-   (The Moderns)." In his *Murder for Pleasure: The Life and Times of the Detective Story*. New York: D. Appleton-Century, 1941.
Born in the United States, Carr is considered a British writer "by residence and subject matter." Haycraft classes Carr as one of the liveliest and most readable of writers with a "unique sense of the macabre," who produces novels that are sometimes thought to be too ingenious. A sketchy, incomplete biography; a letter to his American publisher about his family's experiences during the Blitzkrieg in World War II is quoted.

Herzel, Roger. "John Dickson Carr." In *Minor American Novelists*, edited by Charles Alva Hoyt. Carbondale: Southern Illinois University Press, 1970.
The defects in a work of literature, flat characters, implausible plots, the author's misleading the reader, are both justifiable and necessary in Carr's detective stories. Describes the way Carr's novels are really two stories: what appears to happen and what really happens. Notes that only in *The Burning Court* (1937) does an ending in a Carr novel violate the basic premise behind his work, that the forces of reason must explain the unknown.

Kingman, James. "John Dickson Carr and the Aura of Genius." *The Armchair Detective* 14 (Spring, 1981): 166-167.

Improbabilities and coincidences in *The Problem of the Green Capsule* (1939) and *The Crooked Hinge* (1938) may be "beyond rational possibility" but are overlooked by most readers conditioned to the ingenious explanations in Carr's detective novels. Kingman finds that the central flaw in *The Crooked Hinge* lies in the description, or rather lack of physical description, of one character, yet the novel is considered a masterpiece. Warning: The solution to the mystery is revealed.

Miller, Edmund. "Stanislaw Lem and John Dickson Carr: Critics of the Scientific Worldview." *The Armchair Detective* 14 (1981): 341-343.

Compares and contrasts the work of two dissimilar writers who seem "to find a critical focus for [their] fantasy in dissatisfaction with the neat rationalism of the scientific worldview." Lem shows statistical problems to be ridiculous; Carr (in *The Burning Court*, 1937) demonstrates how "a gothic solution to a problem may be more intellectually satisfying than a rational solution also available."

Nevins, Francis M., Jr. "The Sounds of Suspense: John Dickson Carr as a Radio Writer." *The Armchair Detective* 11 (October, 1978): 335-338.

An adaptation of *The Burning Court* (1937) was the first episode of *Suspense* (June 17, 1942), possibly the longest-running dramatic series on American radio. Lists the twenty-two scripts Carr himself wrote for *Suspense* (October 27, 1942-June 22, 1943) with notes on casts and plots. Additional lists of scripts for *Cabin B-13* and comments on Carr as narrator of *Murder by Experts*.

Panek, LeRoy L. "John Dickson Carr." In his *Watteau's Shepherd's: The Detective Novel in Britain, 1914-1940*. Bowling Green, Ohio: Bowling Green University Popular Press, 1979.

A discussion of Carr's work divided according to detective hero. The Henri Bencolin novels represent Carr's apprenticeship; the two transitional novels, *Poison in Jest* (1932) and *The Bowstring Murders* (1933), present new characterizations and points of view; the Dr. Fell novels and H. M. Merrivale stories are treated separately with profiles of each detective. Categories of detective plots are discussed. Omits discussing historical novels and most other works published after 1939.

Routley, Erik. "And a Large Supporting Cast." In his *The Puritan Pleasures of the Detective Story*. London: Victor Gollancz, 1972.

Carr's contribution to detective literature was to establish it as a serious form of writing. Routley believes that a gift for character and a sense of the macabre and sense of humor characterize Carr's work from the beginning. A virtuoso, but not an inventor, predictable as P. G. Wodehouse, Carr is as much of a craftsman, although sometimes he appears to be lecturing the reader.

Symons, Julian. "The Golden Age: The Thirties." In his *Bloody Murder: From the Detective Story to the Crime Novel, a History*. Rev. ed. New York: Viking Press, 1985.
Carr was unique among detective-story writers in devoting himself to the locked-room puzzle. His solutions may be improbable, but not necessarily impossible. His major flaw lies in building the whole story around the puzzle and leaving no room for characterization. What readers remember is the puzzle, not the people.

RAYMOND CHANDLER

Biography

Bruccoli, Matthew, ed. *Chandler Before Marlowe: Raymond Chandler's Early Prose and Poetry, 1908-12*. Columbia: University of South Carolina Press, 1973.
While little of Chandler's apprentice work is very good, it does demonstrate that the ideas and manner of the detective novels will be found in the early work. Bruccoli collects poetry, essays, and sketches, as well as book reviews originally published in England, and adds brief critical notes. Foreword by Jacques Barzun.

Chandler, Raymond. *The Notebooks of Raymond Chandler and English Summer: A Gothic Romance*. Edited by Frank MacShane. New York: Ecco Press, 1976.
In common with other writers, Chandler kept a series of notebooks in which he recorded daily events, progress on his work, private thoughts, and observations. Only two of these survive, and selected portions have been collected by MacShane. Includes "Twelve Notes on the Mystery Story" and a short story that Chandler intended to expand to novel length. Illustrated with facsimile pages from his notebooks.

_____ . *Raymond Chandler Speaking*. Edited by Dorothy Gardiner and Katherine Sorley Walker. Boston: Houghton Mifflin, 1962.
A collection of letters and articles by Chandler in which he speaks his mind about the world of writing, mystery novels, films, publishing, famous crimes, and cats. Chandler's correspondents were publishers, editors, and other writers. Includes the first four chapters of the unfinished Philip Marlowe novel "The Poodle Springs Story." Illustrated with five photographs. Indexed.

_____ . *Selected Letters of Raymond Chandler*. Edited by Frank Mac-Shane. New York: Columbia University Press, 1981.
Having established himself as a serious writer, Chandler "turned to letter writing as a means of communicating" with the outside world when he could not sleep. MacShane explains that Chandler's correspondents were mostly publishers, agents, magazine editors, or professional critics of crime fiction, seldom other writers. His topics included "his childhood in England, the position of the writer in Hollywood, his current reading, what it takes to be a novelist, or the mores of southern California." Letters written from 1937 to 1959 are included.

Gilbert, Michael. "Autumn in London." In *The World of Raymond Chandler*, edited by Miriam Gross. New York: A & W Publishers, 1978.

An account of three visits Chandler made to England between 1955 and 1958 and five years of correspondence and friendship with Gilbert, his solicitor. Gilbert includes excerpts from the letters and relates anecdotes about Chandler's tax problems and his longing to move to England "without being disastrously shattered by taxes and so forth."

Gross, Miriam, ed. *The World of Raymond Chandler*. New York: A & W Publishers, 1978.
Fourteen articles by scholars and associates of Raymond Chandler examine his life and his literary career and discuss the paradoxes in his character: the mixture of toughness and sentimentality and the mastery of the hard-boiled style combined with his romanticism. Lavishly illustrated with photographs of Chandler and scenes from films based on his work. Most of the essays are listed individually in this bibliography.

Homberger, Eric. "The Man of Letters (1908-1912)." In *The World of Raymond Chandler*, edited by Miriam Gross. New York: A & W Publishers, 1978.
Since little is known about Chandler's years in England and since he is not mentioned in chronicles of the times, one can only speculate about that period in his life. Based on Chandler's early writings (1908-1912) and the intellectual climate of the day, Homberger indicates what life for a reviewer and essayist might have been. Suggests that Chandler transferred the world of literary culture he left behind him in England to the dialogue in his Philip Marlowe stories.

Lambert, Gavin. "A Private Eye: Raymond Chandler." In his *The Dangerous Edge*. London: Barrie & Jenkins, 1975.
Chandler was "a quiet man who loved cats and idealized his motherly wife," according to Lambert. Under her protection, he could imagine Philip Marlowe, a man who walked the mean streets unprotected. Marlowe was Chandler's opposite and idealized self. Biographical details and analysis of the major short stories and novels.

MacShane, Frank. *The Life of Raymond Chandler*. New York: E. P. Dutton, 1976.
Rather than dealing with Chandler as a writer of detective stories in the context of the popular fiction of his day, MacShane treats him as a mainstream novelist, Chandler's own view of himself. A liberal use of Chandler's letters allows the author to tell his own story. Includes a basic checklist of Chandler's writings according to the dates of the original publication as book or magazine story. Illustrated. Index.

Marling, William. *Raymond Chandler*. New York: Twayne, 1986.
According to Marling, Chandler's perspective enabled him to push the limits

of the detective story further than anyone could have imagined. "A poet in his youth, he introduced style into the genre and showed, as poets know, that metaphor is an expression of mythic impulse." Covers Chandler's life and the history of detective fiction and of the pulp magazines. Examines his short fiction and novels but omits discussion of his screenplays. Selected bibliography and index.

Norman, Frank. "Friend and Mentor." In *The World of Raymond Chandler*, edited by Miriam Gross. New York: A & W Publishers, 1978.
A personal account. It was Natasha and Stephen Spender who arranged for Chandler to meet Frank Norman, author of the prison memoir *Bang to Rights* in 1958. Never completely sober during their brief friendship, Chandler was impressed by the way Norman argued with the waiter at the Café Royale and the fact that Norman's writing lacked "damned literary nonsense."

Powell, Dilys. "Ray and Cissy." In *The World of Raymond Chandler*, edited by Miriam Gross. New York: A & W Publishers, 1978.
Meeting Chandler at a party after having read his books with pleasure, Powell found him to be on the defensive, partly from a belief that the English citizens he encountered might look down on him, partly on behalf of his wife, whom he believed he needed to protect. Powell suggests that Cissy Chandler lived on in the image Chandler created of her, "the adored creature to be consulted, encouraged, constantly and proudly displayed."

Commentary

Barzun, Jacques. "The Illusion of the Real." In *The World of Raymond Chandler*, edited by Miriam Gross. New York: A & W Publishers, 1978.
In his famous essay, "The Simple Art of Murder," Chandler claimed that literature dealt mostly with reality but failed to define what he meant by realism. According to Barzun, Chandler's type of story is no more "real" than the gentle, classical form, and his statements about Philip Marlowe, the true hero-detective, reveal him to be a "sentimental tale-spinner."

Binyon, T. J. "A Lasting Influence?" In *The World of Raymond Chandler*, edited by Miriam Gross. New York: A & W Publishers, 1978.
While there is a superficial similarity between Chandler's novels and the typical private-eye novel, the only real connection Binyon sees is their use of his advice on plotting. Discusses Thomas B. Dewey, Harold Q. Masur, William Campbell Gault, Ross Macdonald, John D. MacDonald, Peter Israel, Andrew Bergmann, and Robert B. Parker as exercises in Chandler pastiche.

Bruccoli, Matthew J. "Afterword: Raymond Chandler and Hollywood." In *The Blue Dahlia*, by Raymond Chandler. Carbondale: Southern Illinois University Press, 1976.
Chandler earned a considerable amount of money while on the payrolls of Paramount Pictures, Warner Bros., Metro-Goldwyn-Mayer, and Universal studios, but was uncomfortable working under their "mandatory collaborative system." Bruccoli discusses Chandler's own scripts as well as the attempts by others to film his novels. He was not proud of *The Blue Dahlia*, in spite of the success the film enjoyed.

Cawelti, John. "Hammett, Chandler, and Spillane." In *Adventure, Mystery and Romance: Formula Stories as Art and Popular Culture*. Chicago: University of Chicago Press, 1976.
Cawelti notes that in *Farewell, My Lovely* (1940) Chandler uses the detective-story formula to deal with themes such as "romantic illusion," "destructive innocence," and "the conflict between individual moral feeling and the collective routines of society." According to Cawelti, Chandler's characters achieve depth because his themes are serious and Philip Marlowe is believable because of the serious significance and human complexity of many of the characters he meets.

Davies, Russell. "Omnes Me Impune Lacessunt." In *The World of Raymond Chandler*, edited by Miriam Gross. New York: A & W Publishers, 1978.
Davies thinks that Philip Marlowe is not a "hyperactive hero," but that it is difficult to explain how he can be distinguished from other private eyes in fiction; Chandler's verbal gymnastics are not enough of an explanation. His combination of "soul-baring" and "reticence," with the latter triumphing, make him the interesting figure he is. Davies considers "English Summer" as an example of what Chandler's writing would be like without Philip Marlowe.

Durham, Philip. *Down These Mean Streets a Man Must Go: Raymond Chandler's Knight*. Chapel Hill: University of North Carolina Press, 1963.
Durham believes that Raymond Chandler's role in developing the "objective technique" in American literature is significant. A romantic in a world of unrelieved violence, Chandler wrote in a genre in which love had no place. Includes a biographical chapter. Discusses the short stories for *Black Mask*, the early novels, a portrait of Los Angeles as Chandler saw it, the screenwriting, Philip Marlowe's development as hero, and Chandler's technique as a writer. Bibliography includes reviews of Chandler's works. Checklist of Chandler's titles through 1962, including paperback and foreign-language editions.

Eames, Hugh. "Philip Marlowe—Raymond Chandler." In his *Sleuths, Inc.: Studies of Problem Solvers*. Philadelphia: J. B. Lippincott, 1978.

The difficulties Philip Marlowe encounters are part of his "own special problem: his compulsion, unvoiced but always there, to be a decent human being."
Eames gives a brief historical survey of Los Angeles and the Los Angeles
Police Department with reference to Joseph Wambaugh's 1975 novel, *The
Choirboys*, as a source. Notes that Marlowe is able to solve the problems of
other people but never his own. Contrasts Marlowe with Sherlock Holmes and
pays some attention to details of Chandler's life.

Houseman, John. "Lost Fortnight." In *The World of Raymond Chandler*, edited by
Miriam Gross. New York: A & W Publishers, 1978.
When Paramount Pictures needed a film for Alan Ladd to star in, Chandler
obliged by turning a half-completed novel into *The Blue Dahlia* (1946). Houseman, the producer of the film, explains that, in spite of not having an ending to
the story at a crucial point in its composition, Chandler completed the job, the
film was completed ahead of time, and the studio made a considerable amount
of money. Houseman and Chandler remained friends for thirteen years.

James, Clive. "The Country Behind the Hill." In *The World of Raymond Chandler*,
edited by Miriam Gross. New York: A & W Publishers, 1978.
James discusses Chandler's style, from the "overcooked metaphors" to his
knack for slang and the quiet effects that succeed in presenting the dialogue
inside Philip Marlowe's head. Chandler continued to refine his technique,
mainly through Marlowe's personality. He is at his best in *The Lady in the
Lake* (1943), but even in *Playback* (1958) there are moments worth appre-
ciating.

Knight, Stephen. " '. . . a hard-boiled gentleman'—Raymond Chandler's Hero."
In his *Form and Ideology in Crime Fiction*. Bloomington: Indiana University
Press, 1980.
Knight contrasts Chandler to Dashiell Hammett. Hammett avoided formula
writing while Chandler created a constant hero with a more uniform direction.
The patterns that shaped the meanings in his texts were repeated in both form
and content, a classic example of the way illusion operates in popular fiction.
Chandler believed that style was the main method of raising crime fiction to an
artistic level. Analyzes *Farewell, My Lovely* (1940) and notes how Chandler's
short stories were utilized in his novels.

Luhr, William. *Raymond Chandler and Film*. New York: Frederick Ungar, 1982.
Examines Chandler's influence upon the film style known as *film noir* and
those trends in the film industry that made that style possible. Describes
Chandler's years in Hollywood, his "turbulent relationship" with the studios
and with Billy Wilder, John Houseman, and Alfred Hitchcock. Analyzes
Chandler's own screenplays and the films based on his fiction. Illustrated with
a filmography and a selected bibliography.

Mason, Michael. "Marlowe, Men, and Women." In *The World of Raymond Chandler*, edited by Miriam Gross. New York: A & W Publishers, 1978.
Discusses Philip Marlowe's character. The general effect of Chandler's ambivalence about Marlowe's relationship with women is that the novels are not as clear about good and evil as the author claimed. The women in the Marlowe novels are homicidal; the men are likable (even Moose Malloy in *Farewell, My Lovely*). Warning: The murderer in each novel is identified.

Moffat, Ivan. "On the Fourth Floor of Paramount: Interview with Billy Wilder." In *The World of Raymond Chandler*, edited by Miriam Gross. New York: A & W Publishers, 1978.
Chandler worked with director Billy Wilder, on the script for the film of James M. Cain's *Double Indemnity*. While their relationship was strained, they worked well together. Wilder believes that the experience with screenwriting spoiled Chandler for the lonely life of writing novels. He thinks that Chandler's novels were not as well plotted as Dashiell Hammett's but that there was "a kind of lightning" on every page.

Parker, Robert B. Introduction to *Raymond Chandler's Unknown Thriller: The Screenplay of "Playback."* New York: Mysterious Press, 1985.
A biographical sketch precedes a discussion of the difficulties Chandler had in turning his screenplay *Playback* into a Philip Marlowe novel. By using Marlowe as narrator—"a frame defined by the sardonic and sentimental first-person narrator"—he had to abandon most of the original story. Parker finds that this study of one of Chandler's failures helps readers appreciate all the more the technique that went into his more successful work.

Pepper, James. Preface to *Raymond Chandler's Unknown Thriller: The Screenplay of "Playback."* New York: Mysterious Press, 1985.
Pepper describes how, in 1947, Chandler's original story editor at Paramount Pictures and later executive producer at Universal-International arranged for him to write an original screenplay at a salary of four thousand dollars per week. Chandler wrote *Playback* with deliberate care, but the project had to be canceled due to financial considerations. The original draft in the Raymond Chandler Archive, University of California at Los Angeles, has now been supplemented by this final, superior draft found in the Universal studio archives.

Ruhm, Herbert. "Raymond Chandler: From Bloomsbury and the Jungle—and Beyond." In *Tough Guy Writers of the Thirties*, edited by David Madden. Carbondale: Southern Illinois University Press, 1968.
Ruhm explains how Chandler mastered the American idiom of slang, wisecrack, and hyperbole, and used it to describe the world of urban California

with wit and vigor. His masterpieces are *Farewell, My Lovely* (1940) and *The Little Sister* (1949), but in *The Long Goodbye* (1953) he wrote a novel of character and came closest to his goal of a realistic novel with murders. Ruhm considers Chandler's image of America to be the image of the last frontier.

Skenazy, Paul. *The New Wild West: The Urban Mysteries of Dashiell Hammett and Raymond Chandler*. Boise, Idaho: Boise State University Press, 1982.
Skenazy considers Chandler's major contributions to the American detective story to be his subverting reality to the romantic quest and his developing "a tone of weariness highlighted by the shocking simile." Chandler's use of titles and the names of characters to indicate the underlying medieval romantic tradition is contrasted with Dashiell Hammett's materialism. Discusses the significance of the emphasis on perception in Chandler.

Speir, Jerry. *Raymond Chandler*. New York: Frederick Ungar, 1981.
An overview of Chandler's life and work. Chapter 1 is a brief biography; chapters 2 through 4 cover the seven Philip Marlowe novels in the order of their publication. Chapter 5 examines the short stories and how they contain the raw material of the novels. Chapter 6 discusses Marlowe; chapter 7 covers Chandler's style. The final chapter attempts to understand the author's "black vision" of a "perverse world." Bibliography, index.

Spender, Natasha. "His Own Long Goodbye." In *The World of Raymond Chandler*, edited by Miriam Gross. New York: A & W Publishers, 1978.
Spender describes Chandler's last years, when his wife was dying: his alcoholism, his depression, and his suicide attempts. She notes that *The Long Goodbye* (1953) contains self-portraits of Chandler in Terry Lomax, Roger Wade, and Philip Marlowe himself. Chandler's childhood legacy of "Victorian values" was never eliminated, only altered, by changes in his environment. A tough stance was the only defense against corruption.

Symons, Julian. "An Aesthete Discovers the Pulps." In *The World of Raymond Chandler*, edited by Miriam Gross. New York: A & W Publishers, 1978.
Symons suggests that Chandler was by temperament a romantic aesthete, who sometimes overstated his claims for the type of detective story he chose to write. Had he not decided to treat the form as seriously as possible, he could never have justified writing detective fiction at all. The pulps shaped him, but the novels allowed him the freedom to develop and to express himself.

Thomson, James W. "Murder with Honor: Raymond Chandler." *The New Republic* 179 (July 22, 1978): 28-31.
Thomson contrasts Chandler's technique with that of Dashiell Hammett. While Hammett perfected the first-person objective narrative technique for his

stories, in which the neutral observer sees and records actions but makes no attempt to interpret, Chandler chose to concentrate more on character than on violence. Philip Marlowe faces death regularly but never becomes calloused by the frequency of the encounter. Suggests that the bitterness in the later novels reflects changes in Chandler's own life.

Wolfe, Peter. *Something More Than Night: The Case of Raymond Chandler*. Bowling Green, Ohio: Bowling Green University Popular Press, 1985.
Wolfe notes that Chandler's "lack of staying power" weakened individual works as well as his entire writing career, yet he has become a classic by depicting with immaculately crafted sentences a hero who "moves in a corrupt, brutal world armed only with his code of honor." Detailed analysis of Philip Marlowe as hero, the California setting, the short stories, and the seven novels. Wolfe weaves what others have said of Chandler into a general overview of critical attention. Bibliographic notes. No index.

LESLIE CHARTERIS
(Leslie Charles Bowyer Yin)

Biography

"Leslie Charteris." In *Twentieth Century Authors*, edited by Stanley J. Kunitz and Howard Haycraft. New York: H. W. Wilson, 1942.

An autobiographical statement by Leslie Charteris commenting on the variety of experiences that went into the writing of the Saint stories as well as some of the more personal aspects of his life up to the 1940's. Brief assessment by the editors of Charteris' work and an expansion on some personal details of his life. Selected list of his works through 1942 with brief references to magazine articles about him. Includes a photograph of Charteris.

"Leslie Charteris." In *Twentieth Century Authors: First Supplement*, edited by Stanley J. Kunitz. New York: H. W. Wilson, 1955.

A response and corrections by Leslie Charteris to the account of his life and career that appeared in the 1942 edition of *Twentieth Century Authors*. Brings the record up to date on his marriages and divorces. Notes plans for future episodes in the career of the Saint. Selected list of titles in the Saint series from 1943 to 1955.

Lofts, W. O. G., and Derek Adley. *The Saint and Leslie Charteris*. Bowling Green, Ohio: Bowling Green University Popular Press, 1972.

A biography of Charteris that concerns primarily those aspects of his life regarding his writing of the Saint stories. Chapters devoted to the television series featuring Roger Moore, Charteris' correspondence, the collection of his papers at Boston University, and the commercialization of the character in comics, bubble-gum cards, and jigsaw puzzles. Bibliography of Charteris' work in book and periodical appearances. No index.

Lundin, Bo. "Leslie Charteris." In *Twentieth Century Crime and Mystery Writers*, edited by John M. Reilly. New York: St. Martin's Press, 1980.

A brief catalog of personal details of Charteris' life along with some facts of his literary career, followed by an extensive checklist of crime novels, collections of short stories, screenplays, and other publications. Concludes with approximately one thousand words of commentary assessing Charteris' place in crime fiction.

Commentary

Adrian, Jack. Introduction to *The Saint in New York*, by Leslie Charteris. London: J. M. Dent, 1984.

Adrian discusses Charteris' early development as a writer and his borrowing of melodramatic paraphernalia from Edgar Wallace, light dialogue from Dornford Yates, geniality and brutality from Sapper, later acquiring his own pace, action, color, and enthusiasm. *The Saint in New York* (1935) was his first full-length novel designed as a novel, and not a reconstruction from three novelettes published originally in *The Thriller*. In it, Charteris achieved his own style and stopped imitating others.

Butler, William Vivian. *The Durable Desperadoes*. London: Macmillan, 1973.
After a number of false starts with novels featuring other characters, Charteris created Simon Templar, and the editor of a British weekly *(The Thriller)* hired him to write a regular series of novelettes about the character. Butler notes changes in the character from the earliest stories to those in *The Thriller*, down to the "Anglo-American" Saint that appeared when Charteris was living in the United States and the figure in the stories written just prior to the beginning of the television series. Suggests at least four variations and discusses the stories.

Charteris, Leslie. "The Saint." In *Meet the Detective*, compiled by Cecil Madden. New York: Telegraph Press, 1935.
A lighthearted account of the possible origin of the Saint in the stickfigures Charteris used to illustrate a serial in a magazine he produced for his parents when he was ten years old. A self-directed study of burglary while he was a law student at Cambridge led to Charteris' writing his first novel. The Saint, he believes, is not a detective but an adventurer who enjoys the adventure and believes in romance.

DelFattore, Joan. "Leslie Charteris." In *Dictionary of Literary Biography*, edited by Bernard Benstock and Thomas F. Staley, vol. 77. Detroit: Gale Research, 1988.
Surveys Charteris' career as a writer, discussing his early work in some detail and noting the development of Simon Templar into a major crime-fiction hero. Traces changes in style and substance in the series from 1928 to 1971. Comments on film and television adaptations and briefly discusses Charteris' own revisions of adaptations by others of the television scripts for book publication. Bibliography of book publications, 1927-1972. Illustrations.

Shibuk, Charles. "Notes on Very Early Leslie Charteris." *The Armchair Detective* 4 (July, 1971): 230-231.
Describes the editorial contents and physical appearance of *The Thriller*, a British weekly with the subtitle *The Paper with a Thousand Thrills*. Annotated bibliography of eleven novelettes by Leslie Charteris from the magazine, with corresponding data on book publication in the Saint saga. An additional nine stories are listed in *The Armchair Detective* letter columns in the issues for January, 1972, and April, 1972.

Watson, Colin. "With Thy Quire of Saints for Evermore . . ." In his *Snobbery with Violence: Crime Stories and Their Audience*. London: Eyre & Spottiswoode, 1971. Reprint. New York: Mysterious Press, 1988.

Watson suggests that since, as a character, the Saint has appeared in so many stories over such a span of time, he can be used as a subject for studying changes in popular tastes, contrasting the qualities considered heroic by a mass audience in 1930 and those considered heroic today. The early Simon Templar was interchangeable with Bulldog Drummond; the later Simon Templar is more liberal and less homicidal.

G. K. CHESTERTON

Biography

Barker, Dudley. *G. K. Chesterton: A Biography*. New York: Stein & Day, 1973.
A brief, readable biography scrupulously fair to its subject, but considered by some critics to be unconvincing in its presentation of new evidence to explain Chesterton's nervous collapse as a student. Briefly discusses the Father Brown stories, which Barker believes deteriorate in quality as the character changes from a simple, intuitive priest to a deductive detective and mouthpiece for Chesterton's social and religious views. The central idea for each story remains sound even so. Brief checklist of titles. Index.

Chesterton, G. K. *The Autobiography of G. K. Chesterton*. New York: Sheed & Ward, 1936.
Posthumously published, Chesterton's account of his own life pays little attention to the people and events around him, concentrating instead on his opinions. The material is arranged thematically instead of chronologically. As such Chesterton barely touches on his own writings until the final chapter, when he discusses the significance of having a detective like Father Brown seem so featureless.

——————— . "A Defense of Detective Stories." In *The Art of the Mystery Story*, edited by Howard Haycraft. New York: Simon & Schuster, 1947. Reprint. New York: Grosset & Dunlap, 1961.
Probably the earliest serious application of the critical method to the detective story. Chesterton sees it as a legitimate form of art and as an expression of some of the "poetry of modern life," with civilization as a form of rebellion and the policeman as an agent of social justice.

Dale, Alzina Stone. *The Outline of Sanity: A Biography of G. K. Chesterton*. Grand Rapids, Mich.: Wm. B. Eerdmans, 1982.
A corrective to the biographers who place too much emphasis on Cecil Chesterton's 1908 account of his brother's life and opinions. Dale considers Father Brown to have brought lasting fame to Chesterton by preserving the author's personality and ideas in those "moral concerns told like fairy tales." The stories represent Chesterton at his most characteristic and present his "conviction that God comes to man, not man to God." Critics disagree on the value of Dale's book.

Ffinch, Michael. *G. K. Chesterton*. San Francisco: Harper & Row, 1986.
A thematic, rather than chronological, account of Chesterton's life and work.

Chesterton himself considered the Father Brown stories as potboilers, written for the money they earned. The first story, "The Blue Cross," may well be the best, but "The Invisible Man" has provoked the most comment. "The point of Father Brown was that he should appear pointless, . . ." and, in that, Ffinch echoes Chesterton. Illustrated. Selected list of works. Index.

Leitch, Thomas M. "G. K. Chesterton." In *Dictionary of Literary Biography*, edited by Bernard Benstock and Thomas F. Staley, vol. 70. Detroit: Gale Research, 1988.
Even if Chesterton had not created Father Brown, his detective stories would stand as significant in the historical development of the genre. He insisted on the "conceptual unity of the form" and that the secret should always be a simple one. Leitch discusses Chesterton's essays on detective fiction and briefly covers the Father Brown stories as well as most of his other detective fiction. Brief biographical details. Bibliography. Illustrations.

Ward, Maisie. *Gilbert Keith Chesterton*. New York: Sheed & Ward, 1943.
Possibly the definitive biography, this book covers Chesterton's childhood, schooldays, friendships, theological developments, family life, and editing and writing careers. Contains the text of many of his letters. His Father Brown stories are discussed only briefly. His contribution to the genre was in creating detection "in which the mind of a man means more than his footprints or cigar ash, even to the detective." Illustrated. Bibliography. Index.

Commentary

Conlon, D. J., ed. *G. K. Chesterton: A Half Century of Views*. New York: Oxford University Press, 1987.
More than fifty writers comment on the public and private life of G. K. Chesterton in this anthology of essays. Chesterton had an "ability to appreciate the obvious" and to point out to others what they had missed. His was a multifaceted personality that needs refocussing to be appreciated. Only those essays on the Father Brown stories are listed in this bibliography.

Gardner, Martin. Introduction to *The Annotated Innocence of Father Brown*, by G. K. Chesterton. New York: Oxford University Press, 1987.
Contrasts Father Brown with the hard-boiled school of detective fiction; the latter appears to have replaced fantasy with reality, while the former retains it. Parallels between Father Brown and Sherlock Holmes are drawn by Gardner (Father Brown's Dr. John Watson is Flambeau), who predicts that Chesterton's stature as writer and thinker will only increase.

Haycraft, Howard. "England: 1890-1914 (The Romantic Era)." In his *Murder for Pleasure: The Life and Times of the Detective Story.* New York: D. Appleton-Century, 1941.

Chesterton created one of the most famous detective characters, Father Brown, and put him in stories that are not really detective stories. By deductive standards, Haycraft contends, they are failures, since Father Brown achieves his results by instinct. Haycraft's assessment is that Chesterton's chief contribution may be in perfecting the metaphysical detective story.

Hollis, Christopher. *G. K. Chesterton.* New York: Longmans, Green, 1954.

A brief survey of Chesterton as a writer. According to Hollis, it is Father Brown's character that impresses readers. His method of detection is psychological or theological, and many of the plots of the stories "turn on characteristically Chestertonian criticisms of the modern world." The critics who think that he uses word tricks merely to show off do not understand the nature of the paradox as Chesterton sees it.

Hynes, Samuel. "A Detective and His God: G. K. Chesterton." *The New Republic* 190 (February 6, 1984): 39, 41-42.

Chesterton may have created Father Brown as a sort of literary joke, an anti-Holmes, according to Hynes, but soon came to recognize the implication of having a priest as a detective to express God's law against God's enemies. Discusses the "nightmare of meaninglessness" that is at the center of the stories. (Review of *The Father Brown Omnibus*, 1983; *The Penguin Complete Father Brown*, 1981; and *The Outline of Sanity*, 1982; a biography of G. K. Chesterton, by A. S. Dale.)

Knox, Ronald. "Chesterton's Father Brown." In *Chesterton: A Half Century of Views*, edited by D. J. Conlon. New York: Oxford University Press, 1987.

Knox, a detective-story writer himself, sees that Father Brown possesses no expert knowledge of arcane matters beyond that of the human heart. He does not see things as a psychologist, but as a moralist. Discusses and disputes the charges that the stories are improbable and judges them by the canons of the detective art to demonstrate that they are more than detective stories: They are a Chesterton manifesto.

Lambert, Gavin. "Final Problems. G. K. Chesterton." In his *The Dangerous Edge*. London: Barrie & Jenkins, 1975.

Lambert notes that bold, theatrical acts in Chesterton's life were a mask for his extreme nervous tension. The toy theater of the author's childhood is the key to the atmosphere of his detective stories, all artificially devised with the real world distorted into ominous shapes and shadows. Discusses reasons that the Father Brown stories never develop into a cohesive whole like the Sherlock Holmes cycle.

Lowndes, R. A. W. "G. K. Chesterton's Father Brown." *The Armchair Detective* 9 (June, 1976): 184-188, 235.

Discusses the creation of Father Brown when Chesterton met Father (later Monsignor) John O'Connor and discussed their opposing views on vice and crime. Lowndes scrutinizes "The Blue Cross" closely and surveys the rest of the series in a sweeping overview. Suggests that the appeal of Father Brown lies in how the stories relate to general motivation and behavior. They may be heavy in paradox, but this tests the wits and stimulates thoughts about appearance and reality.

Porter, Thomas E. "Gilbert Keith Chesterton." In *Twelve Englishmen of Mystery*, edited by Earl F. Bargainnier. Bowling Green, Ohio: Bowling Green University Popular Press, 1984.

Porter explains how Chesterton's adaptation of the detective formula emphasizes the personal qualities of his hero, Father Brown. Discusses the qualities represented in the titles of the Father Brown series (*The Innocence of Father Brown*, 1911; *The Wisdom of Father Brown*, 1914; and *The Incredulity of Father Brown*, 1926) and how innocence, wisdom, and incredulity are represented in the stories themselves. Discusses Father Brown's character and the tales as parables.

Price, R. G. G. "A Check-up on Chesterton's Detective." In *G. K. Chesterton: A Half Century of Views*, edited by D. J. Conlon. New York: Oxford University Press, 1987.

A lighthearted account of Father Brown's life and personality compiled by Price from a reading of some fifty Father Brown stories. Specific details about his educational background, ecclesiastical appointments, and relationship with the police are given. Father Brown was born in Essex and had a sister whose daughter was named Elizabeth Fane. Speculates about the date of "The Mistake of the Machine."

Robson, W. W. "Father Brown and Others." In *G. K. Chesterton: A Centenary Appraisal*, edited by John Sullivan. New York: Barnes & Noble Books, 1974.

Robson believes that the Father Brown stories deserve to be taken seriously. Many are variations on Edgar Allan Poe's "The Purloined Letter," but they share the characteristics of imagination and moral seriousness with Charles Dickens' *The Mystery of Edwin Drood* (1870). Believes that Father Brown's secret is being able to identify with the murderer; thus, he is true to traditional theology as well as to the detective-story tradition.

Routley, Erik. "The Fairy Tale and the Secret." In his *The Puritan Pleasures of the Detective Story*. London: Victor Gollancz, 1972.

An analysis of the Father Brown stories, but this time with the emphasis placed on the unusual attitude toward violence found in them. Routley thinks that Chesterton raises such awkward questions in his stories that it is impossible to dismiss them as being trivial examples of the writer's art.

_____ . "The Mystery of Iniquity." In his *The Puritan Pleasures of the Detective Story*. London: Victor Gollancz, 1972.
Routley describes Father Brown as the first detective character produced by an author who had already established himself as a man of letters. Discusses the presence of moralism in the stories, which is that of the common man and not that of the sophisticated theologian. Discusses several stories and reveals some of their solutions.

Sullivan, John, ed. *G. K. Chesterton: A Centenary Appraisal*. New York: Barnes & Noble Books, 1974.
On the occasion of the centennial of Chesterton's birth, John Sullivan, his official bibliographer, collects essays by writers, scholars, and personal acquaintances, which survey his work in general, but particularly his fiction and his verse. They focus on his personality, the relationship between art and propaganda, his achievement, and his influence overseas.

Symons, Julian. "The Short Story: The First Golden Age." In his *Bloody Murder: From the Detective Story to the Crime Novel, a History*. Rev. ed. New York: Viking Press, 1985.
Chesterton's essential view of the detective story, that it expressed the poetry of city life, is found in his essay "A Defense of Detective Stories," according to Symons. In spite of having written other detective stories, Chesterton's reputation rests on the Father Brown collections. At his best, his stories contain a paradox about the nature of man and the way that reality appears to be fantasy.

Ward, Maisie. *Return to Chesterton*. New York: Sheed & Ward, 1952.
Not so much a new biography or commentary of Chesterton as a supplement to Ward's 1943 biography, *Gilbert Keith Chesterson*. Includes unpublished letters, verses, and other works of Chesterton, long and short, as well as memories and anecdotes of those who knew him. Discusses the origins of Father Brown.

Wills, Garry. "Pattern in Pantomime." In his *Chesterton, Man and Mask*. New York: Sheed & Ward, 1961.
Chesterton may have denigrated the detective story in 1900, but he came to its support later in his own stories. Wills suggests that the Father Brown stories eventually came to revolve about the idea of humility as the root of knowledge, which is not so much theology as common sense. Chesterton's clues are really symbols, and the moral significance in the tales prevent the anticlimax found in the usual detective novel.

AGATHA CHRISTIE
(Agatha Mary Clarissa Mallowan)

Biography

Christie, Agatha. *An Autobiography.* New York: Dodd, Mead, 1977.
Begun in 1950, this autobiography was completed some fifteen years later. Not a strictly chronological arrangement, it presents what Christie wanted to remember of a life lived the way she wanted to live it and in a world she remembered the way she wanted it to be. Does not refer to her famous disappearance of 1926 but does include information on her writing and her characters. Illustrated. Indexed.

_____ . *Come, Tell Me How You Live.* New York: Dodd, Mead, 1974.
Originally published in 1946, this is an account of Agatha Christie's experiences while accompanying her archaeologist husband in Iraq and Syria. Anecdotes cover how to pack for such travels and the people they met. Comments on six thousand years of an unchanging way of life in the Middle East. Begun before World War II, the account was revised during the four years spent in wartime London. No references to her writing. Illustrated with photographs taken in the Middle East.

Gilbert, Michael. "A Very English Lady." In *Agatha Christie: First Lady of Crime*, edited by H. R. F. Keating. New York: Holt, Rinehart and Winston, 1977.
A well-illustrated biographical sketch of Agatha Christie that analyzes the more exciting aspects of what must have seemed on the surface a most uneventful life—her mysterious disappearance in 1926 and her travels with her archaeologist husband, Max Mallowan. Gilbert considers unfounded the charge that her disappearance was a publicity stunt.

Hughes, Dorothy B. "The Christie Nobody Knew." In *Agatha Christie: First Lady of Crime*, edited by H. R. F. Keating. New York: Holt, Rinehart and Winston, 1977.
Hughes examines the six novels Christie wrote under the pseudonym Mary Westmacott and discusses her reasons for writing them. According to Hughes, some of the best of her writing is contained in the Westmacott novels. In them, Christie tried to understand herself and her world. Beginning with *Unfinished Portrait* (1934) they are her fictionalized autobiography.

Mallowan, Max. *Mallowan's Memoirs.* New York: Dodd, Mead, 1977.
The autobiography of archaeologist Max Mallowan, Agatha Christie's second husband. Briefly discusses Christie the person, their life together, her books

(with some comments on the Westmacott novels), in which she expressed the "supreme art of telling a story," and her plays. Considers the psychology and insight into human nature she put into her books to have the most appeal for Agatha Christie's readers.

Morgan, Janet. *Agatha Christie: A Biography*. New York: Alfred A. Knopf, 1985.
The authorized biography, based on Christie's correspondence, manuscripts, "plotting books," photograph albums, scrapbooks, diaries, address books, receipts, and accounts as well as on interviews with members of her family, her friends, and her acquaintances. Discusses how she developed her ideas and examines the reasons for her appeal. No bibliography or notes. Illustrated with photographs, some of which are unique to this book. Indexed.

Murdoch, Derrick. *The Agatha Christie Mystery*. Toronto: Pagurian Press, 1976.
Murdoch looks for clues to Christie's popularity and success in her private life, the way she constructed her mystery stories and her other writing. Against a background of the literary traditions of the detective story and its critics, he suggests that part of her secret was in her ability to write what the majority of her readers wanted to read—a good puzzle, with some humor, a real surprise, and the reassurance that everything would end all right. Illustrated with scenes from motion pictures based on her work. Indexed.

Osborne, Charles. *The Life and Crimes of Agatha Christie*. New York: Holt, Rinehart and Winston, 1983.
A chronological publishing history of Agatha Christie's books, mysteries, and nonmysteries, set against a background of her life. The circumstances under which each book was conceived, written, and published is followed by a description of the book and how it was received by the critics when it was published. Secondary sources are cited and illustrations duplicate few found in other works on Christie.

Robyns, Gwen. *The Mystery of Agatha Christie*. Garden City, N.Y.: Doubleday, 1978.
This biography of Christie concentrates on her life and character without critical assessment of her writing. Based on interviews and contemporary newspaper accounts. Robyns covers the 1926 disappearance more thoroughly than any other account to date. Thirty-two pages of photographs. Index. Notes that Christie's own character remained unaffected by the brief periods of trouble in her life.

Commentary

Allen, L. David. *"The Murder of Roger Ackroyd."* In his *Detective in Fiction*. Lincoln, Nebr.: Cliffs Notes, 1978.

A plot summary of one of Agatha Christie's most interesting, intriguing, and successful novels, with critical comments. Controversial when it was published in 1926, *The Murder of Roger Ackroyd* remains controversial over whether Christie played fair and gave the reader all the clues required to solve the mystery. Allen thinks that the false clues are there in abundance and the task set for the reader is not easy, but the necessary details are plausibly presented.

—————— . *"What Mrs. McGillicuddy Saw!."* In his *Detective in Fiction*. Lincoln, Nebr.: Cliffs Notes, 1978.
A detailed plot summary. Allen thinks that the reader may find difficulty determining just who the murderer is before the solution is revealed at the end, because the physical evidence is downplayed. *What Mrs. McGillicuddy Saw!* (1957; British title: *4.50 from Paddington*) is considered by Allen to be one of the best Jane Marple books.

Bargainnier, Earl F. *The Gentle Art of Murder: The Detective Fiction of Agatha Christie*. Bowling Green, Ohio: Bowling Green University Popular Press, 1981.
Bargainnier presents a literary analysis of Agatha Christie's detective fiction so that readers may better appreciate her skill. Background material on the detective story is followed by chapters on her settings, characters, plots, devices, and themes. The whole is summed up in a chapter on her achievement. Includes notes, a bibliography, and an index of characters, novels, and short-story titles.

Barnard, Robert. *A Talent to Deceive: An Appreciation of Agatha Christie*. New York: Dodd, Mead, 1980. Rev. ed. New York: Mysterious Press, 1987.
A thorough, serious attempt to explain the popularity and success of Agatha Christie. Barnard believes that it is a mistake to discuss the detective story itself, and her work in particular, in the same manner that one studies the mainstream novel. She is a teller of popular tales and should be judged accordingly. Good comprehensive bibliography and short-story index with an annotated list of full-length works. Annotations are evaluative, with no unnecessary detail.

Brand, Christianna. "Miss Marple—a Portrait." In *Agatha Christie: First Lady of Crime*, edited by H. R. F. Keating. New York: Holt, Rinehart and Winston, 1977.
A character sketch of Miss Jane Marple, created (according to Brand) as the very antithesis of Hercule Poirot. Poirot is a show-off, while Miss Marple is modest but has confidence in her own ability. The frailties of old age—failing eyesight, increasing deafness, rheumatism, and arthritis—do not deter her in her adventures.

Crispin, Edmund. "The Mistress of Simplicity." In *Agatha Christie: First Lady of Crime*, edited by H. R. F. Keating. New York: Holt, Rinehart and Winston, 1977.
Crispin is interviewed by Keating. Christie's plots, he believes, were highly sophisticated, not in the manner in which they were plotted but in her sentence structure, choice of words, and punctuation. Yet he finds enough variety in her style to add color to the books. She created tension by her plot construction.

Fitzgibbon, Russell H. *The Agatha Christie Companion*. Bowling Green, Ohio: Bowling Green University Popular Press, 1980.
The first half of this book discusses the detective story in general, Agatha Christie's life, and each of her detectives, major and minor. The second half is a complete bibliography of her works, including paperback editions through 1978. Arranged by series detective or category. Contains an alphabetical list of all titles keyed to the original bibliography, a list of alternate book titles, a "short-story finder" for Christie collections, and an index of characters. Selected bibliography of material about Christie.

Fremlin, Celia. "The Christie Everybody Knew." In *Agatha Christie: First Lady of Crime*, edited by H. R. F. Keating. New York: Holt, Rinehart and Winston, 1977.
Traces the public recognition of Agatha Christie, contrasting the early negative reviews with her rising popularity, her becoming a subject for humorists and cartoonists, the increasing and sustained praise followed by a sense that she was losing her touch, and the triumph of the mock obituaries of her character Hercule Poirot as evidence of Christie's status as a permanent national institution.

Hart, Anne. *The Life and Times of Miss Jane Marple*. New York: Dodd, Mead, 1985.
A biography and character sketch of Miss Marple, who was "born at the age of sixty-five to seventy" in the pages of *The Murder at the Vicarage* (1930) and must have been more than one hundred in *Nemesis* (1971). Details of her career and daily life in the village of St. Mary Mead are found in the twelve novels and twenty short stories that make up the Marple canon. Includes a map of St. Mary Mead and a Miss Marple bibliography.

Haycraft, Howard. "England: 1918-1930 (The Golden Age)." In his *Murder for Pleasure: The Life and Times of the Detective Story*. New York: D. Appleton-Century, 1941.
Haycraft supplies sketchy biographical details, which include the publication of Christie's first book, *The Mysterious Affair at Styles* (1920), the controversy over *The Murder of Roger Ackroyd* (1926), her disappearance in 1926, and her

marriage to Max Mallowan. Hercule Poirot is seen as a champion of theory over matter. Criticizes Christie's too-frequent reliance on the least likely person as suspect. Sets her in the context of the genre.

Jenkinson, Philip. "The Agatha Christie Films." In *Agatha Christie: First Lady of Crime*, edited by H. R. F. Keating. New York: Holt, Rinehart and Winston, 1977.
Survey of films (1928-1974) based on Agatha Christie's stories, most of which never satisfactorily represented their sources. The best of all the adaptations for the screen is Rene Clair's *And Then There Were None* (1945); the most success-ful as a film is *Witness for the Prosecution* (1957); the most popular as a series, the Margaret Rutherford/Miss Marple films (1961-1964); the most stylish and amusing, *The Alphabet Murders* (1966); and the most ambitious, *Murder on the Orient Express* (1974).

Keating, H. R. F. "Hercule Poirot: A Companion Portrait." In his *Agatha Christie: First Lady of Crime*. New York: Holt, Rinehart and Winston, 1977.
Keating traces the career of Hercule Poirot, as chronicled by Agatha Christie, from 1920 to 1974. He suggests that Poirot must have been 130 when he died, having calculated his birth date as 1844 and his retirement from the Belgian police as 1904. Suggests possible specific dates for individual cases and finds it appropriate that Styles St. Mary was the setting for both his first case in England and his last.

_____ , ed. Introduction to *Agatha Christie: First Lady of Crime*. New York: Holt, Rinehart and Winston, 1977.
Briefly surveys Christie's life and achievement. Keating believes that she was not an intellectual but, in reality, an entertainer, producing simple gifts for the spectators, never delivering anything beyond the common stock of human na-ture or writing only to be clever, but creating ingenious plots. Thirteen writers contribute to this collection of essays, and each is listed in this bibliography.

Lathen, Emma. "Cornwallis' Revenge." In *Agatha Christie: First Lady of Crime*, edited by H. R. F. Keating. New York: Holt, Rinehart and Winston, 1977.
When Lord Cornwallis surrendered to George Washington in 1781, it marked the end of British influence in the Colonies. Lathen discusses Agatha Christie's influence on readers in the United States as a renewal of the British influence lost in the eighteenth century. Avid Christie fans should rejoice that there are so many titles to read and reread.

Maida, Patricia, and Nicholas B. Spornick. *Murder She Wrote: A Study of Agatha Christie's Detective Fiction*. Bowling Green, Ohio: Bowling Green University Popular Press, 1982.

Noting the multitude of books about Agatha Christie, the authors claim that they will focus only on her detective fiction, analyzing the components of her work (puzzle, detectives, policemen, environment) to reveal what was unique to her work. Takes up the background of detective fiction, considers Hercule Poirot and Jane Marple separately, briefly looks at the other detectives in her works. Notes, but no bibliography.

Mann, Jessica. "Agatha Christie." In her *Deadlier Than the Male: Why Are Respectable English Women So Good at Murder?* New York: Macmillan, 1981.
A biographical sketch of the writer whose own autobiography was accurate in that it depicted her life as she really saw it, not as it really was. Mann notes that Christie's novels were equally unrealistic, but that is part of their charm. Her characters are like puppets, brought onstage for one performance, but with no life beyond the covers of the book.

Panek, LeRoy L. "Agatha Christie." In his *Watteau's Shepherds: The Detective Novel in Britain, 1914-1940.* Bowling Green, Ohio: Bowling Green University Popular Press, 1979.
Panek agrees with those critics who are at a loss to explain Christie's continued success. He examines her early thrillers for clues to her development as an author of pure detective stories and discovers thriller elements (master criminals and gangsters) throughout her work. Discusses style and point of view as assets in her goal of fooling her readers.

Ramsey, Gordon K. *Agatha Christie: Mistress of Mystery.* New York: Dodd, Mead, 1967.
This was the first book devoted to Agatha Christie. Chapters include a brief discussion of the mystery story as a form, the career of Agatha Christie, mystery writers as social historians, devices of the profession, M. Hercule Poirot, Miss Jane Marple, and a detailed analysis of *The A. B. C. Murders* (1936). Annotated bibliography of works through 1967 and music for nursery rhymes used in Christie's stories. Sixteen pages of photographs.

Riley, Dick, and Pam McAllister, eds. *The Bedside, Bathtub, and Armchair Companion to Agatha Christie.* New York: Frederick Ungar, 1979, Rev. ed. 1986.
A veritable coffee-table book of plot summaries, character lists, and articles on various aspects of Agatha Christie's works, from settings to film adaptations to murder methods. Lavishly illustrated with movie stills and posters, and cover illustrations. First edition contains colored illustrations of movie posters, while the revised edition uses black and white ones. Title index.

Routley, Erik. "Quartet of Muses: First Pair." In his *The Puritan Pleasures of the Detective Story.* London: Victor Gollancz, 1972.

Routley thinks that Christie earned the title "queen of crime" by never working below her high standard. She wrote to amuse readers, not to involve them in a style that did not make excessive demands, working within a pattern that did not allow room for any agonizing self-criticism. Her real secret was how she accomplished this while maintaining professional standards.

Sanders, Dennis, and Leon Lovallo. *The Agatha Christie Companion: The Complete Guide to Agatha Christie's Life and Work*. New York: Delacorte Press, 1984.
An exhaustive compendium of all Christie publications with cross-reference lists according to major series characters. Contains Christie material written for or adapted for stage, film, and television. Background notes on the writing of each book, the critical acceptance, plot summary, principal characters, and first editions noted. Index of titles and characters.

Symons, Julian. *Bloody Murder: From the Detective Story to the Crime Novel, a History*. Rev. ed. New York: Viking Press, 1985.
Agatha Christie inherited the tradition of Sherlock Holmes when she began her career. Symons considers her originality to lie in writing pure puzzle stories in which there is no opportunity for emotional engagement with the characters. Reading her best work of the 1930's is like watching a conjurer at work dealing cards.

——————— . "The Mistress of Complication." In *Agatha Christie: First Lady of Crime*, edited by H. R. F. Keating. New York: Holt, Rinehart and Winston, 1977.
According to Symons, it is Christie's plot construction that sets her apart from other crime writers. Her facility with handling the devices of a detective-story plot is evident from her earliest novel, *The Mysterious Affair at Styles* (1920). Her plots are based on a simple circumstance that becomes elaborated and concealed. Discusses *The Murder of Roger Ackroyd* (1926), *The A. B. C. Murders* (1936), and *Ten Little Niggers* (1939; also as *And Then There Were None* and *Ten Little Indians*) as examples of her originality in constructing puzzles.

Toye, Randall. *The Agatha Christie "Who's Who."* New York: Holt, Rinehart and Winston, 1980.
This biographical dictionary lists more than two thousand characters who appear in Christie's novels and short stories. Each item includes a biographical sketch drawn from material in the story or stories in which the character appears. Included is a bibliography of Christie's fiction, arranged chronologically. The titles of the Hercule Poirot, Ariadne Oliver, and Jane Marple series as well as Christie's plays and nonmysteries are listed in the appendixes. Illustrated with drawings.

Trewin, J. C. "A Midas Gift to the Theatre." In *Agatha Christie: First Lady of Crime*, edited by H. R. F. Keating. New York: Holt, Rinehart and Winston, 1977.

Surveys the twelve full-length and three one-act plays written by Christie between 1930 and 1962, including one published, but not produced onstage. Over the years, she confided secrets of denouement that critics and playgoers agreed not to divulge. Trewin admits that there is no easy explanation for the continued success of *The Mousetrap*, which opened in London's West End as *Three Blind Mice*. Illustrated with photographs of productions and of Charles Laughton as Hercule Poirot.

Walter, Elizabeth. "The Case of the Escalating Sales." In *Agatha Christie: First Lady of Crime*, edited by H. R. F. Keating. New York: Holt, Rinehart and Winston, 1977.

Walter describes Christie's relationship with her publishers, Collins, from the day they published *The Murder of Roger Ackroyd* (1926). A thorough professional, Christie delivered her typescripts and proofs on time and only objected to editing which rearranged her sentences in spoken dialogue or did not observe her preference in spelling. One of the world's best-selling writers, Christie was remarkably modest.

Watson, Colin. "The Message of Mayhem Parva." In *Agatha Christie: First Lady of Crime*, edited by H. R. F. Keating. New York: Holt, Rinehart and Winston, 1977.

As escapist literature, Agatha Christie's work is certainly an escape from boredom. Watson notes the character created by Marie Belloc Lowndes that was so similar to Hercule Poirot and speculates on why he was not the success that Poirot was. Notes that solving the puzzle in the Christie story made the world seem safer—it cancelled out the death that had come before.

Weaver, William. "Music and Mystery." In *Agatha Christie: First Lady of Crime*, edited by H. R. F. Keating. New York: Holt, Rinehart and Winston, 1977.

Weaver explains that Agatha Christie's books present music in a somewhat ambivalent way. It is never stressed, yet it exists just beneath the surface: nursery rhymes, old folk songs, a verse of a psalm, the opera, or plots or themes from operas. The answer, he thinks, must lie in Agatha Christie's enjoyment of music. She once studied voice in Paris and wanted to become a concert pianist.

Wynne, Nancy Blue. *An Agatha Christie Chronology*. New York: Ace Books, 1976.

A very personal annotated bibliography, arranged in order of original publication date, with novels and short-story collections listed separately. Contains alphabetical listing of short stories with sources; short stories in anthologies;

chronological checklists of all titles, all Poirot Books, all Miss Marple Books, all Tuppence and Tommy books, all Ariadne Oliver books, and all Superintendent Battle books. Lists nonmystery titles, omnibus volumes, and plays by Christie. Alphabetical listing (with publication information and title changes) for all books, exclusive of paperback editions. No index.

WILKIE COLLINS

Biography

Davis, Nuel Pharr. *The Life of Wilkie Collins*. Urbana: University of Illinois Press, 1956.

Considers much of Collins' work to be autobiographical and draws conclusions about certain aspects of his life from this premise. Davis draws on more of Collins' letters than any previous writer; he uses memoirs, reviews of Collins' work, and contemporary accounts to present a clear portrait of him as a man as well as a novelist. Notes, selected bibliography, and index. Introduction by Gordon N. Ray who sees Collins as having a solid position in the ranks of Victorian English novelists.

Dickens, Charles. *Letters of Charles Dickens to Wilkie Collins*, edited by Laurence Hutton. New York: Harper & Brothers, 1892. Reprint. New York: Kraus Reprint, 1969.

The collected letters of Charles Dickens addressed to Wilkie Collins from shortly after their meeting, in 1851, to 1870. Collins' own letters do not survive as Dickens burned most of his correspondence and insisted that his correspondents burn his letters to them. Discusses *The Moonstone* and Collins' work in general.

Robinson, Kenneth. *Wilkie Collins, a Biography*. New York: Macmillan, 1952.

The first full-length biography of Collins. Based on S. M. Ellis' *Wilkie Collins, Sheridan Le Fanu, and Others* (1931), as well as on Collins' published and unpublished letters. Robinson discusses Collins' complex personality and attempts to explain why he avoided publicity and was as much of a mystery to the world as the well-kept secrets upon which his stories depend. Much information on his working methods. Brief primary and secondary bibliography. Illustrated. Indexed.

Commentary

Allen, L. David. *"The Moonstone."* In his *Detective in Fiction*. Lincoln, Nebr.: Cliffs Notes, 1978.

Not really a novel of detection, *The Moonstone* (1868) is still a forerunner of the modern detective novel. Allen thinks that Collins' concern is with delineating character and brings the story to focus on the theft of the diamond only in the latter portion of the novel. Plot summary demonstrates how suspense is created through Collins' method of characterization. Allen considers the solution to be logically achieved.

Ashley, Robert Paul. *Wilkie Collins*. London: Arthur Barker, 1952.
A brief biography and critical study that attempts to correct the "misrepresentation and slipshod scholarship" Ashley has found published about Collins to date. Suggests that there may be a basis for considering Collins more than the "master sensationalist" of literature. Examines each of the novels in turn. Classes Collins as a storyteller and the "grandfather of detective fiction." Includes bibliographical notes on sources, a chronology of Collins' life, and a brief checklist of his works. Index.

Bedell, Jeanne F. "Wilkie Collins." In *Dictionary of Literary Biography*, edited by Bernard Benstock and Thomas F. Staley, vol. 70. Detroit: Gale Research, 1988.
Contains biographical details accompanied by a critical survey of Collins' major works in suspense and mystery: *Mr. Wray's Cash-Box: Or, the Mask and the Mystery* (1852), *Basil: A Story of Modern Life* (1852), *Hide and Seek: Or, The Mystery of Mary Grice* (1854), *After Dark* (1856), *The Queen of Hearts* (1859), *The Woman in White* (1860), *No Name* (1862), *The Moonstone* (1868), and others. Writing before the genre had established its formulas and traditions, Collins established significant plot techniques that influenced the development of the form. Extensive bibliography. Illustrations.

_____ . "Wilkie Collins." In *Twelve Englishmen of Mystery*, edited by Earl F. Bargainnier. Bowling Green, Ohio: Bowling Green University Popular Press, 1984.
Bedell considers Collins' greatest contribution to suspense fiction to be his skill in blending romance with realism and the exotic with the mundane. Briefly surveys Collins' accomplishments against a background of his own life. He wrote original, exciting, and suspense-filled novels that "offered richly detailed pictures of Victorian life and subversive, challenging criticism of Victorian society."

Haycraft, Howard. "The In-Between Years (Development)." In his *Murder for Pleasure: The Life and Times of the Detective Story*. New York: D. Appleton-Century, 1941.
Haycraft considers Collins to have been equal to Charles Dickens in characterization, but he considered Dickens to be superior in plot construction. The only time Collins failed was when he tried to imitate Dickens. Haycraft points out that Collins did not really write detective fiction as such but novels of his

times with detective themes. Discusses detective motifs in *The Moonstone* (1868) and the basis for humor in Collins.

Lambert, Gavin. "Enemy Country: Wilkie Collins." In his *The Dangerous Edge*. London: Barrie & Jenkins, 1975.
Discusses *The Woman in White* (1860) and *The Moonstone* (1868) against a background of the mystery of Collins' life and personality. Lambert notes the two basic themes to the thriller that Collins introduced: the isolated hero who is determined to solve the mystery even at the risk of his own life and the innocent man who must overcome the evidence against him. Has high praise for *The Moonstone*.

Lonoff, Sue. *Wilkie Collins and His Victorian Readers: A Study in the Rhetoric of Authorship*. New York: AMS Press, 1982.
This book is confined to an examination of Collins' novels and his statements in prefaces and letters of his theories of fiction writing. Attention is paid to the audience for which Collins wrote, a specifically Victorian readership, whom he endeavored to please. The nature of the bond between author and reader was part of the literary climate in which he worked. Particular attention paid to *The Woman in White* (1860) and *The Moonstone* (1868).

Marshall, William H. *Wilkie Collins*. New York: Twayne, 1970.
A critical survey of Collins as a writer and the part that his development had to do with the development of the English novel. A minor novelist, Collins clearly understood what he was doing and was able to produce major works. Considers him as a novelist writing for the mass reading public during the growth of literacy. Marshall comments on each novel in turn. Selected bibliography indicates original publication information for the short fiction and serial fiction. Lists uncollected works.

Ousby, Ian. "Wilkie Collins and Other Sensation Novelists." In his *Bloodhounds of Heaven: The Detective in English Fiction from Godwin to Doyle*. Cambridge, Mass.: Harvard University Press, 1976.
Ousby concentrates on *The Moonstone* (1868) in his discussion, noting how the mystery depends on the difficulty with which people view one another correctly, as indicated by the shifting viewpoint. The solution is more complex than might be imagined as disturbing truths become revealed. Collins introduces a major theme in the fallibility of the police in the person of Sergeant Richard Cuff.

Page, Norman, ed. *Wilkie Collins: The Critical Heritage*. Boston: Routledge & Kegan Paul, 1974.
A collection of contemporary reviews of Collins' novels from 1850 to 1889,

taken from nineteenth century periodicals or letters written by nineteenth century literary figures. Introduction discusses the publishing history of his novels and his purpose as a writer. Appendix lists Collins' principal works. Selective bibliography and selective index.

Peterson, Audrey. *Victorian Masters of Mystery: From Wilkie Collins to Conan Doyle*. New York: Frederick Ungar, 1984.
Collins earned the title of "father of English mystery fiction" with his ingenuity in building his plots and investing them with mystery. Peterson briefly covers Collins' life and his early works and follows with a more detailed consideration of *The Woman in White* (1860), *No Name* (1862), *Armadale* (1866), and *The Moonstone* (1868). Concludes with a brief look at the later novels. Traces the development of Collins' most successful formulas.

Phillips, Walter C. *Dickens, Reade, and Collins, Sensation Novelists: A Study in the Conditions and Theories of Novel Writing in Victorian England*. New York: Columbia University Press, 1919. Reprint. New York: Russell & Russell, 1962.
Among the earliest critics to treat Charles Dickens seriously as a conscious artist, Phillips explores the mutual influences of Collins and Charles Dickens and the debt they shared to the gothic tradition. Surveys the use of the sensational in English prose fiction and the background of the nineteenth century publishing world.

Sayers, Dorothy L. *Wilkie Collins: A Critical and Biographical Study.* Toledo, Ohio: Friends of the University of Toledo Libraries, 1977.
For at least thirty-six years, Dorothy L. Sayers had planned on writing a biography of Wilkie Collins and had gathered material for it. Five chapters of Sayers' manuscript, covering the years 1824 to 1855, found in a collection of her papers in the Humanities Research Center, University of Texas at Austin, have been published here. Introduction and notes by E. R. Gregory. Illustrations from early editions of Collins' work and facsimile manuscript pages.

Starrett, Vincent. Introduction to *The Moonstone*, by Wilkie Collins. New York: Heritage Press, 1959.
Starrett discusses Collins' plan for writing *The Moonstone* (1868), his characters, some incidents from his life, the publication and reception of the novel, quoting passages from Collins' notes. By modern standards *The Moonstone* must seem old-fashioned, but it was fresh and original in 1868. Starrett conveys the excitement of the reader of the original serial as he waited for the next installment.

_____ . Introduction to *The Woman in White*, by Wilkie Collins. New York: Heritage Press, 1964.

According to legend, Collins was inspired to write *The Woman in White* (1860) on seeing a beautiful young woman one evening in London. Starrett mentions some other possible sources for his inspiration, discusses Collins' outstanding use of atmosphere, his creation of character, and the publication and reception of the novel. Concludes with a brief biographical sketch.

Stewart, J. I. M. Introduction to *The Moonstone*, by Wilkie Collins. Baltimore: Penguin Books, 1966.
One of the most perfectly plotted works of fiction, *The Moonstone* (1868) demonstrates structure, proportion, and narrative tempo superbly suited to its conclusion. Stewart discusses Sergeant Richard Cuff as an example of Collins' ability to delineate character. Biographical details concentrate on Collins' friendship with Charles Dickens, their interest in the theater, and Collins' use of opium. Assesses Collins' achievement in general and considers *The Moonstone* his masterpiece.

Symons, Julian. "Dickens, Collins, Gaboriau: The Pattern Forms." In his *Bloody Murder: From the Detective Story to the Crime Novel, a History*. Rev. ed. New York: Viking Press, 1985.
Collins' merits are principally within the field of melodrama. Symons discusses *Hide and Seek: Or, The Mystery of Mary Grice* (1854), *The Woman in White* (1860), and *The Moonstone* (1868), as well as some of Collins' short stories. Considers *The Woman in White* superior as a novel of character and incident, but believes that Sergeant Richard Cuff brings a touch of reality to an otherwise romantic story.

_____ . Introduction to *The Woman in White*, by Wilkie Collins. Baltimore: Penguin Books, 1974.
Collins was "an odd blend of the respectable and the raffish" whose life-style "offended Victorian proprieties." In some detail, Symons discusses the inspiration for *The Woman in White* (1860), his best novel—its characteristics and the circumstances of its publication. Considers Collins' skill to be in constructing plots and in creating real characters that keep his melodrama from being ridiculous.

JOHN CREASEY

Biography

Briney, Robert E., and John Creasey. "A John Creasey Bibliography." *The Armchair Detective* 2 (October, 1968): 5-22.
The first comprehensive bibliography of Creasey's works. Lists first British and American editions, as of September, 1968, and summarizes his output by series detective. Includes price of each edition and titles of books projected through 1970. Arranged chronologically by date of first publication. The Toff series is the longest, with fifty-four titles.

Greenhouse, Linda. "John Creasey, Author, Is Dead: Specialized in Mystery Novels." *The New York Times*, June 10, 1973, sec. 1: 65.
An obituary. Creasey's statistics as a writer, his rate of writing, and his twenty-eight pen names are displayed. The seventh of nine children, Creasey was reared in poverty, left school at fourteen to support himself as a clerk and factory worker while writing at night. Deeply interested in politics, he was an unsuccessful candidate for Parliament in 1950. Critics were cool to him for the most part, but his successful combination of plot and character made him popular with his readers.

Lachman, Marvin S. "John Creasey." In *Dictionary of Literary Biography*, edited by Bernard Benstock and Thomas F. Staley, vol. 70. Detroit: Gale Research, 1988.
The author of more than five hundred crime novels, Creasey was as famous for the quality of his work as for its quantity. Lachman surveys Creasey's major series and comments on his style. Considers the Gideon series, written under the pseudonym, J. J. Marric, to be his best work and perhaps the best police-procedural series of all. Biographical details note his activity in British politics and social causes. Twelve-page bibliography.

"Obituary: John Creasey." *The Times* (London), June 11, 1973: 16. Reprint. In *Obituaries from the Times, 1971-1975*, compiled by Frank C. Roberts. Westport, Conn.: Mackler Books, 1978.
Creasey was "almost certainly" the most prolific author of crime novels. At the time of his death, he had published 560 titles. Inspired by reading Sapper's Bulldog Drummond series (1920-1937), Creasey published his first novel in 1932. Fascinated by the commercial side of writing, he worked closely with his publishers and agents, studying the market and adapting his style to the prevailing fashion. He believed seriously in his role as an entertainer.

Commentary

Boyles, John. "A Word for John Creasey: J. J. Marric's *Gideon's Risk*." *The Armchair Detective* 11 (July, 1978): 282-283.
The books Creasey wrote as J. J. Marric are praised by Boyles for their artistic realism in portraying police work through George Gideon and his officers in Scotland Yard's Criminal Investigation Department. *Gideon's Risk* (1960) is discussed as representative of the entire Gideon series. Considers the portrayal of character, the economic use of details, and the links that knit together the strands of plot as contributing to the success of the series.

Butler, William Vivian. *The Durable Desperadoes*. London: Macmillan, 1973.
Discusses the economics of writing and publishing thrillers. Creasey's first novel, *Seven Times Seven* (1932) was derived from Bulldog Drummond and the Saint, but attracted the attention of *The Thriller* editor Monty Haydon and led to the creation of that "aristocratic Saint," the Toff (Richard Rollison). Butler covers the development of the Toff, the Baron (John Mannering), and Department Z. Touches on some other topics, in particular the stories written about the wartime service of these characters.

Creasey, John, and Allen J. Hubin. "John Creasey—Fact or Fiction? A Candid Commentary in Third Person." *The Armchair Detective* 2 (October, 1968): 1-5.
Describes Creasey's career, his working methods, especially the need to revise his novels for a new printing to keep them up to date. Contains statistics on the number of words published through July, 1968. Notes Creasey's greater emphasis on sociological themes after 1951. Hubin, editor and publisher of *The Armchair Detective*, describes a visit by Creasey to his Minnesota home. Creasey considers his best novel to be *Look Three Ways at Murder* (1964; a Roger West story).

Dove, George N. "John Creasey." In his *The Police Procedural*. Bowling Green, Ohio: Bowling Green University Popular Press, 1982.
Creasey's contributions to the police procedural, the Roger West series, and the Gideon books do not contain any masterpieces, but there are no failures. Dove sees Creasey's policemen as human beings first and policemen second, but he believes that the reader gets deeper into Gideon than into West. Traces the development of the police procedural in Creasey from the Great Policeman theme.

Harvey, Deryk. "The Best of John Creasey." *The Armchair Detective* 7 (November, 1973): 42-43.
Harvey discusses the strengths and weaknesses of Creasey's novels written at different periods in his career. Considers Roger West to be one of his first

original creations and *Gideon's Day* to owe something to Creasey's having seen Jack Webb's *Dragnet* television series. Suggests that the entire Gideon series plus *Murder, London—South Africa* (1966), *Policeman's Dread* (1962), *Look Three Ways at Murder* (1964), and *The Crime Haters* (1960) as candidates for a short list of Creasey's best work.

"How to Be the Most." *Newsweek* 53 (February 2, 1959): 85-86.
An interview with John Creasey, who admits that the only way to make a living as a writer is to publish more than two books a year. By the time he published his first book at twenty-three he had collected 740 rejection slips. Describes his "time-consuming" pace, writing novels in six or twelve days each, during which he writes five thousand or ten thousand words a day. Believes that the more he produces the better he gets. Photograph of Creasey at age fifty.

EDMUND CRISPIN
(Robert Bruce Montgomery)

Biography

Crispin, Edmund. Introduction to *Best Detective Stories*, edited by Edmund
Crispin. London: Faber & Faber, 1959.
Crispin considers the detective story to be in a healthy state, in spite of the
predictions by the critics of its demise. Believes that the whole art of the
orthodox detective story depends on the artificial nature of its plot. Any part
that overshadows the plot will weaken the structure, and any attempt to elevate
the form by means of characterization or plausibility will fail.

Montgomery, Robert Bruce. "Edmund Crispin." *The Armchair Detective* 12
(Spring, 1979): 183-185.
An informal autobiography written for his publisher, Walker. Montgomery
reveals that reading John Dickson Carr's *The Crooked Hinge* (1938) showed
him what could be done with the detective story. An interest in the theater,
books, and music explains Montgomery's becoming a composer as well as a
storyteller. Agrees with Jacques Barzun's distinction between the novel and the
tale in detective fiction. Indicates that he has been married recently and plans
to resume writing crime fiction.

Wallace, Frances J. "Edmund Crispin." *Wilson Library Bulletin* 23 (June, 1949):
750.
A biographical sketch of Bruce Montgomery, alias Edmund Crispin, who
writes erudite detective stories featuring Gervase Fen, Oxford don. It was
Charles Williams, the writer, who encouraged young Montgomery to develop
a plot idea into the novel *Obsequies at Oxford* (1944; British title: *The Case of
the Gilded Fly*). Comments on the critical reception of his detective stories
and his ability to combine the form with Wodehousian farce and social satire.

Commentary

DeMarr, Mary Jean. "Edmund Crispin." In *Twelve Englishmen of Mystery*, edited
by Earl F. Bargainnier. Bowling Green, Ohio: Bowling Green University Popular Press, 1984.
Influenced by an earlier generation of writers, Crispin wrote detective stories
that were distinctively his own in style. DeMarr describes the characteristics of
his work, his use of recurring characters (Gervase Fen, Detective-Inspector
Humbleby, Sir Richard Freeman, Wilkes), and the backgrounds which Crispin
knew so well and could depict with a fine, satiric pen.

Routley, Erik. "Politeness and Protest." In his *The Puritan Pleasures of the Detective Story*. London: Victor Gollancz, 1972.
Edmund Crispin wrote like a master and was better at creating characters than was Michael Innes. Routley considers no writer in the genre to have been so boldly topical in introducing real people and places in his novels. The original of Gervase Fen is hinted at, but not disclosed. *Obsequies at Oxford* (1944; British title: *The Case of the Gilded Fly*) is an example of how "special knowledge" can be mishandled in a detective story. Briefly discusses *Holy Disorders* (1945), *Dead and Dumb* (1947; British title: *Swan Song*), *Love Lies Bleeding* (1948), *Sudden Vengeance* (1950; British title: *Frequent Hearses*), *Buried for Pleasure* (1948), and *The Long Divorce* (1951) as well as the short story "Baker Dies."

Sarjeant, William A. S. "Obsequies About Oxford: The Investigations and Eccentricities of Gervase Fen." *The Armchair Detective* 14 (Summer, 1981): 196-209.
An imaginative character sketch of Gervase Fen based on information Sarjeant found in Edmund Crispin's detective stories. Born in 1903, probably in London, Fen studied at Magdalen College, Oxford, lectured at the University of Milan (1928), became professor of English language and literature, Oxford (1936 or 1937), a Fellow of St. Christopher's College, published an edition of Langland and a book on eighteenth century minor satirists. Comments on his personal life, his appearance and personality, and discusses his associates and investigations.

AMANDA CROSS
(Carolyn G. Heilbrun)

Biography

"Carolyn G(old) Heilbrun (Amanda Cross)." In *Contemporary Authors*, edited by Ann Evory, vol. 1. Detroit: Gale Research, 1981.
A list of personal details in the life of Carolyn G. Heilbrun, who writes crime fiction as Amanda Cross, along with some facts about her literary and academic careers. Contains a checklist of her books in chronological order and is arranged according to by-line, and a brief survey of her achievements as a scholar and a novelist. List of biographical and critical sources in newspapers and magazines.

Cleveland, Carol. "Amanda Cross." In *Twentieth Century Crime and Mystery Writers*, edited by John M. Reilly. New York: St. Martin's Press, 1980.
A brief summary of the personal details of Carolyn Heilbrun's life, along with some facts of her academic and literary career, followed by a short checklist of her works as "Amanda Cross" and those published under her real name. Autobiographical statements explaining her goals in writing detective fiction. Concludes with about 750 words of commentary that surveys her detective fiction and assesses her place in the genre.

Cooper-Clark, Diana. "Amanda Cross." In her *Designs of Darkness: Interviews with Detective Novelists.* Bowling Green, Ohio: Bowling Green University Popular Press, 1983.
A 1981 interview with Carolyn Heilbrun, who used a pseudonym for her detective stories so that there would be no hindrance to her receiving tenure at Columbia University, where she teaches. Building a novel on the framework of a classic in literature has been the pattern of the majority of her detective novels. Comments on her favorite writers inside and outside the genre and differences in approach in depicting male and female characters.

Heilbrun, Carolyn G. *Writing a Woman's Life*. New York: W. W. Norton, 1989.
A discussion of the way in which conventional methods of dealing with the lives of women in literary forms do not capture the "essence of the feminine experience." Suggests a new approach by describing how she used her detective stories, written under the pen name of Amanda Cross, to present a model for the woman looking for "satisfaction and balance in love, friendship, and career."

Commentary

Carter, Steven R. "Amanda Cross." In *Ten Women of Mystery*, edited by Earl F. Bargainnier. Bowling Green, Ohio: Bowling Green University Popular Press, 1981.
Carter identifies Cross's literary ancestor as Dorothy L. Sayers. Like Sayers, she subordinates the puzzles in her novels to portrayals of a "social environment" and a "personal vision." Kate Fansler has developed from being a female version of Lord Peter Wimsey to a complex figure with her own life and system of values. Among the distinctive characteristics of her books are her use of irony and her concern for social justice.

Klein, Kathleen Gregory. "Feminists as Detectives: Harriet Vane, Kate Fansler, Sarah Chayse." *The Armchair Detective* 13 (Winter, 1980): 31-35.
Klein compares five Amanda Cross novels with three by Dorothy L. Sayers and Lynn Meyer's *Paperback Thriller* (1975). Over the forty years spanned by their publication dates (1930-1976), women have emerged gradually to fill roles previously assigned to men. The "silly female as detective" has been replaced by "the competent, capable woman who values herself and believes in her own abilities."

Purcell, J. Mark. "The 'Amanda Cross' Case: Socializing the U.S. Academic Mystery." *The Armchair Detective* 13 (Winter, 1980): 36-40.
What Carolyn Heilbrun has contributed to her persona as Amanda Cross is a "working professional experience" to give her academic detective novels an authoritative air. Purcell finds some limitations in Cross: dialogue that does not make adequate distinction between speakers and characters who must struggle to convince the reader they that are educated.

Wilt, Judith. "Feminism Meets the Detective Novel." *Clues: A Journal of Detection* 3 (Fall/Winter, 1982): 47-51.
Wilt poses the question of whether the classic rules that govern the detective story are broken by the blending of the form with the feminist academic novel that Amanda Cross has titled *Death in a Tenured Position* (1981). The feminist question posed by Amanda Cross is What kind of a person kills women? Comparisons are made with Dorothy L. Sayers' *Gaudy Night* (1935) and Robert B. Parker's *Looking for Rachel Wallace* (1980).

CHARLES DICKENS

Biography

Becker, May Lamberton. *Introducing Charles Dickens*. New York: Dodd, Mead, 1940.
Drawing on Charles Dickens' correspondence and accounts of people who knew him, Becker presents the life of the great English novelist as a story worth the telling. Intended for a young adult readership, the book contains no documentation of sources, no bibliography, and no index. Illustrated with photographs of Dickens and the places associated with his life. Line drawings depict scenes from the account of his life.

Dickens, Charles. *The Letters of Charles Dickens*. Edited by Madeline House and Graham Storey. Oxford, England: Clarendon Press, 1965-
With six volumes published to date, this is the most complete edition of the letters of Charles Dickens in existence. Begun in 1949 under the editorship of Humphry House. The first volume did not appear until after the editor's death. Includes a biographical table of Dickens' life, full identification of all recipients of the letters, illustrations (including facsimiles of Dickens' handwriting), and an index. Expected to consist of twelve volumes, including an index volume.

Ford, George H. "Charles Dickens." In *Dictionary of Literary Biography*, edited by Ira B. Nadel and William E. Fredeman, vol. 21. Detroit: Gale Research, 1983.
A survey of Charles Dickens' publications against the background of his life and the Victorian era. Contains a checklist of his primary works with a good selected list of secondary sources. Well illustrated with photographs, illustrations from the books, and facsimiles of manuscript pages. A good introductory essay to Dickens and his works.

Forster, John. *The Life of Charles Dickens*. 2 vols. New York: E. P. Dutton, 1950.
Originally published in three volumes between 1872 and 1874, this is the earliest reliable biography of Charles Dickens. Written by his friend, John Forster, the book is not without flaws; it omits any mention of Dickens' wife or their separation. There are many good editions of this book; critics often recommend the one-volume edition of 1928, edited by J. W. T. Ley or the 1966 edition, edited by A. J. Hoppe. The edition cited here is in the Everyman Library (vols. 781 and 782) that includes an introduction by G. K. Chesterton. Index.

Hibbert, Christopher. *The Making of Charles Dickens*. New York: Harper & Row, 1967.

A biography and critical study of Charles Dickens that concentrates on his childhood and youth, the first extensive publication of its kind. Covers the period from 1812 to 1845 and Dickens' thirty-third year. Draws on correspondence and other primary and secondary sources. Selective bibliography and detailed index. More than thirty photographs and illustrations.

Johnson, Edgar. *Charles Dickens: His Tragedy and Triumph.* 2 vols. New York: Simon & Schuster, 1952.
A comprehensive and authoritative biography that makes extensive use of Dickens' letters, in which are found "a wealth of psychological observation and comic episode" similar to those that appear in his novels. Extensive section of notes and basic bibliography. Critical comments on Dickens' writings appear as separate chapters from those depicting incidents in his life. Illustrated. Indexed.

Leacock, Stephen. *Charles Dickens: His Life and Work.* Garden City, N.Y.: Doubleday, Doran, 1934.
This account of the life of Charles Dickens does not present any new interpretations, but the author (noted Canadian humorist) does have an enthusiasm for his subject. No documentation of sources and no bibliography. Discusses Dickens' heirs, the disposition of his manuscripts, and the popularity of his writing. Chronology of events and works. Index.

Priestley, J. B. *Charles Dickens: A Pictorial Biography.* New York: Viking Press, 1961.
A brief yet thorough and readable account of the story of Dickens' life written by a noted English novelist and critic. Lavishly illustrated with more than one hundred contemporary photographs, drawings, and illustrations from Dickens' books. Includes a chronology of Dickens' life and notes on the sources of the illustrations., Index. No bibliography of Dickens' works or documentation of sources.

Symons, Julian. *Charles Dickens.* Denver, Colo.: Alan Swallow, 1951.
A brief survey of the personal details of the life of Charles Dickens, along with a succinct yet penetrating discussion of his work. Concludes with a chapter commenting on his achievement as a writer. Written by a noted literary critic and author of crime fiction. No bibliography of Dickens' own publications or documentation of sources. Index.

Commentary

Aylmer, Felix. *The Drood Case.* London: Rupert Hart-Davies, 1964.
Based on a thorough study of the text of *The Mystery of Edwin Drood,*

fragments of Dickens' rough notes, the original drawings made by Charles
Collins, the differences between them and the Luke Fildes illustrations in the
published book. Aylmer creates a complex background plot against which
Dickens' story must be read. Some of it seems to have little relevance to what
Dickens actually wrote. Appendixes include a synopsis of the story and a
reproduction of Dickens' fragmentary notes.

Baker, Richard M. *The Drood Murder Case: Five Studies in Dickens' "Edwin
Drood."* Berkeley: University of California Press, 1951.
Collects articles previously published. Baker covers the question of whether
Edwin Drood was really murdered and argues for John Jasper as the killer.
Discusses the theories about the identity of Dick Datchery, decides on Hiram
Grewgious. Considers works that might have influenced Dickens' writing of
the novel and speculates on what Dickens might have done with other parts of
the plot (besides the murder) left unfinished.

Bengis, Nathan L. "John Jasper's Devotion." *The Armchair Detective* 8 (May/
August, 1975): 165-178, 257-270; 9 (November, 1975): 25-40.
Outlines the early theories about the solution to *The Mystery of Edwin Drood*
(1870) and presents an argument that Drood is not dead, but John Jasper thinks
that he has killed him and Drood has returned in disguise as Dick Datchery.
Bengis admits that this remains a work to tantalize those who delight in
puzzles. Extensive bibliography.

Borowitz, Albert. "Charles Dickens." In *Dictionary of Literary Biography*, edited
by Bernard Benstock and Thomas F. Staley, vol. 70. Detroit: Gale Research,
1988.
A critical survey of Dickens' contributions to crime fiction, which includes his
"imaginative understanding of criminal psychology," his sense of the ways
normal people share destructive impulses with criminals, his relating fictional
crime and punishment to social concerns, and his portrayal of police detectives. Discusses the crime elements in *Oliver Twist* (1837-1839), *Barnaby
Rudge: A Tale of the Riots of '80* (1841), *Martin Chuzzlewit* (1843-1844), *Bleak
House* (1852-1853), *Great Expectations* (1860-1861), *Our Mutual Friend*
(1864-1866), and *The Mystery of Edwin Drood* (1870). Illustrated. Bibliography.

Carr, John Dickson. "John Dickson Carr's Solution to *The Mystery of Edwin
Drood*." *The Armchair Detective* 14 (1981): 291-294.
In a personal letter (here reproduced in full) to Lillian de la Torre (who
provides an introductory note), John Dickson Carr submits his solution to *The
Mystery of Edwin Drood* (1870) based on the suggestion that Dickens intended
to surpass the ingenuity of Wilkie Collins' *The Moonstone* (1868). Carr's

solution was used in a television serial written by John Keir Cross on British television in 1960.

Collins, Philip. *Dickens and Crime*. London: Macmillan, 1964.
Examines the treatment of crime in the nineteenth century and the state of the prison system as background to a proper understanding of Dickens' work. Dickens was able to project himself, imaginatively, into the minds of criminals and to maintain a clear-sighted view of the structure of society. Collins discusses Dickens' fascination with the police as well as what the outcome of *The Mystery of Edwin Drood* (1870) was likely to have been. Assesses the prevailing theories. Extensive notes and bibliography.

Miller, H. Hillis. *Charles Dickens: The World of His Novels*. Cambridge, Mass.: Harvard University Press, 1958.
Miller discusses Dickens' novels from the belief that a single view of life pervades them and can be traced throughout Dickens' life and career. In *Bleak House* (1852-1853), Dickens used detective story techniques to withhold the secret behind the murder of Tulkinghorn until the end. Considers the origins of some basic detective-story traditions to be found in Dickens.

Ousby, Ian. "Charles Dickens." In his *Bloodhounds of Heaven: The Detective in English Fiction from Godwin to Doyle.* Cambridge, Mass.: Harvard University Press, 1976.
Ousby notes that Dickens' use of detectives in his novels represents a common characteristic of nineteenth century sensation novels. *Bleak House* (1852-1853) can be cited as a comprehensive index to the conventions of the genre as they were developing at the time, including a profusion of missing wills, guilty secrets, and dispersed families.

Starrett, Vincent. Introduction to *The Mystery of Edwin Drood*, by Charles Dickens. New York: Heritage Press, 1941.
Describes the events in Dickens' life that preceded and accompanied the writing of *The Mystery of Edwin Drood* (1870). Starrett examines the various theories made about the probable conclusion of the story. Suggests that readers may attach importance to matters in the unfinished story that the author never intended. Considers *The Mystery of Edwin Drood* "its author's most fascinating work and the greatest detective story in the world," because it is unfinished, can never be finished to everyone's satisfaction, and is, therefore, an unending source of enjoyment.

Symons, Julian. "Dickens, Collins, Gaboriau: The Pattern Forms." In his *Bloody Murder: From the Detective Story to the Crime Novel, a History.* Rev. ed. New York: Viking Press, 1985.

Dickens' interest in prison conditions and his attitude toward punishment made it natural for him to extol the police in his articles and books. Symons explains that Inspector Bucket was not the first detective in fiction, or even in Dickens' work, and he performs no "spectacular feats of detection." Rather, as a "shrewd and sympathetic man," he serves as a prototype of many later professional detectives. Brief commentary on *The Mystery of Edwin Drood* (1870).

PETER DICKINSON

Biography

Keating, H. R. F. "Peter Dickinson." In *Twentieth Century Crime and Mystery Writers*, edited by John M. Reilly. New York: St. Martin's Press, 1980.
A Brief summary of personal details of Dickinson's life and some facts about his literary career, followed by a checklist of his works in crime fiction and his books for children. Contains an autobiographical statement on his goals in writing. Brief commentary assessing Dickinson's achievements in the genre.

Commentary

Bargainnier, Earl F. "The Playful Mysteries of Peter Dickinson." *The Armchair Detective* 13 (Summer, 1980): 185-193.
Discusses Dickinson's policeman hero, James (Jimmy) Pibble, who had figured in five detective novels to 1980. According to Bargainnier, Pibble is a little man who shares the anxieties of the readers and worries about causing the deaths of murderers. The consideration of Pibble is followed by a discussion of Dickinson's more offbeat novels that combine the classic British thriller formula with incongruous events. (Some misplaced paragraphs and textual errors are corrected by Bargainnier in a letter in the Winter, 1981, issue of *The Armchair Detective*.)

Dickinson, Peter. "Superintendent Pibble." In *The Great Detectives*, edited by Otto Penzler. Boston: Little, Brown, 1978.
A Who's Who sketch of Pibble, who served in the Metropolitan Police Force from 1933 to 1970, followed by comments by Mike Crewe, the sergeant in *The Glass-Sided Ants' Nest* (1968), and by Peter Dickinson in his own persona. Dickinson began by creating a detective who was the opposite of the standard fictional detective. When Pibble seemed like a real person, he was solid enough for the author to know when he had written enough books about him.

SIR ARTHUR CONAN DOYLE

Biography

Carr, John Dickson. *The Life of Sir Arthur Conan Doyle*. New York: Harper & Brothers, 1949.
This authorized biography of the creator of Sherlock Holmes, by a writer of detective fiction, reads like a story of adventure, sometimes even of melodrama. Dialogue may be imaginary, but Carr claims that when Doyle speaks it is in his own words from letters, notebooks, diaries, or newspaper accounts. Ten pages of illustrations show Doyle at work in his study and reproduce the letter in which he tells his mother of his plans to kill Sherlock Holmes at the end of the first twelve stories. Selected bibliography and inventory of "Biographical Archives" in possession of Doyle family. Indexed.

Doyle, Adrian Conan. *The True Conan Doyle*. London: Murray, 1945.
A pamphlet written by the youngest son of Arthur Conan Doyle to present to the public a correct account of his father's life and character in contrast to the "travesty" presented by Hesketh Pearson in his biography (*Conan Doyle: His Life and Art*, 1943). Attests his father's chivalry as a man, that he himself was the original of Sherlock Holmes, that he was no overnight convert to spiritualism, and that his writing of historical novels required thorough research. Preface by General Sir Hubert Gough.

Doyle, Arthur Conan. *Letters to the Press*. Edited and with an introduction by John Michael Gibson and Richard Lancelyn Green. Iowa City: University of Iowa Press, 1986.
Selected letters, from among the hundreds Doyle wrote to the press during his lifetime, demonstrate his interests in a wide variety of topics. Includes letters written between 1879 and 1930 arranged in chronological order. Brief section of notes to identify individuals and episodes largely forgotten today. Category index followed by index of personal names and subjects. No references to Sherlock Holmes.

—————— . *Memories and Adventures.* Boston: Little, Brown, 1924. Rev. ed. London: Hodder & Stoughton, 1930.
This autobiography of Arthur Conan Doyle covers his student days in Edinburgh, his medical career, his travels around the world, with a chapter of "sidelights on Sherlock Holmes," up to the end of World War I. A final chapter covers his experiences and his belief in psychic phenomena. Revised edition omits chapter 25 (an account of a trip to the Rocky Mountains) and expands the final chapter. Illustrated. Index.

Edwards, Owen Dudley. *The Quest for Sherlock Holmes: A Biographical Study of Arthur Conan Doyle*. Edinburgh: Mainstream, 1983.

Edwards concentrates on Doyle's early life in this interpretive biography, investigating the influences on him as a writer up to the publication of *A Study in Scarlet* (1887), though he refers to many of Doyle's later works. No footnotes or other documentation, but a lengthy section, "Sources, Acknowledgments, and Procedures," explains that Edwards considers much of Doyle's work to be autobiographical. Illustrations do not greatly duplicate those found in other books on Doyle. Indexed.

Hardwick, Michael, and Mollie Hardwick. *The Man Who Was Sherlock Holmes*. Garden City, N.Y.: Doubleday, 1964.

This brief biographical sketch of Arthur Conan Doyle shows how closely he patterned his detective on his own experiences. Covers the creation of Sherlock Holmes, the decision to end the series, Doyle's experiences in the Boer War, his resurrection of Holmes in "The Adventure of the Empty House," and his intervention as detective in the cases of Oscar Slater and George Edalji. No documentation of sources. Illustrations. Index. Largely superseded by *The Complete Guide to Sherlock Holmes* (1987), by Michael Hardwick.

Higham, Charles. *The Adventures of Conan Doyle: The Life of the Creator of Sherlock Holmes*. New York: W. W. Norton, 1976.

Higham emphasizes the personal adventures of Doyle in coming to the rescue of the underdog and suggests that in creating Sherlock Holmes and John Watson he was depicting aspects of his own personality. Suggests origins for the ideas behind his characters and stories. Includes mysteries, historical fiction, and science fiction. Selective bibliography lists unpublished as well as published sources with a checklist of Doyle's books and pamphlets. Illustrations and index.

Lellenberg, Jon L., ed. *The Quest for Sir Arthur Conan Doyle: Thirteen Biographers in Search of a Life*. Carbondale: Southern Illinois University Press, 1987.

This collection of critiques of the accounts of Arthur Conan Doyle's life published through 1983 serves as an overview of scholarship on Doyle over the years. Discusses the autobiographical elements in Doyle's fiction as well as his official autobiography and other autobiographical writings. Critiques of biographies include those by John Lamond, Hesketh Pearson, Adrian Conan Doyle, John Dickson Carr, Michael and Mollie Hardwick, Pierre Nordon, Mary Hoehling, James Playstead Wood, Ivor Brown, Charles Higham, Ronald Pearsall, Julian Symons, and Owen Dudley Edwards. Illustrations. Index.

Nordon, Pierre. *Conan Doyle: A Biography*. New York: Holt, Rinehart and Winston, 1967.

This translation from the original French is more literary critique than biography, but was one of the first surveys to devote attention to Doyle's historical fiction. Discusses Doyle as patriot, lover of justice, and apostle for the cause of spiritualism for the first half of the book. Divides the remainder of the book between a consideration of Sherlock Holmes and that of the other fiction. Bibliography of works by Doyle merely supplements and corrects H. Locke's *A Bibliographical Catalogue of the Writings of Sir Arthur Conan Doyle* (1928). Brief listings of "Biographical Archives" and general sources. Index. Original French edition contains more thorough documentation of sources.

Pearson, Hesketh. *Conan Doyle: His Life and Art*. London: Methuen, 1943. Reprint. New York: Walker, 1961.
Pearson emphasizes Doyle as a man of contradictions, a writer who could create a character such as Sherlock Holmes and yet come to detest him, a Victorian gentleman who could defend his researches in spiritualism, yet a man of the people. Critics have considered this to be a popular biography, readable yet uneven in emphasis. Frontispiece photograph of Doyle in 1930. No documentation of sources or bibliography. Indexed.

Symons, Julian. *Portrait of an Artist—Conan Doyle*. London: Whizzard Press, 1979. Reprint. New York: Mysterious Press, 1987.
A brief, lavishly illustrated biographical account of Doyle as writer and as public figure. Symons divides his account into six sections: creator of Sherlock Holmes, the young man, the public man, crusader, author, war experience, and last years. Selected bibliography of Doyle's books in six categories. Chronology. List of 122 illustrations (photographs, drawings, and facsimiles of letters). Indexed.

Commentary

Baring-Gould, William. *Sherlock Holmes of Baker Street: The Life of the World's First Consulting Detective*. New York: Ckarkson N. Potter, 1962.
Beginning with the perception of Holmes as a real person, Baring-Gould has constructed a full-length biography of William Sherlock Scott Holmes from the time of his birth in 1854 to his death in 1957. Appendices contain "The Chronological Holmes," an arrangement of the stories as the events unfold, not in the order of publication, on which the biography is based, and "The Bibliographical Holmes: A Selective Compilation" of primary and secondary sources, including publications of the Baker Street Irregulars.

_____ , ed. *The Annotated Sherlock Holmes*. 2 vols. New York: Clarkson N. Potter, 1967.
The complete stories of Sherlock Holmes written by Arthur Conan Doyle,

arranged chronologically from Holmes's first case, "The Gloria Scott," in 1874, when he was a university student, to "His Last Bow," during the opening days of World War I. Introduction, notes, and illustrations are designed to illuminate and enhance the enjoyment of the stories and the Victorian world they depict. Bibliography of significant books, pamphlets, and articles on Sherlock Holmes. Index of story titles.

Brend, Gavin. "Oxford or Cambridge." In *The Baker Street Reader: Cornerstone Writings About Sherlock Holmes*, edited by Philip A. Shreffler. Westport, Conn.: Greenwood Press, 1984.
Doyle, through Dr. John Watson's narratives, did not give a detailed account of Sherlock Holmes's life as a young man. Brend discusses the question of which university he attended. Drawing on the information provided by five of the stories that refer to university affairs, he argues for Oxford over Cambridge.

Cox, J. Randolph. "Sir Arthur Conan Doyle." In *Dictionary of Literary Biography*, edited by Bernard Benstock and Thomas F. Staley, vol. 70. Detroit: Gale Research, 1988.
Discusses the development of the Sherlock Holmes stories against a framework of the life of Arthur Conan Doyle and the early history of the detective story. Considers the structure of *The Hound of the Baskervilles* (1902) to be significant in presenting the theme of science versus the supernatural. Assesses Doyle's reputation and the development of the cult of Sherlock Holmes in the activities of the Baker Street Irregulars. Illustrated. Extensive bibliography of Doyle's books, the major biographies, and critical studies.

Doyle, Pj, and E. W. McDiarmid, eds. *The Baker Street Dozen*. New York: Congdon & Weed, 1987.
An anthology of the thirteen Sherlock Holmes stories selected in 1927 by Arthur Conan Doyle as his own favorites among the sixty stories he wrote. Each story is accompanied by an essay by a prominent Sherlockian scholar discussing the story. Includes a short account of Doyle's invitation to readers to submit lists of their favorite stories to the *Strand Magazine* and other lists of "twelve": women in the life of Sherlock Holmes, best films, best radio shows, portrayals of Sherlock Holmes, artists who have depicted Holmes. Contains a directory of Holmes societies. Index.

Eames, Hugh. "Sherlock Holmes—Arthur Conan Doyle." In his *Sleuths, Inc.: Studies of Problem Solvers*. Philadelphia: J. B. Lippincott, 1978.
Discusses the creation of Sherlock Holmes, his original in Dr. Joseph Bell, examples from the canon of Holmes as a solver of problems. As background to an understanding of the contribution of Doyle to detective fiction, Eames discusses the state of crime in the eighteenth century (with particular attention

to the career of Jonathan Wild) and the creation of a professional police force in London in the nineteenth century. Some biographical details on Doyle.

Hardwick, Michael, and Mollie Hardwick. *The Sherlock Holmes Companion*. Garden City, N.Y.: Doubleday, 1963.
As a guidebook for readers of the Sherlock Holmes stories the volume contains a Who's Who of more than two hundred characters from the canon, many accompanied by the original *Strand Magazine* illustrations by Sidney Paget. Includes plots of all sixty stories (without giving away their solutions), a sampler of quotations from the stories under nine categories, an extensive essay on Sherlock Holmes and John Watson, and a brief biographical sketch of Arthur Conan Doyle. Largely superseded by *The Complete Guide to Sherlock Holmes* (1986), by Michael Hardwick.

Harrison, Michael. *In the Footsteps of Sherlock Holmes*. New York: Frederick Fell, 1960.
Describes the appearance of London in the late nineteenth century and those parts that are mentioned in the Sherlock Holmes stories, with frequent comments on incidents in the canon. Almost literally, a walking tour of London related to Doyle's creations. Compares appearances of buildings in Victorian London with their modern-day appearances. Twenty-four pages of illustrations, principally of street scenes. Includes a list of source material. Harrison draws his own conclusions and refers to few other Sherlockian commentaries. Index.

Haycraft, Howard. "Profile by Gaslight." In his *Murder for Pleasure: The Life and Times of the Detective Story*. New York: D. Appleton-Century, 1941.
Describes the creation of Sherlock Holmes and the publishing history of the stories with brief comments on events in the life of Arthur Conan Doyle. Recounts one of Dr. Joseph Bell's diagnostic dialogues to show how closely it resembles a Sherlockian deduction. Explains the significance of Doyle's contribution to detective fiction and discusses the popularity of the character of Holmes and the legend of his reality as a human being.

Keating, H. R. F. *Sherlock Holmes: The Man and His World*. New York: Charles Scribner's Sons, 1979.
In producing this biography of Sherlock Holmes, Keating has presented the facts of the life of the great detective as they appear in the canon, without any fanciful additions or speculations, against a background of the historical and cultural events of the Victorian world. Holmes is seen as a man of his times. Lavishly illustrated with drawings; paintings; and photographs of people, places, and events in Great Britain and its empire from 1872 to 1917. Indexed.

Knox, Ronald A. "Studies in the Literature of Sherlock Holmes." In *The Baker Street Reader: Cornerstone Writings About Sherlock Holmes*, edited by Philip

A. Shreffler. Westport, Conn.: Greenwood Press, 1984.
Originally written in 1912, this essay by Knox uses the Sherlock Holmes stories as a tool to poke fun at the excesses of biblical scholars. By treating Holmes as a real person, Knox created a form of mock scholarship that has served as a model for Sherlockians ever since.

Lambert, Gavin. "Final Problems: Sir Arthur Conan Doyle." In his *The Dangerous Edge*. London: Barrie & Jenkins, 1975.
A biographical and critical study of Arthur Conan Doyle that equates the idealism of Sherlock Holmes with that of his creator but suggests that there was a fascination with the diabolic side of crime as well as with the science of deductive reasoning. Discusses recurring themes in the stories (including those not about Sherlock Holmes) and suggests possible origins for Doyle's ideas.

Ousby, Ian. "Arthur Conan Doyle." In his *Bloodhounds of Heaven: The Detective in English Fiction from Godwin to Doyle*. Cambridge, Mass.: Harvard University Press, 1976.
Discusses the formula that is the basis for the character and methods of Sherlock Holmes and how this originated in Doyle's days in medical school in Edinburgh along with echoes of Edgar Allan Poe and Robert Louis Stevenson. Ousby suggests that the structure of the stories may have been influenced by the standard Victorian biography so popular at the time and that Doyle included aspects of contemporary society designed to appeal to readers of the day.

Rauber, D. F. "Sherlock Holmes and Nero Wolfe: The Role of the 'Great Detective' in Intellectual History." In *Dimensions of Detective Fiction*, edited by Larry N. Landrum, Pat Browne, and Ray B. Browne. Bowling Green, Ohio: Bowling Green University Popular Press, 1976.
Compares Sherlock Holmes and Nero Wolfe as examples of the great detective as a popular version of the scientist and demonstrates how detective fiction reflects cultural attitudes toward the nature and practice of science. Considers Wolfe's procedures to reflect the attitude of modern physics toward the status of objects, while Holmes works from basic assumptions of classical physics.

Rodin, Alvin E., and Jack D. Key. *The Medical Casebook of Doctor Arthur Conan Doyle: From Practitioner to Sherlock Holmes and Beyond*. Malabar, Fla.: R. E. Krieger, 1984.
An extensive study of Arthur Conan Doyle as a practicing physician and medical writer of both fiction and nonfiction. Presents evidence contradicting the popular opinion that Doyle turned to fiction after failing as a physician. Discusses the amount of medical information found throughout Doyle's work.

Extensive consideration of the fiction not about Sherlock Holmes, with appendices of supporting data, references, and an index. Illustrated with photographs, drawings, and facsimiles of publications, most not duplicating those in other books on Doyle.

Routley, Erik. "The Master." In his *The Puritan Pleasures of the Detective Story*. London: Victor Gollancz, 1972.

Discusses the character of Sherlock Holmes, how he was built up over a period of time to the archetypal figure readers remember. Suggests that Doyle was not precise or conscious of the background history of his character and thus left room for the commentaries of the Baker Street Irregulars. Routley contrasts the element of the romantic with the nonromantic in the stories and considers the incidents where Holmes was incorrect in his reasoning.

Shreffler, Philip A., ed. *The Baker Street Reader: Cornerstone Writings About Sherlock Holmes*. Westport, Conn.: Greenwood Press, 1984.

Nearly thirty essays, poems, and puzzles reprinted from publications during the golden age of Sherlockian writings (1910-1960). Examines the literary criticism of Doyle's work, the perception of Sherlock Holmes as a real person, and the doings of the Baker Street Irregulars. Includes a selected bibliography of the most significant of these writings about the writings. Shreffler's introduction puts the material in context. Selected items have been annotated individually in this bibliography. Index.

Starrett, Vincent. "The Baker Street Irregulars." In *The Baker Street Reader: Cornerstone Writings About Sherlock Holmes*, edited by Philip A. Shreffler. Westport, Conn.: Greenwood Press, 1984.

An anecdotal account of the founding of the Baker Street Irregulars (BSI), the purpose of the organization, and of the historical meeting (December 7, 1934) which Starrett attended with Alexander Woollcott and William Gillette. Includes the text of the BSI Constitution and "Buy-Laws" and the establishment of some of the Scion Societies.

————————— . *The Private Life of Sherlock Holmes*. New York: Macmillan, 1933. Reprint. New York: Mysterious Press, 1988.

Considered to be "the first comprehensive biography of the world's greatest detective," this book collects a number of Starrett's articles published previously. Describes the creation and public response to Sherlock Holmes and traces the history of the character. Considers arguments for locating 221b Baker Street, the detective's methods, the untold stories, the actors who have impersonated Holmes on the stage and screen (through 1930), parodies, and burlesques. Includes E. V. Knox's mock examination paper on the life and work of Sherlock Holmes. Selected bibliography. Illustrated. No index.

Stout, Rex. "Watson Was a Woman." In *The Baker Street Reader: Cornerstone Writings About Sherlock Holmes*, edited by Philip A. Shreffler. Westport, Conn.: Greenwood Press, 1984.

With tongue in cheek, Rex Stout, author of the Nero Wolfe stories, demonstrates what the readers of the Sherlock Holmes stories have never suspected, that the great detective's companion was a woman. Stout chooses passages from the stories that support his theory and proceeds to show how the name of the lady can be found hidden in the titles of the stories themselves. Julian Wolff's equally clever rebuttal to this theory follows in this collection of essays.

Symons, Julian. "The Case of Sherlock Holmes." In his *Bloody Murder: From the Detective Story to the Crime Novel, a History*. Rev. ed. New York: Viking Press, 1985.

Discusses the contribution of Doyle under three headings: the character of Sherlock Holmes, the stories and their author, and the myth of Sherlock Holmes. Symons suggests sources for different aspects of Holmes's character, discusses themes and patterns in the stories, criticizes their casual construction, but believes that Doyle played fair with the reader. Finds storytelling skill not technical perfection in the stories.

Tracy, Jack, ed. *The Encyclopaedia Sherlockiana*. Garden City, N.Y.: Doubleday, 1977.

More than thirty-five hundred main entries, eight thousand story citations, and nearly two hundred illustrations explain and enhance the people, places, and events of the world of Sherlock Holmes. Alphabetically arranged with exhaustive cross-references. As much, if not more, sheer information on characters, incidents, and references as in *The Annotated Sherlock Holmes*. Serves to define terms from nineteenth century English society and history that might not be completely clear to modern readers. Includes a bibliography of sources.

Wilson, Edmund. "Mr. Holmes, They Were the Footprints of a Gigantic Hound." In *The Baker Street Reader: Cornerstone Writings About Sherlock Holmes*, edited by Philip A. Shreffler. Westport, Conn.: Greenwood Press, 1984.

When Edmund Wilson questioned the merits of detective fiction in the pages of *The New Yorker*, he was deluged by letters from angry readers. In his own defense, Wilson admits to having rediscovered the delights of the Sherlock Holmes stories and discusses the reasons they remain superior to the works of Doyle's imitators.

Wolff, Julian. "I Have My Eye on a Suite in Baker Street." In *The Baker Street Reader: Cornerstone Writings About Sherlock Holmes*, edited by Philip A. Shreffler. Westport, Conn.: Greenwood Press, 1984.

Besides the problem of finding the correct location on Baker Street of the address represented in the canon as "221b," Sherlockians are concerned about the physical description of the apartment shared by Sherlock Holmes and Dr. John Watson. Wolff presents a floor plan and cites data from a dozen of the adventures in support of his choices.

DAPHNE DU MAURIER

Biography

Bakerman, Jane S. "Daphne du Maurier." In *Twentieth Century Crime and Mystery Writers*, edited by John M. Reilly. New York: St. Martin's Press, 1980.
A brief summary of personal details of du Maurier's life followed by a checklist of her writings, in chronological order and arranged by categories: crime novels, collections of stories, noncrime fiction, plays, and nonfiction. Contains about 250 words, of commentary assessing her achievements as a writer.

Du Maurier, Daphne. *Gerald: A Portrait*. Garden City, N.Y.: Doubleday, Doran, 1935.
A biography of Gerald du Maurier, "one of the most vivid and dominant figures of the English stage," written by his novelist daughter. Includes some anecdotes of the du Maurier family. Written entirely in third person. Daphne du Maurier never uses the personal pronoun, even in scenes in which she appears. Critics find du Maurier's near-obsession with her father a significant factor in her own personal and literary development. A personal memoir, the book contains no documentation of sources and few dates are assigned to events. No illustrations and no index.

_____ . *Myself When Young: The Shaping of a Writer*. Garden City, N.Y.: Doubleday, 1977.
Writing her autobiography at the age of seventy, du Maurier admits to having difficulty remembering recent events when the events of her youth are so vivid. Using diaries kept from 1920 to 1932, she re-creates her memories, thoughts, impressions, and actions from the age of three until she was twenty-five and published her first novel, *The Loving Spirit* (1931). Twenty-three pages of photographs, but no index or checklist of her work. (British title: *Growing Pains: The Shaping of a Writer*, 1977.)

_____ . *The Rebecca Notebook and Other Memories*. Garden City, N.Y.: Doubleday, 1981.
Du Maurier's notebook of ideas for and the original plot outline of the novel *Rebecca* (1931) was written while she was in Egypt in 1937. Twenty-five pages long, it contains brief chapter outlines, examples of dialogue, and an epilogue, much of it considerably different from the final novel. Early short stories are accompanied by some reminiscent passages that describe the author's daily life in later years. British edition omits some stories and essays.

Kelly, Richard. "Daphne du Maurier." In *Critical Survey of Mystery and Detective Fiction*, edited by Frank N. Magill, vol. 2. Pasadena, Calif.: Salem Press, 1988.

Kelly discusses du Maurier's contribution to mystery fiction in terms of her
landmark novels *Jamaica Inn* (1936), *Rebecca* (1938), and *My Cousin Rachel*
(1951) and her short stories "The Birds" and "Don't Look Now." A short
biographical essay precedes extended analysis of her work and how it relates to
the incidents in her life. List of the titles and publication dates of her books
with a selected list of secondary sources.

Straub, Deborah A. "Daphne du Maurier." In *Contemporary Authors*, edited by
Ann Evory, vol. 6. Detroit: Gale Research, 1982.
A list of personal details in the life of Daphne du Maurier, along with some
facts about her literary career. Contains a list of her publications in chronological order and arranged according to categories. Includes reprint editions. Survey of critical responses to her writing with a list of adaptations to film and
television. List of biographical and critical sources in magazines and newspapers from 1931 to 1980.

Commentary

Bakerman, Jane S. "Daphne du Maurier." In *And Then There Were Nine . . . More
Women of Mystery*, edited by Jane S. Bakerman. Bowling Green, Ohio: Bowl-
ing Green University Popular Press, 1985.
Du Maurier combines the Cinderella story with a variety of forms of the
Bildungsroman to impart imagination and action to the literary conventions
and formulas found in *Jamaica Inn* (1936), *Frenchman's Creek* (1941), *My
Cousin Rachel* (1951), *The Scapegoat* (1957), and *The Flight of the Falcon*
(1965). Bakerman considers this combination to be what constitutes the "du
Maurier tradition" in the gothic mystery.

Kelly, Richard. *Daphne du Maurier*. Boston: Twayne, 1987.
In seven chapters, Kelly discusses du Maurier's life and the influence of her
famous actor father, Gerald du Maurier, on her development as a writer.
Examines her early novels in relationship to that influence. Considers her
masterpiece, *Rebecca* (1938), in some detail and traces her development as a
writer of romantic fiction and her use of themes of love, adventure, and
rebellion. Discusses her later, introspective novels that probe the psychological
and historical roots of her identity, surveys her short stories, evaluates her as a
writer, and assesses her contribution to popular culture and literature. Chronology, selected bibliography, and index.

IAN FLEMING

Biography

Bond, Mary Wickham. *How 007 Got His Name.* London: Collins, 1966.
This slim book was written by the wife of James Bond, ornithologist and author of *Birds of the West Indies* (1936), whose name Ian Fleming appropriated for the hero of his spy thrillers. Contains anecdotes of the unexpected notoriety that led to an afternoon spent at Goldeneye, Fleming's home in Jamaica, in 1964. Comments on the merchandise named for the fictional hero. Includes a parody, "On Her Majesty's Ornithological Service," signed "Avian Flemish" (Kenneth C. Parkes). Two photographs, one of the real James Bond with the creator of the fictional James Bond.

"Ian Fleming." In *Counterpoint*, edited by Roy Newquist. Skokie, Ill.: Rand McNally, 1964.
An interview conducted with Fleming in London in October, 1963. Fleming claims that in James Bond he was creating only "an interesting man to whom extraordinary things happen," not a glamorous figure. Discusses the development of the character's personality and why he himself could not be a model for Bond. Includes influences on the character from writers he has read, how he tries to get American dialogue correct, and the need for a return to romantic writing.

Pearson, John. *The Life of Ian Fleming.* New York: McGraw-Hill, 1966.
A substantial account of the life of the creator of James Bond and the relationship of author to character. A journalist colleague of Fleming, Pearson traces Fleming's use of his social life, naval intelligence, and journalism experience in developing Bond. Based on interviews with Fleming's acquaintances and letters in private files. There is no special documentation of sources. Thirty-one photographs. Index.

Zeiger, Henry A. *Ian Fleming: The Spy Who Came In with the Gold*. New York: Duell, Sloan and Pearce, 1965.
A once-over-lightly biography based on superficial research and published the year after Fleming's death. Discusses Fleming's father, Valentine Fleming, and the ideal of service and duty that his son tried to preserve in his own life and writing. One chapter each is devoted to Fleming as journalist, as naval-intelligence officer, his working methods as a writer, and his opinions on suspense fiction. Zeiger speculates on the reason for the popularity of the stories. Illustrated primarily with publicity photographs.

Commentary

Amis, Kingsley. *The James Bond Dossier*. New York: New American Library, 1965.
Discusses the James Bond series, but with little attempt to include Ian Fleming. Amis considers the novels to be complex and ambitious works of fiction depicting a Byronic hero who reflects the fantasies of his readers. Discussion of characters, male and female, the villains, and speculation on why Fleming never received high critical acclaim yet seems irreplaceable. Appendices on science fiction, escape literature, and sadism. Includes a chart organizing basic data on characters and highlights of the books from *Casino Royale* (1954) to *The Man with the Golden Gun* (1965).

Benson, Raymond. *The James Bond Bedside Companion*. New York: Dodd, Mead, 1984.
Discusses the creation of James Bond, the publishing history of the books, and the accompanying publicity and merchandising of the character and its continued popularity into the 1980's. Contains a biographical sketch of Fleming and a prose portrait of James Bond. Each book is discussed separately under headings of plot, style and themes, and characters. Includes continuations of the series by Kingsley Amis and the first three titles by John Gardner. Films covered through 1983. Appendices list books about Fleming, Bond, and the films, weapons used by Bond, and injuries sustained by the character. Illustrated with photographs (many not found in other books on the subject). Index.

Boyd, Ann S. *The Devil with James Bond!* Richmond, Va.: John Knox Press, 1967.
Relates the popularity of the James Bond series to attitudes in the twentieth century, especially the sense of confusion and apathy. Boyd discusses Bond as modern-day Saint George destroying today's equivalents of the Seven Deadly Sins. Considers Fleming not to have been totally serious when he claimed that he wrote the stories only for fun and for the money. Documented citations and bibliographic notes. Contrasts Bond's mission with that of Dietrich Bonhoeffer in *The Cost of Discipleship* (1959).

Cawelti, John G., and Bruce A. Rosenberg. "Bonded Excitement: Ian Fleming." In their *The Spy Story*. Chicago: University of Chicago Press, 1987.
Considers Fleming to be a major figure in the history of the spy story and the writer who most clearly and forcefully expresses the basic heroic spy-story formula. The character of James Bond is discussed in terms of its bringing together the conflicting cultural values of the mid-twentieth century. Cawelti and Rosenberg consider some of Fleming's popularity may be due to the ambiguities in the novels.

Masters, Anthony. "Ian Fleming: The Dashing Spy." In his *Literary Agents: The Novelist as Spy*. New York: Basil Blackwell, 1987.
Covers Fleming's early life, concentrating on aspects of his career as a journalist and naval intelligence officer that influenced his work as a writer. Discusses his experiences in 1941 that supplied Fleming with material for *Casino Royale* (1954) and the original behind the character of Sir Hugo Drax in *Moonraker*.

Panek, LeRoy L. "Ian Fleming." In his *The Special Branch: The British Spy Novel, 1890-1980*. Bowling Green, Ohio: Bowling Green University Popular Press, 1981.
Considers Fleming to be as a minor writer who contributed little by way of character, theme, or setting to the spy story. According to Panek, it was historical accident that was responsible for the popularity of Fleming's novels. Analyzes the books, finds simplistic psychology as the basis for the motivation of the characters, and striking similarities to the hard-boiled detective story.

Pearson, John. *James Bond: The Authorized Biography of 007*. London: Sidgwick & Jackson, 1973.
Written with tongue in cheek but with a completely straight face, this is the life of the "real" James Bond, compiled by the author of the authorized biography of Ian Fleming, who also worked with Fleming at *The Sunday Times*. Interviews between Pearson and Bond bring out the story of the secret agent and the creation of the myth that Ian Fleming depicted in his novels and short stories.

Rubin, Steven Jay. *The James Bond Films: A Behind the Scenes History*. New York: Arlington House, 1983.
A discussion all of the James Bond films from the 1954 version of *Casino Royale*, made for television, to the two from 1983, *Octopussy* and *Never Say Never Again*. Following an account of Fleming's initial encounters with filmmaking, Rubin devotes a chapter to each film, giving all credits and cast lists, discussing plots, and relating anecdotes about the making of the film. Illustrated with scenes from the films, behind-the-scenes photographs, and publicity shots, as well as poster, merchandise, and photographs of fans lined up to see the films. Index.

Van Dover, J. Kenneth. "Ian Fleming." In his *Murder in the Millions: Erle Stanley Gardner, Mickey Spillane, Ian Fleming*. New York: Frederick Ungar, 1984.
Discusses the James Bond series as a phenomenon in which the audience for the films draws readers to the books. Fleming wrote in a literate, accessible prose derived from W. Somerset Maugham and Raymond Chandler. Van Dover traces the creation of James Bond and suggests reasons for his appeal. The

consistency of the series (as a product) depends on a set of stereotypes used sparingly enough to suggest variety. Outlines the standard features present in *Casino Royale* (1954) compared with others in series. Illustrated with photographs from the films.

DICK FRANCIS

Biography

"Dick Francis." In *The Craft of Crime: Conversations with Crime Writers*, by John
C. Carr. Boston: Houghton Mifflin, 1983.
A biographical sketch and assessment of Dick Francis' work, with recommen-
dations on his best efforts, is followed by an interview. Topics covered include
Francis' own racing background as well as his opinions on racing, his characters, and how he chooses names, influences of earlier writers of thrillers on his
work, his career as a journalist, and the help his wife gives him on his books.

Francis, Dick. *The Sport of Queens: The Autobiography of Dick Francis*. New York:
Harper & Row, 1968. Rev. ed. London: Michael Joseph, 1974.
Francis' first book published in England (1957) was this autobiography that did
not appear in the United States until after he had published his first crime
novels. Written while he was a sportswriter, *The Sport of Queens* covers his life
to his retirement from racing. The Harper & Row edition briefly mentions his
career as a writer; the Michael Joseph edition expands the account. Illustrated
with photographs of Francis as a jockey.

"Interview with Dick Francis." In *Designs of Darkness*, by Diana Cooper-Clark.
Bowling Green, Ohio: Bowling Green University Popular Press, 1983.
Francis considers the puzzle in a detective story to be secondary to the things
the hero and the reader learn in the course of the book. He discusses his
characters, plot structures, why he does not consider himself a "full-blown
novelist," and whether his writing has improved. Some personal family notes
are also included. Photographs of Dick Francis.

Commentary

Axthelm, Pete. "Writer with a Whip Hand." *Newsweek* 97 (April 6, 1981): 98, 100.
Review of *Reflex* (1980), a novel that features "moral ambivalence" as well as
controlled violence and a knowledge of horse racing. Discusses Francis as a
"book-a-year man," whose formula is presented so well that his readers are
seldom disappointed with his product. Presents details of his life that inspired
him to begin writing; discusses where his ideas come from and how he works.

Barnes, Melvyn. *Dick Francis*. New York: Frederick Ungar, 1986.
A brief introduction sets Francis' books in the context of other crime fiction
and indicates his critical reception. This is followed by a chapter of biography

(based largely on *The Sport of Queens*, Francis' autobiography), and an analysis of each novel in publishing sequence. The focus is on the hero, each one
identified by profession or relationship within the book (jockey, reluctant peer,
artist, or photographer). The final chapter gives an overall assessment of
Francis' career. Discussion covers novels from *Dead Cert* (1962) to *The Danger* (1983). Bibliography includes novels through *Break In* (1986), short stories,
and articles about Francis. No illustrations. Index.

Bauska, Barry. "Endure and Prevail: The Novels of Dick Francis." *The Armchair
Detective* 11 (July, 1978): 238-244.
Surveys Francis' novels from *Dead Cert* (1962) to *Knockdown* (1974) against a
background of the racing lore in *The Sport of Queens: The Autobiography of
Dick Francis* (1968). Bauska discusses Francis' heroes, the significance of their
names, and the problems they face in the novels. Considers the "typical"
Francis novel to be found more frequently in his early work and that the later
ones focus more on the protagonist, what makes him what he is, and what this
says about Francis' development as a writer.

Gould, Charles E., Jr. "The Reigning Phoenix." *The Armchair Detective* 17 (Fall,
1984): 407-410.
Without discussing any of Dick Francis' novels in particular, Gould uses
passages from his *The Sport of Queens: The Autobiography of Dick Francis*
(1968), to emphasize that what is significant in his work is his own persona.
As a celebrity, Francis is compared to other celebrities whom Gould has met
or has imagined meeting. Like them, Francis' heroes are "only human," but
affirm virtues that make them "more than only human."

Knepper, Marty S. "Dick Francis." In *Twelve Englishmen of Mystery*, edited by
Earl F. Bargainnier. Bowling Green, Ohio: Bowling Green University Popular
Press, 1984.
A chronology of Francis' life and publications through 1983 and the publication of *Banker*, his twenty-first novel. Knepper surveys Francis' work in order
of publication, discussing differences as well as similarities between individual
novels. Considers his use of characters in various professions, few of them
private investigators, which allows him to explore the quality of professional-
ism in people. Contrasts Francis' work with the work of other mystery writers,
including Raymond Chandler and Dorothy L. Sayers, and discusses the significance of his not using a series character.

Stanton, Michael N. "Dick Francis: The Worth of Human Love." *The Armchair
Detective* 15 no. 2 (1982): 137-143.
Stanton uses the occasion of the publication of Francis' nineteenth mystery,
Reflex (1981), to speculate on the appeal of his work to readers. Considers how

Francis has used variations of setting, plot, and psychology while limiting himself to a background of steeplechase racing. Discusses violence, the types of characters he uses, and his combination of recognition and surprise. Francis adheres to a set of values rather than to a formula.

Zuckerman, Edward. "The Winning Form of Dick Francis." *The New York Times Magazine*, March 25, 1984: 40-41, 50, 54, 60, 62, 64.
A profile of Dick Francis written on the occasion of the publication of his twenty-third mystery novel, *The Danger* (1983), observes him watching a race at Hialeah and reviews the basic incidents of his life: his career as a jockey, his marriage, his years as a journalist, his decision to write a novel, and his subsequent success. Discusses the type of research his wife does for him and outlines some of his characters. Publishers' and critics' comments are quoted. Photographs of Francis at work and at the track.

NICOLAS FREELING

Biography

Jeffares, A. Norman. "Nicholas Freeling." In *Twentieth Century Crime and Mystery Writers*, edited by John M. Reilly. New York: St. Martin's Press, 1980.
A brief catalog of personal details in the life of Nicolas Freeling, along with some facts of his career outside literature, followed by a list of his crime novels and uncollected short stories arranged in chronological order from 1962 to 1979. About one thousand words of commentary assessing Freeling's achievement as a writer.

Commentary

Bakerman, Jane S. "Arlette: Nicolas Freeling's Candle Against the Dark." *The Armchair Detective* 16 (Winter, 1983): 348-352.
Discusses the character of Arlette Van der Valk Davidson, featured as hero of three novels by Freeling, *Auprès de Ma Blonde* (1972; British title: *A Long Silence*), *The Widow* (1979), and *Arlette* (1981). Bakerman notes that Freeling uses the widow of his earlier detective, Piet Van der Valk, as a symbol and paradigm of the dependent person transformed into a functioning, independent one.

Dove, George N. "Nicolas Freeling." In his *The Police Procedural*. Bowling Green, Ohio: Bowling Green University Popular Press, 1982.
Considers Freeling's Piet Van der Valk as an atypical policeman in the procedural category of the genre, but one who belongs more to the Great Policeman school. Dove discusses Freeling's style, the reasons for considering Van der Valk to be a maverick as a police detective, the family life of the detective, and why the final novel is really "an extended parable of Fiction and Reality."

Freeling, Nicolas. "Inspector Van der Valk." In *The Great Detectives*, edited by Otto Penzler. Boston: Little, Brown, 1978.
A brief overview of the Van der Valk series with the essential facts of Freeling's life followed by a discussion of Van der Valk as a character, his personality and life within the novels, and an account of how he was created. Freeling explains why, after ten books, he decided to kill the character, and what Van der Valk meant to him as a writer.

R. AUSTIN FREEMAN

Biography

Donaldson, Norman. *In Search of Dr. Thorndyke: The Story of R. Austin Freeman's Great Scientific Investigator and His Creator*. Bowling Green, Ohio: Bowling Green University Popular Press, 1971.
Donaldson intended this biography to be a study of Dr. John Evelyn Thorndyke as a character in the manner of the various studies of Sherlock Holmes but soon discovered that he could not separate the character from the creator. Freeman's life story is accompanied by running commentary on the Thorndyke stories, the characters, and assessments of Freeman's contributions to detective fiction in general. Frequent use of Freeman's letters. Detailed bibliography of first editions of Freeman's books. Illustrated with photographs, including scenes from television adaptations of the stories. Index.

——————. "R(ichard) Austin Freeman." In *Twentieth Century Crime and Mystery Writers*, edited by John M. Reilly. New York: St. Martin's Press, 1980.
A brief list of personal details of Freeman's life and some facts about his medical career, followed by an extensive checklist of his books in order of publication date and arranged by categories. About 750 words of commentary assessing his achievement as a writer.

Freeman, R. Austin. "The Art of the Detective Story." In *The Art of the Mystery Story*, edited by Howard Haycraft. New York: Simon & Schuster, 1947. Reprint. New York: Grosset & Dunlap, 1961.
Freeman considers the satisfaction offered by the detective story to be primarily an intellectual one and describes the way a detective story can be constructed to furnish that satisfaction. Describes the four stages (statement of the problem, production of clues, discovery of solution by the detective, and proof of solution) necessary to the structure of a good detective story.

"R(ichard) Austin Freeman." In *Twentieth Century Literary Criticism*, edited by Dennis Poupard, vol. 21. Detroit: Gale Research, 1986.
A brief survey of the personal details of Freeman's life, along with a discussion of the consensus of critical opinion about the merits of his work and his contribution to detective fiction. Includes a checklist of his principal works, liberal excerpts from sixteen articles and books about Freeman, and additional secondary sources.

Starrett, Vincent. "Good Bye, Dr. Thorndyke!" In his *Books and Bipeds*. New York: Argus Books, 1947.

An obituary notice for R. Austin Freeman, originally published in Starrett's "Books Alive" column in the *Chicago Sunday Tribune*. Discusses Freeman's literary career and recounts some of the personal details of his life. Comments briefly on the appeal of his detective, Dr. John Evelyn Thorndyke, and assesses Freeman's contribution to detective fiction.

Commentary

Bleiler, E. F. Introduction to *The Best Dr. Thorndyke Detective Stories*, by R. Austin Freeman. New York: Dover, 1973.
A brief critical sketch of R. Austin Freeman, in which Bleiler indicates the knowledge and experience that Freeman brought to his writing of detective stories. Comments on some of Freeman's books and writings outside the Thorndyke series and pays attention to his development of the inverted detective story. This collection includes sections from the early books of short stories about Thorndyke and reprints the newly discovered and earliest of all Thorndyke stories, "31 New Inn."

————————— . Introduction to *The Stoneware Monkey* and *The Penrose Mystery*, by R. Austin Freeman. New York: Dover, 1973.
Discusses the Dr. Thorndyke series in the general context of the realistic scientific detective story and contrasts Freeman's work to that of Arthur Conan Doyle. Considers the author's craftsmanship and other qualities that explain why his best work has survived. Contains brief critiques of the two novels from 1936 and 1938 collected in this volume.

Donaldson, Norman. "A Freeman Postscript." In *Mystery and Detective Annual*. Beverly Hills, Calif.: Donald Adams, 1972.
Discusses the fascination of detailed analysis of R. Austin Freeman's works and whether the results repay the effort. Uses examples from *Helen Vardon's Confession* (1922), *Flighty Phyllis* (1928), *Pontifex, Son and Thorndyke* (1931), *Mr.Polton Explains* (1940), and several short stories. Includes an account of a discussion of Freeman with Vincent Starrett.

Freeman, R. Austin. "Dr. Thorndyke." In *Meet the Detective*, introduction by Cecil Madden. New York: Telegraph Press, 1935.
Freeman describes how, as a medical student, his studies in medical jurisprudence impressed him enough to stay in some "pigeonhole" of his mind until he needed it for the writing of the stories about John Evelyn Thorndyke. Discusses his creation of Dr. Thorndyke, his characteristics and his methods. Comments on the roles of Christopher Jervis and Nathaniel Polton in the stories.

Haycraft, Howard. "England: 1890-1914 (The Romantic Era)." In his *Murder for Pleasure: The Life and Times of the Detective Story.* New York: D. Appleton-Century, 1941.

Presents a brief look at Freeman's background, which explains why he left medicine to write detective fiction. Haycraft considers *The Red Thumb Mark* (1907) one of the "undisputed milestones" in detective fiction and finds special significance in *The Singing Bone* (1912), a collection of short stories in which Freeman experimented with the so-called inverted detective story. Discusses Freeman's narrative style.

Heenan, Michael G. "A Note on the Chronology of the 'Dr. Thorndyke' Novels." *The Armchair Detective* 9 (November, 1975): 52-54.

Heenan has examined the Dr. Thorndyke novels by R. Austin Freeman and suggests their proper order of "dramatic date" in contrast to the order of publication. Notes to each of the twenty-one novels indicate his reasoning and cite specific dates in the texts wherever possible. By this method, he traces Dr. Thorndyke's career from about 1901 through 1936 in novels published from 1907 to 1940. Excludes the short-story collections.

McAleer, John. "R. Austin Freeman." In *Dictionary of Literary Biography,* edited by Bernard Benstock and Thomas F. Staley, vol. 70. Detroit: Gale Research, 1988.

In this concise survey, McAleer discusses Freeman's works against a background of his life and the influences upon him as a writer, in particular Alfred Swaine Taylor's book on medical jurisprudence. Describes his working methods and briefly critiques the novels in the Thorndyke series in published sequence. Comments on Freeman's strengths and weaknesses as a writer. Bibliography includes selected uncollected periodical publications. Illustrated.

Nelson, James. Introduction to *The Red Thumb Mark,* by R. Austin Freeman. New York: W. W. Norton, 1967.

A discussion of the merits of Freeman's first Dr. Thorndyke novel, *The Red Thumb Mark* (1907). Compares Freeman's own opinion with that of general readers to discover that the author was unduly modest in his assessment. Some biographical details. This edition is part of The Seagull Library of Mystery and Suspense.

Penzler, Otto. "Dr. Thorndyke." In his *The Private Lives of Private Eyes, Spies, Crime Fighters, and Other Good Guys.* New York: Grosset & Dunlap, 1977.

It is Dr. John Evelyn Thorndyke's catalog of knowledge combined with other bits of his education that allow him to interpret clues correctly, according to Penzler. Discusses Thorndyke's personality, his abilities as a detective, and his background, such as Freeman has given in the stories with no imaginative additions. Describes Thorndyke's office, home, and laboratory at 5A King's Bench Walk. Illustrated. Checklist of the Thorndyke books.

Routley, Erik. "Severe Science." In his *The Puritan Pleasures of the Detective Story*. London: Victor Gollancz, 1972.
Discusses the Dr. Thorndyke stories as imitations of the Sherlock Holmes series adapted to "the early age of electricity." Compares Thorndyke's methods to those of Holmes and finds them less interesting, less flamboyant. Routley believes that so much of the ambiance of the Holmes stories is lacking in Freeman that they retain little interest for the reader. Discusses characteristics of Freeman's style, the content and ideas in the stories, and the methods and character of Dr. Thorndyke.

Stone, P. M. "5A King's Bench Walk." In *Dr. Thorndyke's Crime File*, by R. Austin Freeman. New York: Dodd, Mead, 1941.
From passages of description given by Freeman in his books through 1940, Stone speculates on the actual location and furnishings of Dr. John Evelyn Thorndyke's rooms at the address given in the stories as "5A King's Bench Walk." Discusses Thorndyke, Nathaniel Polton, and Christopher Jervis, and other recurring characters.

Thomson, H. Douglas. "The Realistic Detective Story: R. Austin Freeman." In his *Masters of Mystery: A Study of the Detective Story*. London: Collins, 1931. Reprint. New York: Dover, 1978.
Discusses Freeman's contributions to that type of detective story which depicts the process of deduction with authenticity and plausibility. Thomson considers Freeman to be more successful in his efforts in the short stories than in the novels and notes what he considers serious faults in the books published through 1930.

ÉMILE GABORIAU

Biography

Bleiler, E. F. Introduction to *Monsieur Lecoq*, by Émile Gaboriau. New York: Dover, 1975.

An extensive discussion of Gaboriau's life and work in the context of his times, the mid-nineteenth century. Bleiler identifies Gaboriau's contributions to the detective story and describes the publishing history of his books in their original French editions as well as in translation. Contains an annotated bibliography of original book publications and translations noting which are authentic crime fiction. Identifies five spurious works often attributed to Gaboriau and cites the best individual works in English about Gaboriau. Illustrations of covers of early editions.

Haycraft, Howard. "The In-Between Years." In his *Murder for Pleasure: The Life and Times of the Detective Story*. New York: D. Appleton-Century, 1941.

Basic biographical details about Gaboriau with an account of some publishing practices of nineteenth century Paris that influenced his methods, content, and style of writing. Haycraft notes that Gaboriau used detection as only one of several themes and so did not write true detective novels. Discusses his detectives and his basic contributions. Speculates on the reasons that few people read him today.

Commentary

Murch, A. E. "The Rise of the *Roman Policier*." In her *The Development of the Detective Novel*. New York: Philosophical Library, 1958. Reprint. Port Washington, N.Y.: Kennikat Press, 1968.

Discusses the *roman policier* (crime novel) as developed by Gaboriau from the serial stories of sensational fiction known as *romans feuilletons*. Murch describes the detectives in Gaboriau's novels, discusses his plot structure, and comments on the influence his stories had on subsequent writers of crime fiction. Contrasts Gaboriau's work in book-length stories with the short fiction of Edgar Allan Poe and Arthur Conan Doyle.

Symons, Julian. "Dickens, Collins, Gaboriau: The Pattern Forms." In his *Bloody Murder: From the Detective Story to the Crime Novel, a History*. Rev. ed. New York: Viking Press, 1985.

Wilkie Collins is known to have read Gaboriau's works, and Symons speculates briefly on possible influences of the French writer on his own novels. Describes

Gaboriau's detective, Monsieur Lecoq, and contrasts his sober detection with the "sensational themes" found in the novels themselves. Comments briefly on *L'Affaire Lerouge* (1866; *The Widow Lerouge*, 1873), *Monsieur Lecoq* (1869), and "Le Petit Vieux de Batignoles" ("The Little Old Man of the Batignoles," 1876). Symons considers the latter to be Gaboriau's masterpiece.

Thomson, H. Douglas. "The French Detective Story: Émile Gaboriau." In his *Masters of Mystery: A Study of the Detective Story*. London: Collins, 1931. Reprint. New York: Dover, 1978.
An extensive discussion and consideration of Gaboriau's works. Thomson quotes liberally from *L'Affaire Lerouge* (1866; *The Widow Lerouge*, 1873), *Le Crime d'Orcival* (1867; *The Mystery of Orcival*, 1871), and *Monsieur Lecoq* (1869; English translation, 1879) to demonstrate Gaboriau's style and technique. Lists many of the tricks and ruses introduced by Gaboriau that have become conventions and clichés in detective fiction.

ERLE STANLEY GARDNER

Biography

Fugate, Francis L., and Roberta B. Fugate. *Secrets of the World's Best-Selling Writer: The Storytelling Techniques of Erle Stanley Gardner*. New York: William Morrow, 1980.

Using the notebooks, manuscripts, and correspondence in the Erle Stanley Gardner collection of the Humanities Research Center, University of Texas at Austin, the Fugates have presented a chronicle of Gardner's development as a writer from 1909 to 1969. Appendices contain selected sections of Gardner's "Formulae for Writing a Mystery." Includes facsimile pages of his notes. Selected bibliography. Index.

Gardner, Erle Stanley. "The Case of the Early Beginning." In *The Art of the Mystery Story*, edited by Howard Haycraft. New York: Simon & Schuster, 1947. Reprint. New York: Grosset & Dunlap, 1961.

An anecdotal survey of the early days of the hard-boiled detective story, published by *Black Mask* magazine. Gardner suggests that while Carroll John Daly introduced that type of story it was Dashiell Hammett who developed the style of writing identified with the hard-boiled form. Comments on his own contributions and the differences between the hard-boiled story and the action-detective story.

_____ . "Getting Away with Murder." *The Atlantic Monthly* 215 (January, 1965): 72-75.

Gardner describes his experiences while writing for the pulps, especially *Black Mask* and his stories of Ed Jenkins, the "Phantom Crook"; and his unwillingness to write stories with a situation for his characters that might make it difficult to produce a sequel. Includes anecdotes about writers Carroll John Daly and Dashiell Hammett. Explains why he will never have Perry Mason and Della Street marry.

_____ . "My Stories of the Wild West." *The Atlantic Monthly* 218 (July, 1966): 60-62.

Gardner describes his days writing Western stories for the pulp magazines and the efforts he made to make his backgrounds and local color authentic. Relates anecdotes of how a writer could get the most money for the number of words he wrote and an account of a joke played on one of the editors for the Munsey magazines when he visited Gardner's ranch.

_____ . "Speed Dash." *The Atlantic Monthly* 215 (June, 1965): 55-57.

Gardner's own account of his days as a pulp writer, his writing stories for

Street & Smith's *Top Notch* magazine about Speed Dash, the Human Fly, and
the ideas suggested for the character by his editor and his publisher. Describes
the series, his fan mail, and discusses the plot of one of them, "The Room of
Falling Flies."

Hughes, Dorothy B. *Erle Stanley Gardner: The Case of the Real Perry Mason*. New
York: William Morrow, 1978.
Mystery writer Hughes presents the life of Erle Stanley Gardner, practicing
attorney, champion of the underdog, author of eighty-two Perry Mason novels,
and best-selling writer. Gardner's life is presented through his own words in
his correspondence and other writings. Little critical commentary on his
books. Lavishly illustrated with more than seventy photographs. Includes a
bibliography of more than one thousand publications of Gardner, compiled by
Ruth Moore. Index of titles and personal names.

Johnston, Alva. *The Case of Erle Stanley Gardner*. New York: William Morrow,
1947.
An overview of Gardner's life as a lawyer and writer. Relates anecdotes of
some of his more spectacular successes in court and how they became incidents in his fiction. Bibliography of books published through 1946 and sixteen
pages of photographs of Gardner at work as writer and rancher. Johnston's
book appeared originally as three articles in *The Saturday Evening Post*, October 5-19, 1946.

Krebs, Albin. "Erle Gardner Dies; Mystery Writer, 80." *The New York Times*,
March 12, 1970: 1, 82.
An obituary of Erle Stanley Gardner. Contains statistics of the sales figures of
his books, his founding of the Court of Last Resort, his reputation for being a
champion of the underdog, his working methods, and his admiration for the
law. Basic biographical details. Krebs suggests that Gardner's success was due
to his intricate plots, his happy endings, and his ability to entertain.

Commentary

Hanscom, Leslie. "Man of Mystery." *Newsweek* 55 (January 18, 1960): 53-56.
On the occasion of the publication of Erle Stanley Gardner's one hundredth
book, *The Case of the Waylaid Wolf*, *Newsweek* associate editor Hanscom
assesses the reasons for his large sales and his continued popularity. Describes
his writing habits, considers what lies at the center of Perry Mason's appeal,
and constructs a profile of Mason based on Gardner's sparse descriptive passages. Illustrated. Includes a floor plan of Perry Mason's office suite.

Lachman, Marvin. "The Case of the Unbeaten Attorney: Or, The Secret Life of
Perry Mason." *The Armchair Detective* 4 (April, 1971): 147-151.
A slightly tongue-in-cheek survey of Perry Mason's career compiled by Lach-
man from hints in the novels about his appearance, his relationship to Della
Street, the examples of the lawyer breaking the law for the cause of justice.
Suggests that Perry Mason and Lieutenant Arthur Tragg are really brothers.
Despite the lack of specific references to Mason's age and birthplace in
Gardner's books, Lachman has some speculations to offer.

Morton, Charles W. "The World of Erle Stanley Gardner." *The Atlantic Monthly*
219 (January, 1967): 79-86, 91.
An overview of Gardner's career as a best-selling writer. Morton discusses
some of the reasons for Gardner's success, finding the key to be the amount of
material from his own experience on which he drew for his stories. Describes
Gardner's working methods, the way his stories have been marketed in magazines and books since 1923. Speculates on the reason for his universal appeal
and the impact of the Columbia Broadcasting System television series about
Perry Mason. Some attention is paid to his series of travel books, especially
The Hidden Heart of Baja (1962).

Robbins, Frank E. "The Firm of Cool and Lam." In *The Mystery Writer's Art*,
edited by Francis M. Nevins, Jr. Bowling Green, Ohio: Bowling Green University Popular Press, 1970.
A survey of the stories Gardner wrote under the pen name A. A. Fair about
Bertha Cool and Donald Lam (thirteen titles published between 1939 and 1952,
when this article was originally written). Describes the characters, the type of
cases they investigate, and discusses some of the reasons for the appeal of this
series to readers.

Stewart-Gordon,James. "Unforgettable Perry Mason." *Reader's Digest* 116 (May,
1980): 108-112.
Discusses Erle Stanley Gardner's popularity as a writer and compares his
experiences in court with those of his character Perry Mason. Brief overview of
Gardner's life, the publishing history of the Perry Mason books, the creation of
the Bertha Cool and the Donald Lam books, and the creation of the Court of
Last Resort. Stewart-Gordon synthesizes and condenses material from other
sources into a light, readable account that gives a good sense of Gardner's
accomplishment as a writer.

Van Dover, J. Kenneth. "Erle Stanley Gardner." In his *Murder in the Millions: Erle
Stanley Gardner, Mickey Spillane, Ian Fleming*. New York: Frederick Ungar,
1984.
A survey of Gardner's career as a best-selling writer. Some biographical de-

tails. Van Dover discusses the value to the writer and the reader of the use of a strict formula. Covers Gardner's pulp writing (especially the Lester Leith stories) with close analyses of *The Case of the Velvet Claws*, and *The Case of the Sulky Girl* (the first two Perry Mason novels, which were both published in 1933). Briefer consideration of Gardner's other series: D.A. Selby, Bertha Cool, and Donald Lam.

MICHAEL GILBERT

Biography

Gilbert, Michael. "The British Police Procedural." In *Whodunit? A Guide to Crime, Suspense, and Spy Fiction*, edited by H. R. F. Keating. New York: Van Nostrand Reinhold, 1982.
The author of a series of police procedurals, Michael Gilbert traces the development of the procedural by writers who had little personal understanding of the work of the professional policeman. The best writers of this type of story, he believes, should be policemen themselves, but in reality it is the professional writers and amateurs in police work who have written the best procedurals. Considers what it takes to give the best impression of what policemen think about themselves and their work.

_____ . "The Moment of Violence." In his *Crime in Good Company: Essays on Criminals and Crime-Writing*. London: Constable, 1959.
Gilbert explains the differences between the detective story and the thriller. Considers the latter to be more difficult to write and gives his reasons. The hero of the thriller, he explains, must be seen from within and not from the outside only. Discusses most common errors writers make in depicting violence in fiction.

_____ . "Quantity and Quality." In *Colloquium on Crime: Eleven Renowned Mystery Writers Discuss Their Work*, edited by Robin W. Winks. New York: Charles Scribner's Sons, 1986.
Discusses the use of "technicalese" (the superficial, acquired techniques that adorn a story) and the different ways that detail and description should be used in a detective story and in a thriller to achieve the goals of each form. Gilbert cites specific examples of writers who knew when to extend a description and writers who did not.

_____ . "The Spy in Fact and Fiction." In *The Mystery Story*, edited by John Ball. Del Mar, Calif.: Publisher's Inc., 1976.
Gilbert compares the work of the real-life spy to the game he played in his childhood known as *L'Attaque*, then discusses the development of intelligence operations and traces the progress of the spy story from John Buchan and Erskine Childers through Eric Ambler, Ian Fleming, and John le Carré to Len Deighton. Some reflections on contemporary political events that might inspire good spy stories.

Commentary

Dove, George N. "Michael Gilbert." In *Twelve Englishmen of Mystery*, edited by
    Earl F. Bargainnier. Bowling Green, Ohio: Bowling Green University Popular
    Press, 1984.
    Dove classifies Gilbert's fiction into five categories: professional detection,
    professional intelligence (or counterintelligence), amateur detection, amateur
    intelligence, and the social theme/suspense novel. While using some characters
    in more than one story, Gilbert has no recurring characters who always play
    major roles. Discusses more than twenty books briefly and considers Gilbert's
    craftsmanship and ability to deal with serious themes that reinforce the mys-
    tery and its solution.

Gilbert, Michael. "Patrick Petrella." In *The Great Detectives*, edited by Otto Penz-
    ler. Boston: Little, Brown, 1978.
    A brief sketch of Gilbert's achievements as a writer is followed by Gilbert's
    own account of the early life of Patrick Petrella from his birth to Spanish and
    English parents to his joining the ranks of the Metropolitan Police. Discusses
    Petrella's qualities as a character and as a professional policeman and explains
    how the idea for Petrella came to him while he was in church, listening to a
    sermon.

Heilbrun, Carolyn. "Who Did It? Michael Gilbert." *The New York Times Book
    Review* 87 (September 12, 1982): 9, 24.
    A review of *End-Game* (1982) and *Mr. Calder and Mr.Behrens* (1982), by
    Gilbert. The omnivorous reader of detective stories does not reread the books,
    Heilbrun claims. It is the smaller group of real connoisseurs who read fewer
    authors but enjoy returning to the presence of their favorites. Briefly suggests
    reasons that Gilbert should belong to the group of favorite authors, including
    his plotting and dialogue. Wonders why his books are not better known.

GRAHAM GREENE

Biography

Costa, Richard Hauer. "Graham Greene." In *Dictionary of Literary Biography*, edited by Bernard Oldsey, vol. 15. Detroit: Gale Research, 1983.
An extensive survey of Greene's publications against the background of his life and literary career. Lavishly illustrated with photographs of Greene, the covers of his books, and pages of his manuscripts. Contains a selected bibliography of his books, screenplays, and periodical publications in chronological order by date of publication. Extensive bibliography of secondary sources. This article has been brought up to date by Costa in the *Dictionary of Literary Biography Yearbook* for 1985.

De Vitis, A. A. *Graham Greene*. Rev. ed. Boston: Twayne, 1986.
Primarily a critical study of Greene's works. Includes some personal details of his life. Surveys Greene's works in order of publication as well as thematically. Includes a chronology of his life, a section of bibliographic notes, a selected primary bibliography, and an annotated secondary bibliography. Index.

Greene, Graham. *A Sort of Life*. New York: Simon & Schuster, 1971.
Critics have said that Greene's autobiography conceals more than it reveals. It ends just as his first novel, *The Man Within* (1921), has been published. Final chapter comments briefly on some of the later books, including *Orient Express* (1932; British title: *Stamboul Train*), and reprints some diary excerpts. Childhood, attempted suicide, psychoanalysis at sixteen, schooldays at the University of Oxford, involvement in the Secret Service, and apprenticeship as a journalist are some of the incidents covered.

——————— . *Ways of Escape*. New York: Simon & Schuster, 1980.
This second volume of Greene's autobiography picks up where *A Sort of Life* (1971) ended, with the publication of *The Man Within* (1929), and takes his story to 1978. Greene candidly discusses his own writing and the people he has met; he also covers the inspirations and circumstances under which each book was written. Describes his experiences with drugs and his experiences with filmmaking, especially the writing of the treatment for *The Third Man*. Includes sections of travel diaries kept in Africa, Cuba, Vietnam, and Mexico.

Hindman, Kathleen B. "Graham Greene." In *Dictionary of Literary Bibliography*, edited by Stanley Weintraub, vol. 13. Detroit: Gale Research, 1982.
A survey of Greene's work as a dramatist against the background of his life. Lavishly illustrated with photographs of Greene during a rehearsal for one of his plays, a production of one of the plays, and the program book for his first

play. Includes a selected bibliography of his works in chronological order and arranged by categories with a brief bibliography of secondary sources.

Sherry, Norman. *The Life of Graham Greene*. Vol. 1, 1904-1939. New York: Viking Press, 1989.
Based on correspondence, diaries, and personal interviews, this is the first full-length biography of Graham Greene. Sherry made personal visits to the locales in Greene's novels and talked with the people Greene put into his fiction. Divided into eight sections; the biography takes Greene through the publication of *The Power and the Glory* (1939). Extensive bibliographic notes, seventy-eight photos, fifteen line illustrations. Index.

Commentary

Calendrillo, Linda T. "Role Playing and 'Atmosphere' in Four Modern British Spy Novels." *Clues: A Journal of Detection* 3 (Spring/Summer, 1982): 111-119.
Calendrillo uses the examples of John Buchan's *The Thirty-nine Steps* (1915), Graham Greene's *The Confidential Agent* (1939), John le Carré's *The Spy Who Came in from the Cold* (1963), and Joseph Conrad's *The Secret Agent* (1907) to show how the protagonist changes roles, how he responds to the role changes, and what the effect of the physical surroundings or atmosphere is on characterization and theme.

Cawelti, John G., and Bruce A. Rosenberg. "At a Crossroads: Eric Ambler and Graham Greene." In their *The Spy Story*. Chicago: University of Chicago Press, 1987.
Discusses the ways in which Greene's work, like Eric Ambler's, transformed the spy story and was itself transformed by the changing formulas. Cawelti and Rosenberg contrast Ambler, who began his career by writing spy stories, with Greene, who came to the field after writing several mainstream novels. Examines *The Confidential Agent* (1939), *The Honorary Consul* (1973), and *The Human Factor* (1978) to show how Greene has merged the spy genre with the mainstream novel.

Christopher, J. R. "A Detective Searches for a Clue to *The Heart of the Matter*." *The Armchair Detective* 4 (October, 1970): 32.
Christopher examines Greene's novel *The Heart of the Matter* (1948), normally classed as a serious novel and not as an entertainment, to determine what qualities it possesses that might place it in the second category. Christopher lists detective-story motifs (including reversal of situations) contained in Greene's novel and identifies characters whose roles match those more standard to detective fiction.

Lambert, Gavin. "The Double Agent: Graham Greene." In his *The Dangerous Edge*. London: Barrie & Jenkins, 1974.

Beginning with an account of Greene's serious nightmares, Lambert shows how these relate to the themes in his so-called serious fiction as well as his entertainments. Demonstrates how the entertainments and other fiction are part of a whole and not separate entities. Extensive discussion of *This Gun for Hire* (1936; British title: *A Gun for Sale*), *The Confidential Agent* (1939), and *The Ministry of Fear* (1943). Divides Greene's fiction into overlapping categories with consideration of themes, characters, and point of view.

Macdonald, Andrew, and Gina Macdonald. "Graham Greene." In *Dictionary of Literary Biography*, edited by Bernard Benstock and Thomas F. Staley, vol 77. Detroit: Gale Research, 1988.

A survey of Greene's entertainments discussed in the order of their publication against a background of Greene's own life and compared with his other writings. Recurring themes, the flawed but human and likable central characters, and Greene's comments on his own work are covered. Extensive bibliographies of his own publications (1925-1985) and books and articles about him. Illustrated.

Masters, Anthony. "Graham Greene: The Abrasive Spy." In his *Literary Agents: The Novelist as Spy*. New York: Basil Blackwell, 1987.

Masters describes Greene's own experiences as a "reasonably efficient intelligence officer" under Stewart Menzies of MI6 and traces the influences on his own writing, particularly *The Confidential Agent* (1939), *The Ministry of Fear* (1943), *The Third Man* (1950), *Our Man in Havana* (1958), and *The Human Factor* (1978) in which the themes of duplicity and betrayal are demonstrated most clearly.

Nelson, Bill. "Evil as Illusion in the Detective Story." *Clues: a Journal of Detection* 1 (Spring, 1980): 9-14.

A discussion of the nature of evil as presented in two novels, Wilkie Collins' *The Moonstone* (1868) and Graham Greene's *Brighton Rock* (1938). The surface revelation of the way evil can be controlled is only one of Nelson's considerations. Both Collins and Greene destroy or attack illusions, but their goals appear to be different.

Panek, LeRoy L. "Graham Greene." In his *The Special Branch: The British Spy Novel, 1890-1980*. Bowling Green, Ohio: Bowling Greene University Popular Press, 1981.

Espionage, as such, plays only a secondary role in Greene's spy stories, according to Panek. Greene is more concerned with themes of commitment, conscience, individual will, betrayal, and alienation. Discusses *Orient Express* (1932; British title: *Stamboul Train*), *This Gun for Hire* (1936; British title: *A*

Gun for Sale), *The Confidential Agent* (1939), *The Ministry of Fear* (1943), *The Quiet American* (1955), *Our Man in Havana* (1958), *The Honorary Consul* (1973), and *The Human Factor* (1978).

Sandoe, James. "Dagger of the Mind." In *The Art of the Mystery Story*, edited by Howard Haycraft. New York: Simon & Schuster, 1947. Reprint. New York: Grosset & Dunlap, 1961.

Discusses the subcategory of "psychological thriller" and examines the work of several writers whose books fit that description. Writers included: Joseph Sheridan Le Fanu, Patrick Hamilton, Margaret Millar, Cornell Woolrich, Eric Ambler, and Graham Greene. Close attention paid to *Brighton Rock* (1938) and *The Confidential Agent* (1939).

Wolfe, Peter. *Graham Greene: The Entertainer*. Carbondale: Southern Illinois University Press, 1972.

This was the first full-length study of Greene's entertainments as opposed to his serious fiction. Individual chapters are devoted to analyzing the novels from *Orient Express* (1932 British title: *Stamboul Train*) to date of the study, covering style, technique, structure, and characterization. They are discussed as entertainments and serious literature. Uses references and quotations from other critics to present an overview of Greene's critical reception.

DASHIELL HAMMETT

Biography

Hammett, Dashiell. "From the Memoirs of a Private Detective." In *The Art of the Mystery Story*, edited by Howard Haycraft. New York: Simon & Schuster, 1947. Reprint. New York: Grosset & Dunlap, 1961.

Hammett recalls some experiences of the eight years he spent as a private detective for the Pinkerton Detective Agency. Contains twenty-nine numbered vignettes and observations originally published in *The Smart Set* for March, 1923, at the same time that he was beginning to sell his hard-boiled detective fiction to *Black Mask* magazine.

Hellman, Lillian. Introduction to *The Big Knockover: Selected Stories and Short Novels by Dashiell Hammett*, edited by Lillian Hellman. New York: Random House, 1966.

A personal account of Hellman's friendship with Dashiell Hammett, who was her "closest . . . most beloved friend." Hellman explains why she will never write a biography or a critical study of Hammett. Anecdotes from their life together demonstrate aspects of Hammett's character, personality, personal opinions, ideas about the writer's life, and his last days.

Johnson, Diane. *Dashiell Hammett: A Life*. New York: Random House, 1983.

This is the first biography of Hammett written with the cooperation of his family and his friend Lillian Hellman. Based on letters and interviews, Johnson's book devotes little critical attention to Hammett's writings, concentrating instead on the facts of their publication. Liberal quotations from his letters. Reprints "From the Memoirs of a Private Detective" in its entirety. Select bibliography. Notes. Illustrated. Index.

Layman, Richard. *Shadow Man: The Life of Dashiell Hammett*. New York: Harcourt Brace Jovanovich, 1981.

This is the first extensive biography of Hammett. Written without "assistance and without hindrance" of Hammett's "most trusted friend" Lillian Hellman and based on official records and interviews with family, friends, and associates of Hammett, Layman's scholarly book presents fact and not speculation. Describes the publishing history of Hammett's books and stories, offers critical assessment, and cites the contemporary reception of most titles. Chronology. Illustrations. Appendices include bibliography, the full text of Hammett's testimony before United States Second District Court, before Judge Sylvester Ryan, July 9, 1951. Index.

Nolan, William F. *Dashiell Hammett: A Casebook*. Santa Barbara, Calif.: McNally & Loftin, 1969.

This is the first book published about Hammett and is part biography, part publishing history of his novels and stories, part critical assessment of his works and his place in the history of the detective story, and part bibliography. Nolan discusses the five novels and the short stories about the Continental Op, Hammett's scripts for the "Secret Agent X-9" comic strip, and the movie versions of his books. "A Dashiell Hammett Checklist" includes his radio work and the motion pictures. Secondary bibliography. Index.

_____ . *Hammett: A Life at the Edge*. New York: Congdon & Weed, 1983.

Nolan expands and updates the material used in his earlier book, *Dashiell Hammett: A Casebook* (1969).

Based on interviews, a study of unpublished manuscripts, and a close reading of Hammett's stories. Nolan pursues his subject like a private detective investigating a mystery. Includes informal critical discussion of the books and stories, along with the incidents of Hammett's life. Contains illustrations of manuscript pages, and early magazine and book editions, photographs of people who knew Hammett, and locations of places mentioned in the novels. Selected bibliography, and notes. Index.

Symons, Julian. *Dashiell Hammett*. New York: Harcourt Brace Jovanovich, 1985.

A critical, biographical survey of the man who "created the first truly American crime novels." Symons puts Hammett in the context of the development of crime fiction and discusses the short stories and the major novels against the outline of his life. Lavishly illustrated with photographs from Hammett's life, magazine covers and pages, book jackets, scenes from movies based on the books, and places in San Francisco represented in *The Maltese Falcon* (1929). Chronology, notes, selected bibliography. Index.

Commentary

Bentley, Christopher. "Murder by Client: A Reworked Theme in Dashiell Hammett." *The Armchair Detective* 14 (Winter, 1981): 78-79.

Discusses *The Maltese Falcon* (1929) as an example of the way Hammett occasionally reused the characters and situations of some of his short stories with greater sophistication in a novel. Traces the material used in *The Maltese Falcon* to "The Whosis Kid," "The House on Turk Street," "The Girl with the Silver Eyes," and "The Gutting of Couffignal," but especially "Who Killed Bob Teal?" from which liberal excerpts are given.

Cawelti, John G. "Hammett, Chandler, and Spillane." In his *Adventure, Mystery, and Romance: Formula Stories as Art and Popular Culture*. Chicago:

University of Chicago Press, 1976.
Hammett is considered unique as a writer of formula stories in not using the same detective or the same story repeatedly. Cawelti questions the claim that Hammett's stories are particularly realistic. Discusses, compares, and contrasts *Red Harvest* (1927) and *The Maltese Falcon* (1929). Considers Hammett to have used a formula story to explore aspects of belief and illusion. Claims that his contribution is his "powerful vision of life."

Dooley, Dennis. *Dashiell Hammett*. New York: Frederick Ungar, 1984.
A critical survey of Hammett's work set against the backdrop of his life. Dooley attempts to take a fresh look at the writing without reference to the opinions of other critics. Fully half of the book discusses Hammett's short stories. A chapter is devoted to each of the five novels with a summary of Hammett's accomplishments and his contribution to detective fiction. Dooley considers the best of Hammett to be a standard against which other writers may be measured. Bibliographic notes and selected bibliography. Index.

Durham, Philip. "The *Black Mask* School." In *Tough Guy Writers of the Thirties*, edited by David Madden. Carbondale: Southern Illinois University Press, 1968.
An account of the founding of *Black Mask* magazine, how the hard-boiled American detective and the myth of the special attitude toward violence were created in its pages, and what made Hammett's stories so distinctive. Discusses many of the Continental Op stories and explains how they prepared the way for Hammett's most successful work in his novels.

Eames, Hugh. "Sam Spade—Dashiell Hammett." In his *Sleuths, Inc.: Studies of Problem Solvers*. Philadelphia: J. B. Lippincott, 1978.
Discussion of *The Maltese Falcon* (1929) and the character of Sam Spade combined with a somewhat rambling, informal, interpretive account of Hammett's life and career as private detective and writer of detective fiction. Eames considers Hammett's background as a detective before he became a writer to be significant to an understanding of him as a writer and includes an account of the history of the Pinkerton Detective Agency, for which Hammett worked.

Edenbaum, Robert I. "The Poetics of the Private Eye: The Novels of Dashiell Hammett." In *Tough Guy Writers of the Thirties*, edited by David Madden. Carbondale: Southern Illinois University Press, 1968.
Discusses the characteristics of the Hammett tough-guy hero, free of sentiment, free of the fear of death, and free of temptations from money or sex. Demonstrates how this hero is developed in *Red Harvest* (1927), *The Dain Curse* (1928), *The Maltese Falcon* (1929), *The Glass Key* (1930), and *The Thin Man* (1932). Considers *The Maltese Falcon* to be the most significant novel in this development.

Finch. G. A. "From Spade to Marlowe to Archer: An Essay." *The Armchair Detective* 4 (January, 1971): 107-110.

Compares the character of Sam Spade to Philip Marlowe and Lew Archer and demonstrates what each figure contributed to the development of the hard-boiled detective story. Finch examines *The Maltese Falcon* (1929) closely to demonstrate Hammett's use of adjectives that contribute to his style in making Sam Spade a completely persuasive figure. Notes that Hammett's own background as a private detective lends significant authenticity to his writing.

Hagemann, E. R. "From 'The Cleansing of Poisonville' to *Red Harvest.*" *Clues: A Journal of Detection* 7 (Fall/Winter, 1986): 115-132.

A thorough examination of the differences between the *Black Mask* magazine serial "The Cleansing of Poisonville" and its book version as Hammett's first novel *Red Harvest*. In a set of charts, Hagemann indicates the many alterations that make two different novels out of the two versions. Argues for the superiority of the pulp-magazine version over the Knopf edition, which shows evidence of a heavy editorial hand.

Hammett, Dashiell. Introduction to *The Maltese Falcon*. New York: Modern Library, 1934.

A brief account of how *The Maltese Falcon* (1929) was written, the sources of some parts of its basic structure in something Hammett had read and in two short stories he had written with which he was not satisfied. Describes the origins of some of the characters: Wilmer, Brigid O'Shaughnessy, Lieutenant Dundy, Tom Polhaus, Iva Archer, Effie Perine, and Casper Gutman. Hammett claims that Sam Spade is what most private detectives would like to be.

Haycraft, Howard. "America: 1918-1930 (The Golden Age)." In his *Murder for Pleasure: The Life and Times of the Detective Story*. New York: D. Appleton-Century, 1941.

Discusses Hammett's contribution to the detective story. Haycraft contrasts Hammett with his popular contemporary S. S. Van Dine and claims that his significance as an innovator is equal to that of Arthur Conan Doyle. Comments on the popularity of Hammett's five novels and his origins as a pulp writer. Concludes with some basic biographical information.

Malin, Irving. "Focus on 'The Maltese Falcon': The Metaphysical Falcon." In *Tough Guy Writers of the Thirties*, edited by David Madden. Carbondale: Southern Illinois University Press, 1968.

Malin considers Hammett's technique in writing flat, impersonal prose that conveys a toughness of style to be symbolic of a deep truth beneath the surface of the stories. Notes the ways in which Sam Spade shares archetypal qualities with mythic heroes and demonstrates how Hammett's dialogue, characters, and action convey "metaphysical subtleties."

Marcus, Stephen. Introduction to *The Continental Op*, by Dashiell Hammett. New York: Random House, 1974.
A biographical sketch of Dashiell Hammett is followed by a discussion of *The Maltese Falcon*, novel (1929) and movie (1941), focussing on the "Flitcraft episode" as a key to Hammett's vision. Marcus considers Hammett to have had a consistency and coherence in his work that represented an "authentic imaginative vision" of his art. Constructs a prototypical case for the Continental Op to demonstrate this thesis.

Occhiogrosso, Frank. "Murder in the Dark: Dashiell Hammett." *The New Republic* 177 (July 30, 1977): 28-30.
Occhiogrosso considers the Continental Op to be a more significant character than Sam Spade or Nick and Nora Charles, and the stories that Hammett wrote about him to be the best in the hard-boiled tradition. Discusses Hammett's innovations in the detective story, his characters, his style, and the variations on a theme to be found in his work. Argues for the Op as one of the most memorable figures in American literature.

Raubicheck, Walter. "Stirring It Up: Dashiell Hammett and the Tradition of the Detective Story." *The Armchair Detective* 20 (Winter, 1987): 20-25.
Raubicheck examines the short stories about the Continental Op and demonstrates how most of them have the same structure as the traditional, classic detective story written by Edgar Allan Poe and Arthur Conan Doyle: statement of the problem, production of clues, the solution, and the explanation. Hammett's innovations lie in the manner in which these are presented. The Op achieves results by "stirring things up."

Reilly, John M. "Sam Spade Talking." *Clues: A Journal of Detection* 1 (Fall/ Winter, 1980): 119-125.
Reilly finds a relationship between nineteenth and twentieth century American fiction in considering the differences between vernacular American speech in the prose of Mark Twain and the speech of Sam Spade in *The Maltese Falcon* (1929). Discusses the significance of Hammett's narrating the novel in third person with Spade as manipulator, revealing his character through his speech.

Symons, Julian. "The American Revolution." In his *Bloody Murder: From the Detective Story to the Crime Novel, a History*. Rev. ed. New York: Viking Press, 1985.
A survey of Hammett's novels and how they represent a change from earlier detective stories in style and tone. Symons considers the novels to be superior

to the short stories. Speculates on reasons for Hammett's career as a writer being so short and relates that to those other aspects of life (including politics) that occupied more of his time.

——————— . "Dashiell Hammett: A Writer and His Time." In his *Critical Observations*. New York: Ticknor & Fields, 1981.
Discusses Hammett under three headings: the rise and fall of a legend (biographical sketch that suggests the reasons Hammett stopped writing in 1934), his style of writing and the similarities with that of Ernest Hemingway (comments on the short stories and *Red Harvest*, 1927), and his art (the structure of his books as a series of dialogues and confrontations).

Wolfe, Peter. *Beams Falling: The Art of Dashiell Hammett*. Bowling Green, Ohio: Bowling Green University Popular Press, 1980.
A comprehensive survey of Hammett's writings. Wolfe considers the short stories to be significant contributions to American literature as well as to detective fiction. Discusses Hammett's use of detective-story conventions (the dying message, misdirection, and the clue so obvious that no one can see it). Discusses each novel at length in turn but considers *The Maltese Falcon* (1929) to be the best.

CYRIL HARE
(Alfred Alexander Gordon Clark)

Biography

"Alfred Alexander Gordon Clark (Cyril Hare)." In *Contemporary Authors*, edited by Hal May, vol. 112. Detroit: Gale Research, 1985.
Contains exactly 136 words of personal and professional detail about Alfred Alexander Gordon Clark, who wrote detective novels and short stories under the pen name Cyril Hare. Refers to his detectives, Inspector Mallett and Francis Pettigrew, and mentions some of the titles of the books in which they appear. Cites two sources for biographical and critical information, both of which are cited in this bibliography as well.

Brooks, William S. "Cyril Hare: Alfred Alexander Gordon Clark." In *Critical Survey of Mystery and Detective Fiction*, edited by Frank N. Magill, vol. 2. Pasadena, Calif.: Salem Press, 1988.
Describes the principal series characters in Hare's detective stories and assesses his general contribution to the genre. A brief biographical sketch is followed by an extended analysis of his major novels. Includes lists of titles and dates of publication of Hare's major publications with a brief bibliography of secondary sources.

Hare, Cyril. "The Classic Form." In *Crime in Good Company*, collected by Michael Gilbert. London: Constable, 1959.
A biographical sketch of Cyril Hare, written by Michael Gilbert, is followed by Hare's own description of the essentials of the English detective story: a crime, a detective to unravel the crime, and a criminal to be unmasked at the end. Discusses what the writer can do to make the solution feasible, how characters should be portrayed, the importance of background, the type of detective to use, and the purpose of detective fiction.

Shibuk, Charles. "Cyril Hare." In *Twentieth Century Crime and Mystery Writers*, edited by John M. Reilly. New York: St. Martin's Press, 1980.
A brief outline of personal details of the life of Alfred Alexander Gordon Clark, who wrote crime fiction as Cyril Hare, along with a list of his novels, collected short stories, uncollected short stories, and other writings arranged in chronological order and by categories. Contains about 750 words of commentary assessing his achievement as a writer.

Commentary

Bargainnier, Earl F. "The Detective Fiction of Cyril Hare." *The Armchair Detective* 17 (Winter, 1984): 26-33.
A survey of Hare's nine detective novels with some biographical information (especially the origin of his pseudonym). Bargainnier begins by discussing the general characteristics of Hare's work, touches only briefly on the short stories, examines *An English Murder* (1951), and then considers the novels about Francis Pettigrew and Inspector Mallet, separately and together. Includes a checklist of the books. Illustrated with covers from 1980's paperback editions. (Some errors occur; the date of Hare's death is given as 1957 instead of 1958.)

Carpenter, Richard. "Cyril Hare: Master of the Classic Detective Story." *Clues: A Journal of Detection* 8 (Fall/Winter, 1987): 89-112.
Carpenter classes Cyril Hare as one of those classic British writers of detective fiction who combine delicate and subtle plots with interesting characters and a "richly evoked setting." Discusses all these characteristics as they are demonstrated in the novels and short stories. Notes Hare's emphasis on fine points of law and his use of irony. Comments on Francis Pettigrew. Considers *Tragedy at Law* (1942) to be Hare's masterpiece.

Gilbert, Michael. "Introduction: Cyril Hare." In *Best Detective Stories of Cyril Hare*. London: Faber & Faber, 1959. Reprint. New York: Walker & Co., 1961. Reprinted as *Death Among Friends and Other Detective Stories*, by Cyril Hare. New York: Harper & Row, 1984.
Gilbert describes how he discovered Cyril Hare's detective stories while in a prisoner-of-war camp in Italy during World War II and his subsequent meeting with the writer. Follows this with a biographical sketch and a discussion of Hare's short stories, which Gilbert finds readable at all times due to their "smoothness and technique." Describes the stories as falling into three categories: stories with legal backgrounds, stories about murder, and stories about other crimes.

Shibuk, Charles. "Cyril Hare." *The Armchair Detective* 3 (October, 1969): 28-30.
A biographical sketch of Cyril Hare is followed by an annotated bibliography of his novels and the collection of short stories, arranged in the order of their first publication. Annotations include variant titles, paperback reprint information, a brief and perceptive evaluation of each novel by Shibuk or by other critics. The entry for the posthumous collection of short stories indicates contents, the name of the detective (if any), and magazine appearances in *Ellery Queen's Mystery Magazine*.

Steiner, T. R. "Cyril Hare (Alfred Alexander Gordon Clark)." In *Dictionary of*

Literary Biography, edited by Bernard Benstock and Thomas F. Staley, vol. 77. Detroit: Gale Research, 1988.

A critical survey of Hare's nine detective novels in the order of publication, accompanied by a brief biographical sketch. Steiner explains what makes his work distinctive and why *An English Murder* (1951), so conventional a detective story, should be his most successful novel. Brief consideration of his short stories. Includes a bibliography of Hare's books and selected periodical appearances. Illustrated with first-edition jackets from two of Hare's novels.

Strout, Cushing. "Murder with Manners: Cyril Hare." *The New Republic* 177 (July 30, 1977): 34-36.

Considers that Cyril Hare's detective fiction to be for fastidious readers and discusses his narrative technique, point of view, use of misdirection, close reasoning, and the other virtues that his stories possess which distinguish them from other examples of the formal detective story. Indicates that Hare's theories of how detective fiction should be written have been put to practical use in his own stories.

PATRICIA HIGHSMITH

Biography

Highsmith, Patricia. "Not-Thinking with the Dishes." In *Whodunit? A Guide to Crime, Suspense, and Spy Fiction*, edited by H. R. F. Keating. New York: Van Nostrand Reinhold, 1982.
Highsmith explains the source of her ideas: a situation of surprise or coincidence or a theme. Discusses her working methods: how many hours a day to write, how many words, particularly under ideal conditions, when not to think about the work. Decides that it is impossible to explain how to write a book, that it is better just to write it. Photograph of Highsmith and a manuscript page from *People Who Knock on the Door* (1983).

"Interview with Patricia Highsmith." In *Designs of Darkness*, edited by Diana Cooper-Clark. Bowling Green, Ohio: Bowling Green University Popular Press, 1983.
Highsmith talks about her writing, her philosophy of life, her prime purpose to entertain, not to make a point or be an intellectual. Discusses her views on murder as a social problem, her interest in guilt, her experiences of being "categorized" as a writer by her publishers and her readers. Comments on many of her novels, but particularly on *Strangers on a Train* (1949). Photograph of Highsmith.

Richardson, Maurice. "Simenon and Highsmith: Into the Criminal's Head." In *Crime Writers*, edited by H. R. F. Keating. London: British Broadcasting Corporation, 1978.
Discusses the works of Georges Simenon and Patricia Highsmith as examples of modern crime writers whose stories are entertaining yet serious contributions to literature. The biographical sketch contributes more personal information about Highsmith's life and family than can be found in most other sources.

Straub, Deborah A. "(Mary) Patricia Highsmith." In *Contemporary Authors*, edited by Linda Metzger and Deborah A. Straub, vol. 20. Detroit: Gale Research, 1987.
A brief catalog of personal details of the life of Patricia Highsmith, along with some facts about her career as a writer. Contains a list of books in chronological sequence, 1950 to 1987. Commentary assessing her achievement as a writer, notes on adaptations of her stories into motion pictures, and biographical and critical sources in newspapers and magazines.

Commentary

Highsmith, Patricia. *Plotting and Writing Suspense Fiction*. Boston: The Writer, 1972.

Highsmith presents the essentials of suspense fiction and its particular characteristics and shows what techniques a writer can use in plotting and writing. Discusses her own experiences in writing: ideas, development, plotting, writing the first draft, overcoming problems, writing the second draft, revising. Explains in detail how she planned and wrote *The Glass Cell* (1964).

Hubly, Erlene. "A Portrait of the Artist: The Novels of Patricia Highsmith." *Clues: A Journal of Detection* 5 (Spring/Summer, 1984): 115-130.

Discusses those novels of Patricia Highsmith that feature characters who create works of art. Hubly defines art in the broadest sense to include writing, acting, and forgery. Explains that by examining these artists the reader can explore the major themes of Highsmith's stories, such as the nature of identity, a real versus an imagined world. Compares *A Suspension of Mercy* (1965), *The Tremor of Forgery* (1969), and *The Talented Mr. Ripley* (1955).

Klein, Kathleen Gregory. "Patricia Highsmith." In *And Then There Were Nine . . . More Women of Mystery*, edited by Jane S. Bakerman. Bowling Green, Ohio: Bowling Green University Popular Press, 1985.

Highsmith's extension of the limits of the crime novel began with *Strangers on a Train* (1949), which can be read as a model for her later work. Bakerman considers that the theme of the capacity for crime and violence in ordinary people suggests a duality in their personalities. Explains why readers may become alienated by some of her characters.

Symons, Julian. "Crime Novel and Police Novel." In his *Bloody Murder: From the Detective Story to the Crime Novel, a History*. Rev. ed. New York: Viking Press, 1985.

Considers Patricia Highsmith to be the most important modern crime novelist because she is able successfully to combine plot, character, and environment in her work. Symons concentrates his discussion on *Strangers on a Train* (1949), *Lament for a Lover* (1954; British title: *The Blunderer*), *The Two Faces of January* (1964), *Those Who Walk Away* (1967), and the four novels about Tom Ripley.

TONY HILLERMAN

Biography

Hillerman, Tony. "Mystery, Country Boys, and the Big Reservation." In *Colloquium on Crime*, edited by Robin W. Winks. New York: Charles Scribner's Sons, 1986.
Hillerman describes why it is important for him to be a storyteller and not an artist. In some detail he explains how he wrote his first novel *The Blessing Way* from countless revisions of the first chapter to the final version of the last one. Discusses the difficulty and the joy of writing, how he feels about the Navajo and why he returned to the Joe Leaphorn and Jim Chee stories after trying the Great American Novel in *The Fly on the Wall*.

Holt, Patricia. "PW Interviews: Tony Hillerman." *Publishers Weekly* 218 (October 24, 1980): 6-7.
Hillerman is interviewed at home in Albuquerque on the occasion of the publication of *People of Darkness*. Comments on the influence of reading detective novels (especially those by Arthur Upfield), his career in journalism, and his decision to become a writer. Considers his purpose to be instruction as well as entertainment, since he uses detective fiction to show aspects of ancient Indian customs that are still alive and significant.

Parker, Betty, and Riley Parker. "Hillerman Country." *The Armchair Detective* 20 (Winter, 1987): 4-8, 10-14.
A biographical sketch and discussion of the locale in Tony Hillerman's detective stories, interspersed with notes on the plots of seven titles. Hillerman is interviewed about his decision to incorporate Indian mythology in his novels, he comments on which of his books he thinks is the best and why he likes writing mysteries. Illustrated with photographs of the Southwestern United States and a map of the territories used in his books.

Taylor, Bruce. "Interview with Tony Hillerman." *The Armchair Detective* 14 (Winter, 1981): 93-95.
An interview conducted in 1978, preceded by a brief biographical sketch. Hillerman comments on his decision to write about the Navajo culture, his choice of characters as determined by the plot, crime writers who have influenced his own writing, and his working methods. He claims that he writes so slowly he is not likely to become a full-time writer.

Commentary

Bakerman, Jane S. "Joe Leaphorn and the Navajo Way: Tony Hillerman's Detective Fiction." *Clues: A Journal of Detection* 2 (Spring/Summer, 1981): 9-16.

Among the greatest strengths of Hillerman's detective novels is his ability to show how difficult it is to live in a society made up of people of multiple ethnic backgrounds. Bakerman considers Joe Leaphorn's knowledge of anthropology to be one factor that makes this possible and plausible. Discusses *The Blessing Way* (1970), *Dance Hall of the Dead* (1973), and *Listening Woman* (1977).

_____ . "Tony Hillerman's Joe Leaphorn and Jim Chee." In *Cops and Constables*, edited by Earl F. Bargainnier and George N. Dove. Bowling Green, Ohio: Bowling Green University Popular Press, 1986.

On the surface, Hillerman's detective novels give the reader adventure, danger, and heroism, but they also make the reader think and feel. Bakerman discusses the major police detectives in the novels, Joe Leaphorn and Jim Chee, how they reflect the cultural background of the American Indian of the Southwest and how their actions present realistic accounts of policemen at work. Notes that the stories can be read as social criticism.

Quirk, Thomas. "Justice on the Reservation." *The Armchair Detective* 18 (Fall, 1985): 364-366, 368-370.

Discusses the ways in which Hillerman's detective novels present the conflict between federal jurisdiction and tribal jurisdiction. Quirk describes the factual, legal background to Hillerman's stories with examples from the United States Supreme Court decisions, the *New Mexico Statutes*, and the *Navajo Tribal Code*. Focusses his discussion on *Dance Hall of the Dead* (1973).

CHESTER HIMES

Biography

Becker, Jens Peter. "Chester (Bomar) Himes." In *Twentieth Century Crime and Mystery Writers*, edited by John M. Reilly. New York: St. Martin's Press, 1980.
A brief list of the personal details of Chester Himes's life, along with a list of his awards and followed by a list of his publications in chronological order and arranged by category. Includes about one thousand words of commentary assessing his achievement as a writer of crime fiction.

Campenni, Frank. "Chester Himes." In *Dictionary of Literary Biography*, edited by Jeffrey Helterman and Richard Layman, vol. 2. Detroit: Gale Research, 1978.
A brief biography of Himes that relates the themes of his writing to the incidents in his life. Discusses his autobiography and his mainstream novels before commenting on the detective novels that Campenni considers "symbolic fantasies, surrealist allegories of lives in chaos." Assesses Himes's achievement as a writer. Checklist of his works in chronological sequence with some secondary sources listed. Photograph of Himes.

Goldsworthy, Joan. "Chester Himes." In *Contemporary Authors*, edited by Deborah A. Straub, vol. 22. Detroit: Gale Research, 1988.
A brief list of personal details in the life of Chester Himes, along with a survey of his career as a convict and as a writer. Contains a list of his books in chronological order and arranged according to category. Excellent survey of critical response to his writing with citations for film versions of his crime fiction. List of biographical and critical sources in books, magazines, and newspapers. Includes obituary notices.

Himes, Chester. *Autobiography*. Vol. 1, *The Quality of Hurt*; vol. 2, *My Life of Absurdity*. Garden City, N.Y.: Doubleday, 1972, 1976.
This is an intensely personal account of the life of expatriate novelist and mystery writer Chester Himes. Expresses his bitterness toward the United States. The second volume describes his career as a writer of detective fiction and has been criticized for devoting space to irrelevant matters.

Mok, Michael. "PW Interviews: Chester Himes." *Publishers Weekly* 201 (April 3, 1972): 20-21.
An interview with Chester Himes on the occasion of the publication of the first volume of his autobiography, *The Quality of Hurt* (1972). Himes explains that the Harlem in his books is Harlem as he sees it and is not intended to represent any official segment of the black community. Comments on his writing, on revolution, and the significance to American blacks of his crime stories.

Reckley, Ralph. "Chester Himes." In *Dictionary of Literary Biography*, edited by Trudier Harris, vol. 76. Detroit: Gale Research, 1988.

An extensive survey of the works of Chester Himes as an Afro-American writer against the background of his life. More emphasis on his novels of protest than on his detective novels. Lavishly illustrated with photographs of Himes as a child and as a young man, and in his mature years. Includes a checklist of Himes's fiction with a good selected bibliography of secondary sources.

Commentary

Berry, Jay R., Jr. "Chester Himes and the Hard-Boiled Tradition." *The Armchair Detective* 15, no. 1 (1982): 38-43.

Describes the tradition and viewpoint of the hard-boiled detective story. Berry considers that Himes began working strictly within that tradition in his first detective novels, then went beyond its limits. Berry finds the presence of violence in Himes's Harlem novels to be their core of reality. Discusses *For Love of Imabelle* (1957), *The Crazy Kill* (1959), *All Shot Up* (1960), *The Heat's On* (1966), *Blind Man with a Pistol* (1969), but reserves most of his attention for *Cotton Comes to Harlem* (1965).

Campenni, Frank J. "Black Cops and/or Robbers: The Detective Fiction of Chester Himes." *The Armchair Detective* 8 (May 1975): 206-209.

Himes began his stories of Grave Digger Jones and Coffin Ed Johnson on commission for a French publisher because he was desperate for money. Campenni considers that this hastily written hack work may outlive Himes's more serious novels of the black experience. Discusses the prevailing motifs of violence, the symbolic comic touches, and the odd assortment of characters in the stories. Checklist of the nine detective novels.

Lundquist, James. *Chester Himes*. New York: Frederick Ungar, 1976.

A dust-jacket blurb calls this the first book-length study of Chester Himes, but Stephen Milliken's *Chester Himes: A Critical Appraisal* (1976) appeared the same year. Lundquist deals with Himes's life in his first chapter, devotes two chapters to his serious fiction and one to his detective fiction, which he discusses in the context of the hard-boiled tradition. Describes *The Crazy Kill* (1959) and *Blind Man with a Pistol* (1969) in detail to demonstrate how Himes developed as a writer. Includes a bibliography of Himes's novels and a selected bibliography of works about him.

Milliken, Stephen F. "The Continental Entertainer: The Detective Novellas, *Pinktoes*." In his *Chester Himes: A Critical Appraisal*. Columbia: University of Missouri Press, 1976.

Discusses the detective fiction in a chapter along with one of the serious novels, *Pinktoes* (1961). While Chester Himes had published several works of serious fiction, it was his detective novels set in Harlem that earned for him a sizable readership, a measure of prosperity, and his first significant literary award, the Grand Prix. Milliken discusses the themes and characters in the detective fiction, concentrating on the images of Coffin Ed Johnson and Grave Digger Jones, noting the consistencies and inconsistencies of presentation.

Nelson, Raymond. "Domestic Harlem: The Detective Fiction of Chester Himes." In *Dimensions of Detective Fiction*, edited by Larry N. Landrum, Pat Browne, and Ray B. Browne. Bowling Green, Ohio: Bowling Green University Popular Press, 1976.

Himes referred to his stories of crime and violence with police detectives Grave Digger Jones and Coffin Ed Johnson as his "Harlem Domestic" series. Nelson considers the series to be an imaginative history of changing attitudes, social and psychological, of black Americans in the 1950's and 1960's. Discusses the novels from *For Love of Imabelle* (1957) to *Blind Man with a Pistol* (1969) as representing Himes's own changing attitudes, from optimism to frustration.

Reilly, John M. "Chester Himes' Harlem Tough Guys." *Journal of Popular Culture* 9 (Spring, 1976): 935-947.

Discusses Himes's nine novels of Harlem from *For Love of Imabelle* (1957) to *Blind Man with a Pistol* (1969) as a cycle with coherent themes about life in black America. Reilly examines the plots and characters of each book in turn, indicates how the characters of Coffin Ed Johnson and Grave Digger Jones develop as the plots become more complex. Considers that the books belong more to the school of "tough guy" novels than to the tradition of detective stories.

MICHAEL INNES
(John Innes Mackintosh Stewart)

Biography

Innes, Michael. "Death as a Game." *Esquire* 63 (January, 1965): 55-56.
A lighthearted account of how Innes began writing detective novels and his experiences with attitudes about the respectability of the genre for readers and writers. Innes considers the form to be essentially artificial, a "paper game," and gives substantial reasons for his belief. Comments on *Seven Suspects* (1936; British title: *Death at the President's Lodging*), *The Case of the Journeying Boy* (1949), *A Night of Errors* (1947), and membership in the Detection Club.

Stewart, J. I. M. "J. I. M. Stewart." In *Contemporary Authors: Autobiography Series*, edited by Adele Sarkissian, vol. 3. Detroit: Gale Research, 1986.
Stewart describes his childhood, his student days, his family background, his interest in books and reading as a series of pictures that should ultimately explain how and why he writes the way he does. Admits that his attitude toward the detective story is heterodox and explains the rules of the game as he tried to follow them. Reconstructs the writing of his first detective novel and comments on the writing of his mainstream novels, especially the Staircase in Surrey series. Another version of the material in this article appears in *Myself and Michael Innes*, by J. I. M. Stewart, 1988.

_____ . *Myself and Michael Innes*. New York: W. W. Norton, 1988.
An anecdotal autobiography that Stewart describes as a series of pictures that show his life. Divided into three sections: "Childhood," "School and University," and "Working Life," it is only in the latter that he discusses his writing of detective stories as "Michael Innes." Includes a chapter "Excursus on the Detective Story," in which he discusses the methods of Arthur Conan Doyle, Agatha Christie, and Dorothy L. Sayers. Well illustrated with family photographs. Brief index.

Commentary

Bakerman, Jane S. "Advice Unheeded: Shakespeare in Some Modern Mystery Novels." *The Armchair Detective* 14 (Spring, 1981): 134-139.
Discusses the use of Shakespearean themes in four mystery novels (*The Daughter of Time*, 1951, by Josephine Tey; *Bullets for Macbeth*, 1976, by Marvin Kaye; *A Little Less Than Kind*, 1963, by Charlotte Armstrong; and

Hamlet, Revenge!, 1937, by Michael Innes). Bakerman comments on Innes' use of quotation as a unifying device, of the use of a double-mystery (a novel-within-a-novel), the characterizations, and the value to an appreciation of the novel of the reader's being familiar with the text of Shakespeare's *Hamlet*.

Haycraft, Howard. "England: 1930-   (The Moderns)." In his *Murder for Pleasure: The Life and Times of the Detective Story*. New York: D. Appleton-Century, 1941.

This is certainly the earliest critical appraisal of "Michael Innes" to appear in a book. Haycraft quotes a letter from Innes about his early life, his teaching position at Adelaide University, and his opinions of his own detective stories. Haycraft discusses the merits of Innes' first three novels *Seven Suspects* (1936; British title: *Death at the President's Lodging*), *Hamlet, Revenge!* (1937), and *Lament for a Maker* (1938).

Innes, Michael. "John Appleby." In *The Great Detectives*, edited by Otto Penzler. Boston: Little, Brown, 1978.

The editor's brief discussion of Appleby and his creator is followed by Innes' interpretive essay on his detective's personality and background. Discusses his creation of the character and his writing of the first novel (on a trip by sea from England to Australia), the importance of the great house as a setting, and the purpose of Aristotle's Unities of time, place, and action.

Neville, John D. "Michael Innes." *Clues: A Journal of Detection* 5 (Fall/Winter, 1984): 119-130.

A brief overview of J. I. M. Stewart's novels written as Michael Innes. Neville classifies Innes' work into categories based on inner themes of recurring motifs. Cites critics' comments on Innes' books, discusses John Appleby and his family, and draws some comparisons with Ngaio Marsh. Checklist of the detective fiction arranged in chronological order through *Lord Mullion's Secret* (1981.) All this in only twelve pages.

Panek, Leroy. "The Novels of Michael Innes." *The Armchair Detective* 16 (Spring, 1983): 116-130.

Discusses Innes' literary products, detective novels, thrillers, and popular novels, noting prevailing themes and traditions that he used, rejected, or altered in his own writing. Panek considers that Innes' variety of forms as well as his "sense of construction and plotting" have kept his novels fresh in spite of the quantity he wrote and calls Innes' novels escapist reading for cultivated readers. Bibliographic notes. Photographs of Innes and covers of several modern paperback editions of his novels.

Routley, Erik. "Politeness and Protest." In his *The Puritan Pleasures of the Detective Story*. London: Victor Gollancz, 1972.

Discusses detective-story writers published by Victor Gollancz: Michael Innes, Edmund Crispin, Joanna Cannan, and John Bingham. Routley classes Innes among those who "celebrate the academic" in the genre and discusses his style, characters, and backgrounds. In his interpretation, Routley considers what makes Innes memorable and why his stories are so entertaining.

Scheper, George L. *Michael Innes*. New York: Frederick Ungar, 1986.
The first full-length critical survey of the forty mystery novels of Michael Innes, whom Scheper considers "the most literate and civilized detective-story writer now living," for instead of realism, Innes presents "detective novels of manners." Scheper begins with a chapter of biography followed by critical studies of representative novels grouped into categories: Appleby stories, thrillers, Oxford stories, novels about art and artists, and country-house settings. Sums up Innes' achievement. Comprehensive bibliography includes books published under his real name John Innes Mackintosh Stewart. Index.

Symons, Julian. "The Golden Age: The Thirties." In his *Bloody Murder: From the Detective Story to the Crime Novel, a History*. Rev. ed. New York: Viking Press, 1985.
Only a brief discussion. Symons classes Michael Innes in the first rank of detective-story writers who treat the form as an elaborate and literate game. His strengths lie in the high spirits and amusing dialogue of his books, not in their puzzles. Brief comments on Inspector Appleby as a character and the spy stories and thrillers.

P. D. JAMES

Biography

Bannon, Barbara A. "PW Interviews: P. D. James." *Publishers Weekly* 209 (January 5, 1976): 8-9.

Having published six mystery novels and won two awards for her work, James is considered a significant writer in the field. Bannon's interview brings out the basic information about her background, her decision to be a writer, her working methods, and her view of her detectives, Adam Dalgliesh and Cordelia Gray. Discusses her work in the criminal department of the Home Office.

Cooper-Clark, Diana. "Interview with P. D. James." In *Designs of Darkness*, edited by Diana Cooper-Clark. Bowling Green, Ohio: Bowling Green University Popular Press, 1983.

James discusses the discipline of writing detective fiction that helped her write them as serious novels. Explains some of the differences between the type she writes and the ones written to a strict formula. Comments on the role of the detective, on the homicidal mentality, and how her stories take shape.

Herbert, Rosemary. "A Mind to Write: An Interview with P. D. James." *The Armchair Detective* 19 (Fall, 1986): 340-348.

P. D. James speaks primarily about her book *The Maul and the Pear Tree: The Ratcliffe Highway Murders, 1811* (1971), a work of nonfiction just being published in the United States. Also talks of her pleasure in reading detective fiction, her decision to use Cordelia Gray and not Adam Dalgliesh in some books, her interest in the question of guilt, of death, and how her books depict different aspects of human love.

James, P. D. "A Series of Scenes." In *Whodunit? A Guide to Crime, Suspense, and Spy Fiction*, edited by H. R. F. Keating. New York: Van Nostrand Reinhold, 1982.

James discusses her writing methods and the practical advantages of working early in the morning, and the satisfaction of working with pen in hand before going to the typewriter. She puts the book together like a jigsaw puzzle, made up of scenes from a film. The mechanics of creation are easier to explain, she thinks, than where she gets her ideas. Photographs of James and a fragment of the second draft of *The Skull Beneath the Skin* (1982).

Salwak, Dale. "An Interview with P. D. James." *Clues: A Journal of Detection* 6 (Spring/Summer, 1985): 31-50.

James is interviewed at her home in London, on July 22, 1982. Forty-two questions on influences of earlier detective-story writers, Adam Dalgliesh, difficulties in writing, her attitude toward her own work, the psychological background of *Innocent Blood* (1980), themes, unsympathetic characters, and inspirations for plots and scenes. Most of her novels are discussed briefly.

Commentary

Bakerman, Jane S. "Cordelia Gray: Apprentice and Archetype." *Clues: A Journal of Detection* 5 (Spring/Summer, 1984): 101-114.
Discusses *An Unsuitable Job for a Woman* as a conventional detective novel and as a divergence from the earlier novels of P. D. James, comparing it to the *Bildungsroman* in mainstream literature. Bakerman then discusses Cordelia Gray's role in the novel to show how this supports her thesis. Suggests that this theme is continued in *The Skull Beneath the Skin* (1982).

Campbell, SueEllen. "The Detective Heroine and the Death of Her Hero: Dorothy Sayers to P. D. James." *Modern Fiction Studies* 29 (Autumn, 1983): 497-510.
Comparisons between Sayers' Harriet Vane novels, *Strong Poison* (1930), *Gaudy Night* (1935), and *Busman's Honeymoon* (1937), and James's Cordelia Gray stories, *An Unsuitable Job for a Woman* (1972), *Innocent Blood* (1980), and *The Skull Beneath the Skin* (1982). Campbell notes the focus on character and theme, issues such as the role of women, "the importance of work, the destructive power of love, and the complex relationships between men and women, parents and children."

Gidez, Richard B. *P. D. James*. Boston: Twayne, 1986.
Describes James's role in revitalizing the detective story with her modern themes; a feminist detective, Cordelia Gray; sympathetic portrayals of homosexuals; and attention paid to the psychology of power and loneliness. Gidez discusses each of James's novels in turn and deals with the best of her short stories, commenting on the detective's role and the settings. Compares *An Unsuitable Job for a Woman* (1972) to Dorothy L. Sayers' *Gaudy Night* (1935). Bibliography and index.

Hubly, Erlene. "Adam Dalgliesh: Byronic Hero." *Clues: A Journal of Detection* 3 (Fall/Winter, 1982): 40-46.
Hubly suggests that placing Adam Dalgliesh in the tradition of the classic detective-fiction hero or seeing him as a departure from that tradition does not fully account for his appeal as a character. Discusses his characteristics and compares him to the heroes of Lord Byron's *Childe Harold's Pilgrimage*, *Lara*, and *Manfred*.

_____ . "The Formula Challenged: P. D. James." *Modern Fiction Studies* 29 (Autumn,1983): 511-521.

Hubly takes sides with the critics who find that P. D. James's detective novels contain elements that challenge the classic detective-story form they most resemble. Discusses the assumptions that are central to the classic form and how James reverses them. Concentrates on *The Black Tower* (1975) with references to other novels to demonstrate the modifications she makes.

Joyner, Nancy Carol. "P. D. James." In *Ten Women of Mystery*, edited by Earl F. Bargainnier. Bowling Green, Ohio: Bowling Green University Popular Press, 1981.

A study of the "developing achievement" of P. D. James with comments on the elements of "content and style that make her writing distinctive." Joyner discusses James's background and influences, the scenes of her crimes, the use of realistic details in her stories, her detectives, and her point of view—"her moral sensitivity and humanistic concerns." Discusses James's first eight novels.

Siebenheller, Norma. *P. D. James*. New York: Frederick Ungar, 1981.

This, the first full-length study of P. D. James discusses her as an author whose works appeal to regular readers of detective fiction as well as to those who only occasionally read the genre. Overview is followed by discussions of her first eight novels, a chapter on Adam Dalgliesh and Cordelia Gray, and chapters on the major themes (alienation, death, the cost of crime, retribution), the other major characters in her novels, and her style. Notes, bibliography, and index.

Smyer, Richard I. "P. D. James: Crime and the Human Condition." *Clues: A Journal of Detection* 3 (Spring/Summer, 1982): 49-61.

Smyer explores the ways James uses the conventions of the traditional detective story to deal with aspects of the human condition. Discusses her flexibility in going beyond those conventions and draws comparisons with works by Arthur Conan Doyle, Dorothy L. Sayers, and other writers. Novels discussed: *Cover Her Face* (1962), *A Mind to Murder* (1963), *Unnatural Causes* (1967), *Shroud for a Nightingale* (1971), *The Black Tower* (1975), *Death of an Expert Witness* (1977), *An Unsuitable Job for a Woman* (1972), and *Innocent Blood* (1980).

Winks, Robin. "P. D. James: Murder and Dying." *The New Republic* 175 (July 1, 1976): 31-32.

Winks proposes P. D. James as a likely candidate to assume the mantle of "queen of detective fiction," worn so long by Agatha Christie. Considers Adam Dalgliesh to be a more interesting character than the characters of the detective novels of James's predecessors, Margery Allingham, Dorothy L. Sayers, or Ngaio Marsh, and praises the realistic details of her first six detective stories.

H. R. F. KEATING

Biography

Clark, Meera. "H. R. Keating: An Interview." *Clues: A Journal of Detection* 4 (Fall/ Winter, 1983): 43-65.

Keating is interviewed on January 10, 1983, at his home in London. Clark asks about his background, his schooldays, his decision to become a writer, his views on detective fiction, why he chose India as a setting for his stories, his working schedule, why he believes he was not really influenced by Teilhard de Chardin, as has been claimed, why he does not describe characters in detail, his mainstream novels, his use of a notebook, and his ear for dialogue.

Keating, H. R. F. "Flying a Bit High." In *Whodunit? A Guide to Crime, Suspense, and Spy Fiction*, edited by H. R. F. Keating. New York: Van Nostrand Reinhold, 1982.

Keating describes the sources for his ideas and how the question of perfection inspired his first Inspector Ghote novel. Explains in some detail the initial planning stages of *The Perfect Murder* (1964), the outline, the need for a subplot and a classic locked-room mystery. Equates the actual writing to leaping from a diving board into cold water. Photograph of Keating and a copy of some his notes for *The Perfect Murder*.

_____ . "H. R. F. Keating." In *Contemporary Authors: Autobiography Series*, edited by Mark Zadrozny, vol. 8. Detroit: Gale Research, 1989.

Keating contrasts the writing of autobiography and the writing of fiction; comments on the importance of understanding one's ancestors to an understanding of oneself; discusses his family, the place of irony as a "major strain" in his books, his years in the army and as a journalist, his marriage, his early novels and the interest in India that lead him to create Ganesh V. Ghote, and his impressions on first visiting the country in 1974. Bibliography of all Keating books through 1988.

Salwak, Dale. "An Interview with H. R. F. Keating." *Clues: A Journal of Detection* 5 (Fall/Winter, 1984): 82-96.

Keating explains how he created Inspector Ghote, why he writes about India and not England, his affinity with the Indian mind, his decision to write about a series detective after a conversation with Margery Allingham, his writing methods, his experiments with mainstream novels, his appreciation of Arthur Conan Doyle, and why he uses his initials and not his full name.

Commentary

Clark, Meera T. "Detective Fiction and Social Realism: H. R. F. Keating's India."
Clues: A Journal of Detection 2 (Spring/Summer, 1981): 1-8.
Comments on the detective story as a form of escape fiction that offers a
"more palatable version of reality" and thus becomes a fiction of social
realism. Clark examines Keating's detective stories as a view of India from the
inside, discussing *Inspector Ghote Breaks an Egg* (1970) in great detail to
demonstrate her point. Sees the theme of his books as an expression of the
responsibility of every human being to define himself or herself through the
right actions.

_____ . "H. R. F. Keating." In *Twelve Englishmen of Mystery*, edited by
Earl F. Bargainnier. Bowling Green, Ohio: Bowling Green University Popular
Press, 1984.
A chronology of significant dates in Keating's career is followed by a survey of
his work that demonstrates how the Inspector Ghote novels may be read as
classic, orthodox detective fiction as well as satirical portraits of life in India.
Traces Keating's "philosophical approach" to his interest in Teilhard de Chardin, the French philosopher-scientist. Contrasts Ghote with other fictional
detectives in a fine thematic study. Includes a checklist of Keating's novels.

Keating, H. R. F. "Inspector Ghote." In *The Great Detectives*, edited by Otto
Penzler. Boston: Little, Brown, 1978.
The editor's comments on Ganesh V. Ghote and Keating's work are followed
by a humorous account of Keating's own observations about Ganesh V. Ghote
in dialect from the point of view of one of Ghote's countrymen. Wonders
where Keating learned so much about India and how his knowledge of Ghote's
personality developed throughout the books he wrote.

Pettersson, Sven-Ingmar. "H. R. F. Keating." *The Armchair Detective* 8 (August,
1975): 277-279, 270.
An overview of Keating's life and work from the point of view of a Swedish
reader. Pettersson comments on possible influences on Keating and concludes
that he is unique. His discussion centers on Inspector Ganesh V. Ghote, the
main character in most of Keating's books, and takes up each novel in turn for
comment. Includes a photograph of Keating and a checklist of his work from
Death and the Visiting Firemen (1959) to *The Underside* (1974).

HARRY KEMELMAN

Biography

Maryles, Daisy. "PW Interviews: Harry Kemelman." *Publishers Weekly* 207 (April 28, 1975): 8-9.

An interview in New York on the occasion of the publication of *Tuesday the Rabbi Saw Red* (1973), of the author who, Maryles notes, laces his suspense novels with dialogues on religion and a portrayal of suburban American Jewish life. Kemelman comments on the creation of Rabbi David Small, the publication schedule of his books, and the response he has had from the Jewish community.

Phipps, Jennie. "His 'Sherlock' a Rabbi." In *Authors in the News*, edited by Barbara Nykoruk, vol. 1. Detroit: Gale Research, 1976.

This interview with Harry Kemelman covers his creation of Rabbi David Small, the idea for his first short story, his teaching of English literature, his own studies in religion, his writing habits, his favorite mystery writers, his hobbies, and his theories on liberal arts education.

Commentary

Kemelman, Harry. Introduction to *The Nine Mile Walk: The Nicky Welt Stories*. New York: G. P. Putnam's Sons, 1967.

One day in his class in English composition, Kemelman asked his students to help in formulating a story. When the students had no ideas, Kemelman relates, he tried it himself. From that experience came the first of the detective stories about Professor Nicky Welt. Describes some of the publishing history of the stories and how they lead to the writing of his first novel, *Friday the Rabbi Slept Late* (1964).

Lachman, Marvin. "Religion and Detection: Sunday the Rabbi Met Father Brown." *The Armchair Detective* 1 (October, 1967): 19-24.

Part 1 is a general discussion of the fictional detectives who have been men (or women) of the cloth. Comments on the instances where fictional detectives created by different writers have appeared in the same story. Part 2 is a pastiche in which G. K. Chesterton's Father Brown and Kemelman's Rabbi David Small meet and solve a mystery together.

Schlagel, Libby. "Today the Rabbi Gets Looked At." *The Armchair Detective* 16, no. 1 (1983): 101-109.

Schlagel considers that Kemelman's series about Rabbi David Small is complete, with the seven novels named for the days of the week, and takes the opportunity to survey the series, not book by book, but thematically. Schlagel describes the rabbi's and Chief of Police Hugh Lanigan's personalities and abilities as detectives. She notes that Kemelman raises interesting questions about the place of organized religion in our lives and discusses his ability as a mystery writer.

Spencer, William David. "Rabbis and Robbers in the Present: The Hectic Week of Rabbi Small." In his *Mysterium and Mystery: The Clerical Crime Novel*. Ann Arbor, Mich.: UMI Research Press, 1989.
Discusses Harry Kemelman's detective, Rabbi David Small, and the series of novels beginning with *Friday, the Rabbi Slept Late* (1964). According to Spencer, the importance of the series lies in its realistic portrayal of a religious professional as well as the message about the relationship of ethics to faith. Notes some of the personal characteristics about Rabbi Small that appear in the books.

RONALD A. KNOX

Biography

Knox, Ronald A. "Detective Fiction." In his *Literary Distractions*. New York: Sheed & Ward, 1958.

Father Knox attempts to define the essence of the detective story to explain its great appeal to readers in search of a good story. Discusses its structure, its characters, something of its history and the rules governing it. Includes nine rules from his famous "Detective Story Decalogue" with comments. Concludes by making some predictions for its future.

_____ . "Detective Story Decalogue." In *The Art of the Mystery Story*, edited by Howard Haycraft. New York: Simon & Schuster, 1947. Reprint. New York: Grosset & Dunlap, 1961.

Knox's Ten Commandments of Detection are referred to in much of the literature about the Golden Age of the detective story. Here they are, reprinted from his introduction to *The Best Detective Stories of 1928* (New York: Liveright, 1929). Knox's comments are designed to ensure that the detective-story author plays fair with the reader.

Waugh, Evelyn. *Monsignor Ronald Knox*. Boston: Little, Brown, 1959.

The definitive biography of Ronald A. Knox, who was essentially a private person, written by his literary executor. Waugh celebrates the writer, priest, translator, author of detective novels and stories, and enthusiastic reader of the same. According to Waugh, Knox considered his six detective novels as intellectual exercises. Refers to them briefly with some indication of their critical reception and how the Roman Catholic church regarded them. Bibliography of Knox's chief publications. Index. British edition contains illustrations.

Commentary

Donaldson, Norman. "Ronald Arbuthnott Knox." *The Armchair Detective* 7 (August, 1974): 235-246.

Knox's detective stories were the least of his many publications, according to Donaldson, but they have an appeal for specialists. Donaldson's article is divided into two parts: "Apostolic Knox" (an account of Knox's life) and "The Detective Novels" (a discussion of each of Knox's six detective novels with references to their critical reception). Donaldson's own response to Knox's detective novels is generally negative.

Kingman, James. "In Defense of Ronald Knox." *The Armchair Detective* 11 (July, 1978): 299.

Kingman lists Knox's accomplishments and tries to explain the generally negative reaction to his detective novels. Comments on Knox's theories of detective fiction and discusses *The Viaduct Murder* (1925) as a demonstration of how those theories were put into practice. Kingman considers Knox to have written good detective novels, but not great ones, but finds much to commend him.

Murray, Brian. "Ronald Arbuthnott Knox." In *Dictionary of Literary Biography*, edited by Bernard Benstock and Thomas F. Staley, vol. 77. Detroit: Gale Research, 1989.

Murray considers that whatever Knox's detective novels may lack in plot and characterization, they are "gracefully written and intelligently conceived." Discusses the six detective novels after a brief biographical sketch of the writer and attempts to account for the general neglect of them by readers. Includes selected bibliography of Knox's books, including his literary criticism, fantasies, and religious writings.

Reynolds, William. "The Detection Club on the Air: 'Behind the Screen' and 'Scoop.' " *Clues: A Journal of Detection* 4 (Fall/Winter, 1983): 1-20.

Reynolds discusses two British Broadcasting Corporation radio serial dramas, the result of the collaboration of several leading names among detective-story writers of the 1930's, including Agatha Christie and Dorothy L. Sayers. Comments on the contributions of each writer in turn, criticizing Ronald Knox's conclusion to "Behind the Screen" as anticlimactic. Includes bibliographical notes with the dates of the original broadcasts.

_____ . "The Detective Novels of Ronald A. Knox." *The Armchair Detective* 14 (Summer, 1981): 275-283.

Reynolds argues that Knox's detective novels, flawed though they may be, combine "clever, fair-play plotting" with something of the author's personality and represent "a coherent view of their times." Discusses each of the six novels, considers *Still Dead* (1934) and *Settled Out of Court* (1933; British title: *The Body in the Silo*) to be very good with the other four equally divided between being either fair or bad. Reynolds is honest in indicating Knox's strengths and weaknesses.

Speaight, Robert. *Ronald Knox: The Writer*. New York: Sheed & Ward, 1965.

Speaight discusses Knox as a professional writer who was aware of his audience. Takes up his work in separate categories, as humanist, detective-story writer, satirist, historian, translator, apologist for the Christian faith, and preacher. Discusses Knox's theory of detective fiction and the first five of his novels in a chapter titled "Who Dunnits." Considers *Settled Out of Court*

(1934; British title: *The Body in the Silo*) the best of the group. Omits any mention of the sixth novel *Double Cross Purposes* (1937). (Published with *Ronald Knox: The Priest*, by Thomas Corbishley, S.J.)

EMMA LATHEN
(Mary Jane Latsis and Martha Henissart)

Biography

Carr, John C. "Emma Lathen." In his *The Craft of Crime: Conversations with Crime Writers*. Boston: Houghton Mifflin, 1983.

Establishes Lathen's place in the modern detective story and discusses John Putnam Thatcher and some prevailing themes in the stories before beginning the actual interview with Martha Hennisart and Mary Jane Latsis. Carr's questions reveal how the two writers met, something of how they collaborate, their experiences with editors and with doing research, and the view of contemporary society that a reader can find in their work.

"Martha Hennissart." In *Contemporary Authors*, edited by Frances Carol Locher, vols. 85-88. Detroit: Gale Research, 1980.

A very brief account of the writing career of Martha Hennissart, who writes crime fiction with Mary Jane Latsis under the pen names of Emma Lathen and R. B. Dominic. Education (Harvard) and city of residence (Boston) are the only items given. Includes a checklist of books in chronological sequence through 1978 and arranged by pen name. Commentary assesses her achievements as writer with selected excerpts form reviews. List of some biographical and critical sources in newspapers and magazines, 1967-1977.

"Mary J(ane) Latsis." In *Contemporary Authors*, edited by Frances Carol Locher, vols. 85-88. Detroit: Gale Research, 1980.

An extremely brief account of some personal details and the literary career of Mary Jane Latsis, who writes crime fiction with Martha Hennissart under the pen names Emma Lathen and R. B. Dominic. Contains little more than her education and city of residence. Includes a list of books in chronological order from 1961 to 1978 and arranged by pen name. Commentary discusses her achievements as a writer with selected excerpts from reviews. List of some biographical and critical sources in newspapers and magazines, 1967-1977.

"Two Lady Writers Make a Killing." *Business Week* no. 2123 (May 9, 1970): 48.

A news story about Emma Lathen, who is as fictitious as her detective hero, John Putnam Thatcher. Discusses the backgrounds of the two women who collaborate under the pseudonym Emma Lathen without naming them. Quoted on reasons for choosing a banker as detective, the two women say that they write social comedies, not classical mysteries. Similarities between names and institutions in their fictional world and some in the real world are noted.

Photograph of the two authors on Wall Street hiding their faces behind copies of two of their novels.

Commentary

Bakerman, Jane S. "A View from Wall Street: Social Criticism in the Mystery Novels of Emma Lathen." *The Armchair Detective* 9 (June, 1976): 213-217.
Bakerman believes that Lathen balances the reassuring predictability of the formula plot with its counterpart, "boring facility," by the quality of her social criticism and her light touch. Surveys the John Putnam Thatcher books thematically to show that how she states her case is as useful to her in making her point as what she says. Indicates examples in *Death Shall Overcome* (1966), where the satire fails by being overdone.

_____. "Women and Wall Street: Portraits of Women in Novels by Emma Lathen." *The Armchair Detective* 8 (November, 1974): 36-41.
Bakerman surveys the major and minor women characters found in Lathen's detective novels featuring John Putnam Thatcher. She considers these characters often "more fully drawn, more able, and generally more nearly real people than is customary in the detective form." Discusses Miss Rose Theresa Corsa, Mrs. Furness (*A Stitch in Time*, 1968), Iris Young, and Joan Hedstrom (*Murder to Go*, 1969) as examples of characters presented in vivid thumbnail sketches.

Bedell, Jeanne F. "Emma Lathen." In *Ten Women of Mystery*, edited by Earl F. Bargainnier. Bowling Green, Ohio: Bowling Green University Popular Press, 1981.
The detective novels of Mary Jane Latsis and Martha Hennisart, writing as Emma Lathen, are a "perfect focus for investigating both sophisticated financial chicanery and plain old-fashioned greed." Bedell discusses characters and themes in sixteen novels about John Putnam Thatcher and five novels about Congressman Benton Safford, written under the pseudonym R. B. Dominic. Together they stand as a record of changing American mores and prove that classic detective fiction is still alive.

Brownell, David. "Comic Construction in the Novels of Emma Lathen and R. B. Dominic." *The Armchair Detective* 9 (February, 1976): 91-92.
To "R. B. Dominic," the political world of Ben Safford is not meaningless and morally chaotic but comic. Brownell compares the fictional worlds of Emma Lathen and Dominic (both pseudonyms for Mary Jane Latsis and Martha Hennisart), finds great similarities in the structures and the attitudes of the central characters, John Putnam Thatcher and Ben Safford, as well as sim-

ilarities between these detective-series situations and the situations found in French farce.

Cawelti, John. "Emma Lathen: Murder and Sophistication." *The New Republic* 175 (July 31, 1976): 25-27.
Cawelti describes the classic detective formula-story in order to demonstrate how Emma Lathen has transformed its basic elements into modern-day terms. Considers John Putnam Thatcher an ideal figure to serve as detective by reason of both his profession and his temperament, and the financial world a natural closed society in which the mystery and its solution can be presented. Suggests that Lathen's sense of moral authority, witty sophistication, and gift for comic satire are among her outstanding talents.

Lawrence, Barbara. "Emma Lathen: The Art of Escapist Crime Fiction." *Clues: A Journal of Detection* 3 (Fall/Winter, 1982): 76-82.
It is the wealth of information about many subjects as well as the sophisticated, urbane characters that make Emma Lathen's detective novels so interesting. Lawrence discusses the ways in which violent death is described to create "a buffer zone" between the fictional situations and the reader so the stories remain diversions as well as intellectually challenging as escape fiction in the sophisticated sense.

Sarjeant, William A. S. "Crime on Wall Street." *The Armchair Detective* 21 (Spring, 1988): 128-130, 132, 134-145.
A survey of the career in fiction of John Putnam Thatcher arranged under seven headings: John Putnam Thatcher and Wall Street, the Sloan Guaranty Trust, Thatcher's Associates, the Secretarial Staff, Thatcher's Friends, Thatcher Himself, Thatcher the Investigator. Ends with a bibliographic record of the published cases of John Putnam Thatcher (nineteen titles, 1961-1982, in order of publication).

JOHN LE CARRÉ
(David John Moore Cornwell)

Biography

Greenway, H. S. D. "Travels with le Carré." *Newsweek* 90 (October 10, 1977): 102.
Describes le Carré's visit to Hong Kong in the winter of 1974 to research the background of the city and the role of the Hong Kong press corps in writing *The Honourable Schoolboy* (1977). Greenway provides humorous anecdotes, comments on the opportunity of reading "various manuscripts" of the novel, and compares Jerry Westerby in le Carré's book with Joseph Conrad's Lord Jim. Photographs of Greenway and le Carré.

le Carré, John. "In England Now." *The New York Times Magazine* October 23, 1977: 34-35, 86-87.
John le Carré describes his unhappy childhood and schooldays of anguish that served as inspiration for parts of *The Honourable Schoolboy* (1977). Le Carré is critical of the education system where preparatory school was a preparation for nothing he encountered in life except receiving empty promises. Briefly mentions his reading: Bulldog Drummond, G. A. Henty, the Biggles stories, Percy Westerman, and Dornford Yates. (Also published as "England Made Me," *Sunday Observer*, November 15, 1977.)

Masters, Anthony. "John le Carré: The Natural Spy." In his *Literary Agents: The Novelist as Spy*. New York: Basil Blackwell, 1987.
A biographical account of David Cornwell who created the name "John le Carré" to sign his spy fiction. Masters discusses incidents that served as inspiration for his fiction and characters from le Carré's life (including his own father) who appear in his novels. Masters is uncertain where Cornwell found his famous pseudonym.

Mathews, Tom. "In from the Cold." *Newsweek* 113 (June 5, 1989): 52-57.
On the occasion of the publication of *The Russia House* (1989), le Carré is the subject of a profile and cover story that surveys his career and notes how the newest novel is a departure in style from his earlier, complex, multilayered work. Illustrated with photos (black and white and color) of le Carré and his family.

Commentary

Barley, Tony. *Taking Sides: The Fiction of John le Carré*. Philadelphia: Open University Press, 1986.

Examines the political insight of le Carré, compares political issues and personal crises in the novels, and explains how the author deals with individual psychology and personal relationships. Barley sets le Carré in the context of the spy story, discusses each novel from *The Spy Who Came In from the Cold* (1963) to *The Little Drummer Girl* (1983) as popular writing, political fiction, and ideology.

Cawelti, John G., and Bruce A. Rosenberg. "The Complex Vision of John le Carré." In their *The Spy Story*. Chicago: University of Chicago Press, 1987.
Traces le Carré's development of the spy story from the classic detective formula of the early George Smiley books to the burnt-out case of Alec Leamas of *The Spy Who Came In from the Cold* (1963) to the complex form in the Smiley-Karla trilogy. Discusses the underlying theme of his books as well as plot, character, narration, and language.

Garson, Helen S. "Enter George Smiley: Le Carré's *Call for the Dead*." *Clues: A Journal of Detection* 3 (Fall/Winter, 1982): 93-99.
Uses le Carré's first novel about George Smiley to demonstrate how atypical he is either as a spy or as a detective when compared to James Bond or Sherlock Holmes. Garson explains how le Carré builds on the structure of *Call for the Dead* (1961) for his other novels. Detailed plot synopsis, character analysis, and Smiley's own life history.

Grella, George. "John le Carré: Murder and Loyalty." *The New Republic* 175 (July 31, 1976): 23-25.
Grella notes the "obsession with the relationship between love and betrayal" as a theme of le Carré's stories. Discusses the novels from *Call for the Dead* (1961) to *Tinker, Tailor, Soldier, Spy* (1974) to show how le Carré has made the spy an appropriate figure for our time with espionage an equally appropriate activity as an explanation for much of our contemporary history.

Kanfer, Stefan. "The Spy Who Came In for the Gold." *Time* 110 (October 3, 1977): 58-60, 67-68, 72.
On the occasion of the publication of *The Honourable Schoolboy* (1977), John le Carré (David Cornwell) is subjected to a biographical and critical analysis by *Time* magazine in the cover story for the issue. Kanfer quickly surveys le Carré's previous work, considers that one of the areas in which he excels is his "sense of place," and discusses *The Honourable Schoolboy* as fictional autobiography. Concludes with an account of le Carré's life. Illustrated with photographs of le Carré and his family. Includes a glossary of espionage jargon.

King, Holly Beth. "Child's Play in John le Carré's *Tinker, Tailor, Soldier, Spy*." *Clues: A Journal of Detection* 3 (Fall/Winter 1982): 87-92.

A detailed analysis of the role of children in le Carré's *Tinker, Tailor, Soldier, Spy* (1974). King believes that the title is symbolic of the way the moral center of the novel is revealed. Contrasts the use of the themes of love and devotion with the capacity for suspicion that prevails in so much of le Carré. Traces links between the child world and the adult world that she finds in the novels to demonstrate her thesis.

_____ . "George Smiley: The Reluctant Hero." *Clues: A Journal of Detection* 2 (Spring/Summer, 1982): 70-76.
The prevailing characteristic of George Smiley is that he survives, both literally and figuratively, in John le Carré's novels. King contrasts him with Alec Leamas, the archetypal spy in *The Spy Who Came In from the Cold* (1963), discusses his role in le Carré's other novels, and argues that it is his conscience, not his actions, that makes him distinctive.

Lewis, Peter. *John le Carré*. New York: Frederick Ungar, 1985.
Lewis devotes his first chapter to le Carré's life and establishes a context for discussing him within the genre of spy fiction. Takes up each novel in turn in chapters 2 through 10, discussing *Call for the Dead* (1961) and *A Murder of Quality* (1962) through *The Little Drummer Girl* (1983). Quotes from interviews with le Carré and comments on themes of rejection, betrayal, and revenge. Bibliography includes le Carré's fiction and nonfiction, as well as selected works about le Carré.

Monaghan, David. "John le Carré and England: A Spy's-Eye View." *Modern Fiction Studies* 29 (Autumn, 1983): 569-582.
For le Carré, the secret world of the spy serves as a microcosm of the larger world of English society by which he illustrates "the various paradoxes in which we live." Monaghan demonstrates ways in which the spy world also functions as an alternative to the real world. Discusses George Smiley and other recurring characters.

_____ . *The Novels of John le Carré: The Art of Survival*. New York: Basil Blackwell, 1985.
Monaghan views the work of John le Carré as a unified phenomenon and addresses both specialist and general reader in this full-length study. Discusses the narrative conventions of each novel from *Call for the Dead* (1961) to *The Little Drummer Girl* (1983), devotes a chapter to George Smiley, and surveys the critical reception of le Carré's work.

Nolan, Richard. "The Spy Fiction of John le Carré." *Clues: A Journal of Detection* 1 (Fall/Winter, 1980): 54-70.
An aversion to Cold War politics and a disillusionment with the spy as hero are

seen by Nolan as major assumptions of le Carré's novels. Discusses *Call for the Dead* (1961), *The Spy Who Came In from the Cold* (1963), *The Looking-Glass War* (1965), *A Small Town in Germany* (1968), *Tinker, Tailor, Soldier, Spy* (1974), *The Honourable Schoolboy* (1977), and *Smiley's People* (1980). Le Carré's expression of his pessimistic political vision in fiction has transformed the spy novel, and Nolan makes some predictions about le Carré's next step.

Panek, LeRoy L. "John le Carré." In his *The Special Branch: The British Spy Novel, 1890-1980*. Bowling Green, Ohio: Bowling Green University Popular Press, 1981.

John le Carré has used the spy novel as a means to explore human identity and the way "men serve institutions and institutions serve men." Panek discusses the structures, narrators, characters, and themes of the spy novels from *Call for the Dead* (1961) to *Smiley's People* (1980). Considers that one of le Carré's objects is to present a history of an imaginary spy organization from World War II to the present.

JOSEPH SHERIDAN LE FANU

Biography

Browne, Nelson. *Sheridan Le Fanu*. New York: Roy Publishers, 1951.
This short work, the first book devoted to Le Fanu since S. M. Ellis' *Wilkie Collins, Le Fanu, and Others* (1931), leans heavily on that source for its details of his life. Browne notes evidence of renewed interest in Le Fanu's work and discusses his life in one brief chapter, followed by one chapter on the novels, one on the short stories and verse, and a final chapter summing up his achievement. Appendix consists of a list of Le Fanu's principal works with the dates of their first publication as books or in periodicals.

McCormack, W. J. *Sheridan Le Fanu and Victorian Ireland*. New York: Oxford University Press, 1980.
In the only extensive critical biography of Joseph Sheridan Le Fanu, McCormack has drawn on printed and manuscript sources for the details of the author's life, and the texts of the original three-decker versions of the novels or the files of the *Dublin University Magazine* where Le Fanu's stories first appeared for his discussions of the fiction. Describes the milieu in which Le Fanu wrote and provides a checklist of his works. Good secondary bibliography. Eight illustrations unique to this volume. Index.

Sherwood, John C. "Joseph Sheridan Le Fanu." In *Critical Survey of Mystery and Detective Fiction*, edited by Frank N. Magill, vol. 3. Pasadena, Calif.: Salem Press, 1988.
Sherwood justifies Le Fanu as a writer of mystery and detective fiction and considers his place to be in that "interregnum" between Edgar Allan Poe and Arthur Conan Doyle. A brief biographical sketch summarizes most of the recorded facts about Le Fanu's life, and an extended analysis of *Checkmate* (1871), *The House by the Churchyard* (1863), *Wylder's Hand* (1864), and *Uncle Silas: A Tale of Bartram-Haugh* (1864) explains his achievements as a novelist. Briefly discusses the short fiction. Contains a list of titles and dates of his principal works of fiction with a selected list of secondary sources.

Stokes, Roy B. "Joseph Sheridan Le Fanu." In *Dictionary of Literary Biography*, edited by Ira B. Nadel and William E. Fredeman, vol. 21. Detroit: Gale Research, 1983.
A general survey of Le Fanu's novels, with only a few references to his short stories, against a background of the few recorded facts about his personal life. Discusses the themes and settings of his works and assesses his achievement as a writer. Illustrated with photographs of Le Fanu and his wife. contains a bibliography of principal publications of Le Fanu and a few secondary sources.

Commentary

Begnal, Michael H. *Joseph Sheridan Le Fanu*. Lewisburg, Pa.: Bucknell University
Press, 1971.
A concise discussion of Le Fanu and his work. Begnal's first chapter covers
biography and Le Fanu's first novel, *The Cock and Anchor* (1845). Chapter 2
covers his gothic tales and chapter 3 his work as a novelist, concentrating on
The House by the Churchyard (1863), *Wylder's Hand* (1864), *Uncle Silas: A
Tale of Bartram-Haugh* (1864), and *Guy Deverell* (1865). Speculates on
whether Le Fanu should be considered an Irish writer (one who contributes
significantly to the progression of Irish literature). Includes selected
bibliography.

Bleiler, E. F. Introduction to *Best Ghost Stories of J. S. Le Fanu*. New York: Dover,
1964.
The introduction is in three sections: a survey of the publishing history of Le
Fanu's most representative work; a discussion of the characteristics of his
stories in which the supernatural is "a natural manifestation," and which
Bleiler traces to Le Fanu's unusual personality; and a brief critical commentary
on the specific contents of this collection. Includes a discussion of Le Fanu's
sources, including Irish folklore.

———————— . Introduction to *Ghost Stories and Mysteries*, by J. S. Le Fanu.
New York: Dover, 1975.
The greatest of Victorian ghost-story writers, Le Fanu produced the most
varied work of the nineteenth century. Bleiler relates the themes of Le Fanu's
stories to aspects of his personality. Discusses the contents of this collection
thematically, noting where and when each story was published originally.
Contrasts the appeal of the short fiction with the long and makes a distinction
between the ghost stories and his tales of mystery.

Bowen, Elizabeth. "*Uncle Silas*." In her *Collected Impressions*. New York: Alfred
A, Knopf, 1950.
Published originally as the preface to a 1947 edition of Le Fanu's novel *Uncle
Silas*, Bowen's essay describes the circumstances surrounding the writing of
the novel, includes some biographical details about the author, discusses the
characters of Silas Ruthyn and Madame de la Rougierre, the "inner, nonpracti-
cal, psychological plot" from which the novel derives its power, the atmosphere, and the probable appeal for the modern reader.

Brownell, David. "Wicked Dreams: The World of Sheridan Le Fanu." *The Armchair Detective* 9 (June, 1976): 191-197.

On the occasion of the publication of the Dover edition of Le Fanu's *Ghost Stories and Tales of Mystery* (1851), Brownell comments on Le Fanu's life and literary career. Discusses Le Fanu's novels, especially *The Cock and Anchor* (1845), *The House by the Churchyard* (1863), *Wylder's Hand* (1864), and *Uncle Silas: A Tale of Bartram-Haugh* (1864). Some of Brownell's discussion is not based on a reading of Le Fanu but on a knowledge of the secondary sources. The focus is mostly on Le Fanu's mysteries. Includes a selected bibliography of Le Fanu's works.

Donaldson, Norman. Introduction to *The Rose and the Key*, by Joseph Sheridan Le Fanu. New York: Dover, 1982.
A biographical sketch of Le Fanu followed by an examination of his fifteen novels, noting which are developed versions of earlier short stories. Discusses characters and structure of *The Rose and the Key* (1871) and the way the structure is designed to heighten the mysteries. Donaldson notes how often Le Fanu makes his female characters (both heroines and villainesses) come to life.

Melada, Ivan. *Sheridan Le Fanu*. Boston: Twayne, 1987.
A brief chapter of biography is followed by chapters on Le Fanu's fiction arranged by categories rather than strictly chronologically: early short fiction, historical novels, *Uncle Silas: A Tale of Bartram-Haugh* (1864; "the quintessence of terror"), novels of suspense, late short fiction, poetry and periodical fiction. Concludes with a chapter on Le Fanu's achievement. Includes a portrait of Le Fanu, notes, and a selected primary bibliography with an annotated list of secondary sources.

Penzoldt, Peter. *The Supernatural in Fiction*. London: Peter Nevill, 1952. Reprint. New York: Humanities Press, 1965.
Part 1 of this study discusses definitions, the structure, and main motifs of the story of the supernatural. Part 2 is made up of chapters on individual writers, including Le Fanu, who introduced the psychic detective, Dr. Martin Hesselius, to English fiction. Penzoldt discusses the characteristics of Le Fanu's fiction and the significance of his influence on other authors in the gothic tradition. Includes extensive bibliographic notes.

Peterson, Audrey. *Victorian Masters of Mystery: From Wilkie Collins to Conan Doyle*. New York: Frederick Ungar, 1984.
Categorizes Le Fanu's fiction as "tales of terror with elements of mystery and suspense." Peterson presents a concise overview of Le Fanu's life and work with a detailed analysis of *Wylder's Hand* (1864) and *Uncle Silas: A Tale of Bartram-Haugh* (1864). Praises a few of the later works but considers most to be inferior to these two novels.

Shroyer, Frederick. Introduction to *Uncle Silas*, by Joseph Sheridan Le Fanu. New York: Dover, 1966.
Discusses the atmosphere of supernatural mystery that pervades *Uncle Silas: A Tale of Bartram-Haugh* (1864) and achieves the effect the author intended. Shroyer describes Le Fanu's literary career and the story of the original publication of the novel, noting the influence he had on other writers, including Arthur Conan Doyle, who borrowed its basic plot for *The Firm of Girdlestone* (1889). Sets *Uncle Silas* in the tradition of gothic fiction.

Sullivan, Jack. *Elegant Nightmares: The English Ghost Story from Le Fanu to Blackwood*. Athens, Ohio: Ohio University Press, 1978.
Nearly one half of Sullivan's book is devoted to Joseph Sheridan Le Fanu. Detailed discussion of "Green Tea" as the "archetypal ghost story" followed by a discussion of Le Fanu's reputation and influence, his development as a writer, and a consideration of the recurring themes and motifs in his short stories. Sullivan finds little in Le Fanu's life to explain his writings.

ELMORE LEONARD

Biography

Dunn, Bill. "*PW* Interviews: Elmore Leonard." *Publishers Weekly* 223 (February 25, 1983): 32-33.

Interviewed on the occasion of the publication of *Stick* (1983), his twenty-second novel, Elmore Leonard reviews his career as advertising copywriter, writer of Westerns, novelist, and screenwriter. Dunn characterizes the basic Leonard novel and gives some examples of his working methods, particularly his use of research interviews. Brief references to titles of some of Leonard's books and screenplays.

Lyczak, Joel M. "An Interview with Elmore Leonard." *The Armchair Detective* 16 (Summer, 1983): 235-240.

Lyczak briefly identifies Leonard in the context of crime fiction before the interview begins. Includes questions on when he first became interested in writing, the authors he read for inspiration, the characteristics of his style, his switch from Westerns to contemporary settings, how he constructs his novels, where he finds his characters, his research for background, and his views on how his work has been adapted for the screen. Bibliography of books published (1953-1983), short stories (1951-1956 and 1982), and screenplays (1970-1982).

Mitgang, Herbert. "Novelist Discovered After Twenty-three Books." *The New York Times* October 29, 1983: 17.

After having published twenty-three novels, Elmore Leonard has begun to receive critical attention for his novel *LaBrava* (1983), as well as for his entire body of work. Mitgang interviews Leonard about his ability to write novels with "narrative drive." Comments on his real-life characters and his use of authentic-sounding dialogue and the filming of his novel *Stick* (1983).

Rubin, Gay. "Hey, Dad . . . It's Clint Eastwood!" In *Authors in the News*, edited by Barbara Nykoruk, vol. 1. Detroit: Gale Research, 1976.

On the occasion of the publication of Elmore Leonard's *Fifty-two Pickup* (1974), the author and his career are the subject of a profile in *The Detroiter* for June, 1974. Comments on his working methods, why he prefers to live and work in Detroit rather than California, and the differences between writing novels and film scripts.

Sutter, Gregg. "Researching Elmore Leonard's Novels." Parts 1/2. *The Armchair Detective* 19 (Winter/Spring, 1986): 4-19, 160-164, 166-172.

A loosely constructed account of the research process for Elmore Leonard's novels by which he acquires the right understanding of his surroundings, the conversations and characterizations of people, written by a man who does some of Leonard's library research, interviews, and field trips. Discusses *Split Images* (1982), *Cat Chaser* (1982), *Stick* (1983), *LaBrava* (1983), and other titles. Illustrated with photographs of Leonard and the places used in his books.

Commentary

Prescott, Peter S. "Making a Killing." *Newsweek* 105 (April 22, 1985): 62-64, 67.
In recognition of having achieved best-seller status with the publication of *Glitz*, Elmore Leonard's career is surveyed. Brief biographical information is followed by a discussion of the reasons that his stories appeal to so many readers, his style, the importance of his characters, the value of not having a unified point of view, and how he makes his situations realistic. Photographs of Leonard as a boy of eight, with his wife in Michigan, and researching a novel in New Orleans.

Sandels, Robert. "Common Criminals and Ordinary Heroes." *The Armchair Detective* 22 (Winter, 1989): 14-20.
Discusses the characteristics of Elmore Leonard's protagonists, comparing the situations in his crime novels with the formulas in the Western and demonstrating the ways the contest between good and evil differs from what the reader may expect. Sandels uses *City Primeval* (1980), *Glitz* (1985), *Cat Chaser* (1982), *Unknown Man No. 89* (1977), *LaBrava* (1983), *Split Images* (1982) and other titles as examples.

Yagoda, Ben. "Elmore Leonard's Rogue's Gallery." *The New York Times Magazine* December 30, 1984: 20, 22, 26, 29.
A profile of Elmore Leonard, who claims that he does not really write mysteries despite winning an Edgar Award from the Mystery Writers of America for *LaBrava* (1982). Yagoda discusses Leonard's use of dialogue and his systematic approach to getting his local color right. Claims that he was more influenced by Earnest Hemingway than by Raymond Chandler, and that his more recent heroes are governed by the sensibility of the detective even when they are not really detectives, and that morality is seldom the point in his stories.

RICHARD LOCKRIDGE and FRANCES LOCKRIDGE

Biography

Filstrup, Chris, and Janie Filstrup. "An Interview with Richard Lockridge." *The Armchair Detective* 11 (October, 1978): 382-393.
Lockridge is interviewed at his home in Tryon, North Carolina, where he is living with his second wife, Hildegarde Dolson. An introduction containing background information is followed by an extensive interview covering his writing methods, alone and with his first wife, Frances; the sources for some of the specialized information in his books; his opinion of hard-boiled detective stories; his favorite mystery writers; and his fan mail.

"Richard Lockridge." In *Contemporary Authors*, edited by Frances Carol Locher, vols. 85-88. Detroit: Gale Research, 1980.
A brief account of personal details in the life of Richard Lockridge, along with some facts about his military service and his career in journalism. Contains a list of books in chronological order, 1932 to 1977, and arranged according to series or by-line. No critical commentary.

"Richard Lockridge, 1898-1982." In *Contemporary Authors*, edited by Hal May, vol. 107. Detroit: Gale Research, 1983.
An obituary of Richard Lockridge, who died on June 19, 1982, in Tryon, North Carolina. Contains an account of the critical response to the books he wrote alone and in collaboration with his first wife, Frances. References to selected titles, obituaries, and other articles in newspapers and magazines in 1982.

"Richard Lockridge." In *Twentieth Century Authors*, edited by Stanley J. Kunitz and Howard Haycraft. New York: H. W. Wilson, 1942.
An account of the personal details of the life of Richard Lockridge and something about his work for *The New Yorker*. Notes the similarities between the style of life enjoyed by Richard and Frances Lockridge and their detective team Gerald and Pam North. Contains a selected list of their principal works through 1942. Includes a photograph of Frances and Richard Lockridge.

"Richard Lockridge." In *Twentieth Century Authors: First Supplement*, edited by Stanley J. Kunitz. New York: H. W. Wilson, 1955.
Brings the story of "the writing Lockridges" up to date with references to the Captain Heimrich series, begun in 1947, and some of the work they have done independently of each other. Selected list of principal works in all categories of writing, together and separately, from 1945 to 1955.

Townsend, Guy M. "Richard and Frances Lockridge." In *Twentieth Century Crime and Mystery Writers*, edited by John M. Reilly. New York: St. Martin's Press, 1980.
A brief catalog of personal details in the lives of Richard and Frances Lockridge, along with some facts of their literary careers. Contains a long list of books and uncollected short stories in chronological order and arranged according to categories. About 750 words of commentary assessing their achievement as writers.

Commentary

Banks, R. Jeff. "Mr. and Mrs. North." *The Armchair Detective* 9 (June, 1976): 182-183.
Banks describes the genesis of Mr. and Mrs. North in a series of *The New Yorker* sketches, from which the characters were transferred to the mystery novels. Discusses the use of backgrounds of book publishing and the theater, some recurring characters (Lieutenant Bill Weigand and Captain Merton Heimrich—the latter achieved his own series), but considers the strength of the series to lie in the humor, also of *The New Yorker* variety. Refers to movie, radio, and television adaptations. Some corrections by Robert E. Briney appear in the following issue of *The Armchair Detective*.

Filstrup, Jane. "Murder for Two: Richard Lockridge." *The New Republic* 179 (July 22, 1978): 35-38.
Filstrup describes the creation of Mr. and Mrs. North and discusses some of the plots, characters, and settings ("Lockridge's New York is a hospitable place for the young, the vigorous, and the virtuous"). Notes the sequences of the novels, with a North story followed by a Captain Heimrich, succeeded by a "chase" story. Discussion of the Heimrich and Lieutenant Shapiro series and some of the characteristics of their personalities that attract readers.

Lockridge, Richard. "Mr. and Mrs. North." In *The Great Detectives*, edited by Otto Penzler. Boston: Little, Brown, 1978.
An editorial introduction provides some information on Frances and Richard Lockridge, while the latter individual provides an account of the creation of Gerald and Pamela North and the collaboration with the former on the detective novels. Discusses their working methods and why he stopped writing the stories following the death of Frances Lockridge. Contrasts the Pam North of the books with the character played in the movies by Gracie Allen.

PETER LOVESEY

Biography

Carr, John C. "Peter Lovesey." In his *The Craft of Crime: Conversations with Crime Writers*. Boston: Houghton Mifflin, 1983.

An introduction to set the stage, with basic biographical data on Lovesey, followed by the actual interview in which Carr asks him about the Victorian period in his works and what crime and police work were really like then. Lovesey discusses his sports journalism, the backgrounds for his Sergeant Cribb stories, Jack the Ripper, and his new novel set in the 1920's, *The False Inspector Dew* (1982).

Cooper-Clark, Diana. "Interview with Peter Lovesey." In her *Designs of Darkness: Interviews with Detective Novelists*. Bowling Green, Ohio: Bowling Green University Popular Press, 1983.

Lovesey talks of Sergeant Cribb, the Victorian age, Victorian sport, Victorian crime, and Victorian literature. He considers Cribb to be a modern man in the Victorian era, that Cribb and Edward Thackeray, his assistant, are really two different aspects of his own character. Expects to return to writing of the Victorian world eventually. Photograph of Lovesey.

Herbert, Rosemary. "The Cosy Side of Murder." *Publishers Weekly* 228 (October 25, 1985): 20, 22, 24, 28, 30-32.

Interviews with several British writers of detective stories. Herbert considers Peter Lovesey to be an "entertaining author" whose Victorian detective Sergeant Cribb is a memorable character. Interviewed at home in England, Lovesey admits that it was his interest in sports (vicariously pursued) that led to his becoming a writer. A study of the nineteenth century for a book on long-distance running, combined with his wife's urging him to enter a contest for a new detective novel, launched him on his career. Comments on the importance of the American market to a British writer.

Lovesey, Peter. "Magician, Actor, Runner, Writer." *The Writer* 101 (January, 1988): 11-13, 46.

A lighthearted account of the ambitions in life that lead Peter Lovesey to become a professional writer. Discusses how the writer can learn to apply personal enthusiasms to the novel or story, how a knowledge of acting methods can be applied to characters to bring them to life, and the importance of pacing.

Commentary

Bedell, Jeanne F. "Peter Lovesey's Sergeant Cribb and Constable Thackeray." In
  Cops and Constables, edited by Earl F. Bargainnier and George N. Dove.
  Bowling Green, Ohio: Bowling Green University Popular Press, 1986.
  Discusses the recurring characters in Lovesey's Victorian detective novels and
  the ways in which the author's understanding of Victorian life dictates the
  characterizations of Sergeant Cribb and Constable Thackeray and their
  methods of detection. Surveys the eight novels in the series from *Wobble to
  Death* (1970) to *Waxwork* (1978). Includes checklist of titles in the endnotes.

Hayne, Joanne Harack. "Peter Lovesey." In *Twentieth Century Crime and Mystery
  Writers*, edited by John M. Reilly. New York: St. Martin's Press, 1980.
  Biographical sketch followed by brief checklist of novels, uncollected short
  stories, and works outside the crime field. Autobiographical statement by
  Lovesey accompanied by approximately five hundred words of critical commentary assessing the author's contribution to crime fiction, especially in his
  historical novels set in Victorian England.

Jayaswal, Shakuntala. "Peter Lovesey." In *Critical Survey of Mystery and Detective
  Fiction*, edited by Frank N. Magill, vol. 3. Pasadena, Calif.: Salem Press, 1988.
  Discusses Lovesey's work in four sections, his principal series characters, his
  general contribution to detective fiction, a short biographical essay, and an
  extended analysis of his detective fiction. Includes a list of titles and publication dates of his books and a selected bibliography on Lovesey's life and work.

Lovesey, Peter. "The Real Inspector Dew." *The Armchair Detective* 17 (Summer,
  1984): 244-248.
  Originally presented as a talk at Mohonk, New York, in March, 1984, Lovesey's
  account describes the murder case of Dr. Hawley Harvey Crippen that inspired
  him to write *The False Inspector Dew* (1982). Attempts to explain the fascination the case holds for people today, particularly in England. Describes Crippen's marriage to Belle Elmore, his meeting with Ethel Le Neve, and the
  circumstances that lead to his murder of his wife and his pursuit by the inept
  Inspector Dew.

ED McBAIN
(Evan Hunter)

Biography

Carr, John C. "Ed McBain." In his *The Craft of Crime: Conversations with Crime Writers*. Boston: Houghton Mifflin, 1983.
Carr's background essay on McBain is followed by an interview in which McBain discusses his days in the navy, how the 87th Precinct series got started, how he chose his pen name, his work on Alfred Hitchcock's film *The Birds*, his reading and research, the difference between serious and genre fiction, themes in his work, the mail he receives from readers, his opinions of other writers, other police procedurals, and the importance of setting his books in an imaginary city and not in New York.

Dahlin, Robert. "*PW* Interviews: Evan Hunter." *Publishers Weekly* 219 (April 3, 1981): 6-7.
His real name was Lombino, but he changed it to Evan Hunter at the suggestion of a publisher. Discusses his working methods, the attractions of writing about young people, and the genesis of the 87th Precinct stories written as Ed McBain. The occasion of the interview was the publication of a novel called *Love, Dad* (1980). Discusses personal relationships, his plans for future books, his experiences writing for the movies.

Dove, George N. "Ed McBain." In *Twentieth Century Crime and Mystery Writers*, edited by John M. Reilly. New York: St. Martin's Press, 1980.
A brief list of personal details in the life of Evan Hunter, who writes crime fiction under the pen name Ed McBain, along with a list of awards received for his writing, his home address, and a long list of his publications in chronological order and arranged by categories and pen names. About 750 works of commentary assessing his achievement as a writer.

Straub, Deborah A., and Jean W. Ross. "Evan Hunter." In *Contemporary Authors*, edited by Ann Evory, vol. 5. Detroit: Gale Research, 1982.
An account of the personal details of the life of Evan Hunter, who writes crime novels under the pen name Ed McBain, followed by some facts about his career as teacher, literary agent, jack of all trades, and writer. Contains a list of his publications in chronological order and arranged according to pen name. The commentary assesses his achievements as a writer. Also includes an interview by Jean W. Ross, conducted by phone, March 3, 1981, in Sarasota, Florida. List of biographical and critical sources in newspapers and magazines from 1954 to 1981.

Voss, Ralph F. "Evan Hunter." In *Dictionary of Literary Biography Yearbook: 1982*,
    edited by Richard Ziegfeld. Detroit: Gale Research, 1983.
    A survey of Evan Hunter's major novels, *The Blackboard Jungle* (1954), *Sons*
    (1969), and *Streets of Gold* (1974), against a background of his life and literary
    career. Contains only a brief examination of the police procedurals about the
    87th Precinct that he writes as Ed McBain. Illustrated with a photograph of
    Hunter, a dust jacket of one of his novels, a page of manuscript, and a scene
    from the film version of *The Blackboard Jungle*. Selected bibliography of his
    books with a list of plays, screenplays, and articles, along with three secondary
    sources.

Commentary

Butts, Dennis. "The Cop and the Machine: Technology and the 87th Precinct
    Novels of Ed McBain." *Clues: A Journal of Detection* 6 (Fall/Winter, 1985):
    99-107.
    Discusses McBain's novels in the general context of the police procedurals and
    the version of realism they present, "the worst aspects of urban society that
    have developed in the postwar period." Butts compares the events in the 87th
    Precinct novels with statistics from the 1969 *Uniform Crime Reports of the U.S.*
    to explain how well the series reflects postwar and contemporary urban crime.
    Examines the use of police technology and forensic evidence in the stories,
    considers *The Heckler* (1960) to be the key book in the series.

Dove, George N. *The Boys from Grover Avenue: Ed McBain's 87th Precinct Novels.*
    Bowling Green, Ohio: Bowling Green University Popular Press, 1985.
    This first book-length study of the police-procedural series of Ed McBain is
    arranged by topic. Dove describes Isola, the city of the novels (based on, but
    not named New York), continues by discussing the time frame of the series.
    Chapters follow that are devoted to the use of police procedures, their relation-
    ship to the public, the criminals, sketches of major and minor recurring charac-
    ters, and McBain's style. Includes a checklist of the novels (1956-1983) with
    statistics related to crime in the stories.

_____ . "Ed McBain." In his *The Police Procedural*. Bowling Green,
    Ohio: Bowling Green University Popular Press, 1982.
    McBain's bright, original writing and his control of his formula, which he
    varies when necessary, are reasons Dove sees for the good reputation of his
    87th Precinct series. A thematic discussion of the series and the elements of
    McBain's style demonstrate the validity of Dove's thesis. Considers that only
    in *Hail to the Chief* (1973) has McBain lost his control.

Knight, Stephen. " '. . . A Deceptive Coolness': Ed McBain's Police Novels." In his *Form and Ideology in Crime Fiction*. Bloomington: Indiana University Press, 1980.
Describes the genesis of the police procedural in Great Britain and United States and the addition of Ed McBain to the roster of writers working in that style. Knight believes that the attitudes of Evan Hunter in *The Blackboard Jungle* (1954) transfer naturally to his 87th Precinct stories, written as Ed McBain. Discusses the first four titles in detail to establish the form, style, and content that McBain repeats throughout the series.

McBain, Ed. "The 87th Precinct." In *The Great Detectives*, edited by Otto Penzler. Boston: Little, Brown, 1978.
Describes the concept of the 87th Precinct series as a family story. The family in this case is the police group and their home is the precinct station. Explains how he tried not to have any individual policeman become the hero, the use of an imaginary city as a setting, himself as observer who speaks for the reader, and about the deaths of some of his characters.

Pronzini, Bill. "The 'Mystery' Career of Evan Hunter." *The Armchair Detective* 5 (April, 1972): 129-132.
A survey of Evan Hunter's mystery fiction from 1952 to 1971, with comments on the 87th Precinct novels as well as books published under the pseudonyms Curt Cannon, Hunt Collins, and Richard Martin. Checklist of all titles including science fiction and short stories arranged according to the author's name that appears on the title page. References to *Manhunt* magazine and David C. Cooke's *Best Detective Stories of the Year* (1954, 1955, 1956, 1957), volumes in which some of Hunter's short stories had their first appearance.

JAMES McCLURE

Biography

Carr, John C. "James McClure." In his *The Craft of Crime: Conversations with Crime Writers*. Boston: Houghton Mifflin, 1983.
A brief biographical sketch and survey of McClure's characteristics as a writer, commenting on the admitted influence on his work of Ed McBain and John D. MacDonald. Interviewed by Carr, McClure speaks in detail about his early life and his writing for television, something about his methods, and his use of poetry and images in his work. Supplies many anecdotes about politics, social life, and apartheid in South Africa, his experiences when he returned to the country for a visit in 1974.

McClure, James. "A Bright Grey." In *Colloquium on Crime*, edited by Robin W. Winks. New York: Charles Scribner's Sons, 1986.
Describes his childhood, his family, growing up in South Africa, his reading, his difficulties in school (failing Afrikaans), experiences as a photojournalist, the move to Great Britain and his early attempts to write, how the idea for his characters Tromp Kramer and Mickey Zondi, came to him, how the stories are written, and the autobiographical elements of *Rogue Eagle* (1976).

Wall, Donald. "An Interview with James McClure." *Clues: A Journal of Detection* 6 (Fall/Winter, 1985): 7-25.
Interviewed at his home in Oxford, McClure talks about how he became interested in writing mysteries and thrillers, the influence on his work of reading Ed McBain and John D. MacDonald, his working schedule, and the advantage of not using much advance planning and of using a series character, and his opinions of other writers of police procedurals.

Commentary

Dove, George N. "James McClure." In his *The Police Procedural*. Bowling Green, Ohio: Bowling Green University Popular Press, 1982.
Discusses McClure's portrayal of the closed society of South Africa and its tensions in his mystery novels, with examples, serious and humorous, from the books. Describes the characteristics of Lieutenant Tromp Kramer and his association with the Bantu Mickey Zondi in terms relating to the way they are portrayed. Dove comments on McClure's "oblique and exacting" prose style and point of view.

Schleh, Eugene. "Spotlight on South Africa: The Police Novels of James McClure." *Clues: A Journal of Detection* 7 (Fall/Winter, 1986): 99-107.

McClure's novels of Lieutenant Tromp Kramer and Detective Sergeant Mickey Zondi are discussed by Schleh in terms of how vividly they portray the system of apartheid in South Africa. Thematically arranged, the discussion makes little mention of the crimes or mysteries the detectives are called on to solve. Checklist of McClure's novels.

Wall, Donald. "Apartheid in the Novels of James McClure." *The Armchair Detective* 10 (October, 1977): 348-351.

Describes the system of apartheid in South Africa and indicates how James McClure had made use of it in his first three detective novels *The Steam Pig* (1971), *The Caterpillar Cop* (1972) and *The Gooseberry Fool* (1974). Discusses the plots and characters, revealing some of the solutions of the mysteries Wall considers "complicated, insightful, and thought-provoking."

White, Jean M. "Wahlöö/Sjöwall and James McClure: Murder and Politics." *The New Republic* 175 (July 31, 1976): 27-29.

White comments on how much a reader can learn of South African apartheid from reading James McClure's novels about Lieutenant Tromp Kramer. Discusses the characters of the detective and his Bantu assistant, Mickey Zondi, quoting sequences of dialogue to indicate how much can be done with a few phrases instead of long, sociological passages.

JOHN D. MacDONALD

Biography

Gindin, James. "John D. MacDonald." In *Twentieth Century Crime and Mystery Writers*, edited by John M. Reilly, 2d ed. New York: St. Martin's Press, 1985.
Provides a brief biographical sketch of MacDonald, as well as a checklist of his works. Offers some discussion of his crime fiction, particularly those works featuring his character Travis McGee.

MacDonald, John D. Foreword to *The Good Old Stuff: Thirteen Early Stories*, by John D. MacDonald, edited by Martin H. Greenberg, Francis M. Nevins, Jr., Walter Shine, and Jean Shine. New York: Harper & Row, 1982.
MacDonald explains the process by which thirteen short stories were chosen for this collection out of the hundreds he had written and published in pulp magazines between 1947 and 1952. Comments on the minor changes made to adjust references that would date the stories or confuse the reader. Reminisces on the circumstances under which they were originally written.

Rollyson, Carl. "John D. MacDonald." In *Critical Survey of Mystery and Detective Fiction*, edited by Frank N. Magill, vol. 3. Pasadena, Calif.: Salem Press, 1988.
A brief but clear biographical sketch of MacDonald's life and work. Contains a bibliography of his works and several pages of discussion of his crime fiction.

Commentary

Abraham, Etta C. "Cops and Detectives." *Clues: A Journal of Detection* 1 (Spring, 1980): 96-98.
A character sketch and discussion of Sheriff Norman Hyzer, protagonist in John D. MacDonald's *The Long Lavender Look* (1970) which demonstrates how the author makes the police appear as persons, not merely functionaries, in his novels. Abrahams compares and contrasts Hyzer's portrayal with that of the other policemen in the story, Lew Arnstead, Deputy Billy Cable, as well as with Travis McGee.

Benjamin, David A. "Key Witness: John D. MacDonald." *The New Republic* 173 (July 26, 1975): 28-31.
Describes the genesis of the Travis McGee series and the serious planning that MacDonald did before he took on the limitations that accompany writing a series of novels about the same character. Benjamin describes the typical McGee story and considers the most obvious reason for the success of the

series to be the characterization of McGee himself. Discusses MacDonald's style, his vignettes of cities, and his use of atmosphere.

Brittin, Norman A. "From the 1940's to the 1980's: John D. MacDonald's Increasing Use of Scatological Language." *Clues: A Journal of Detection* 7 (Spring/Summer, 1986): 49-63.
Dialogue in MacDonald's stories and novels represents prevailing editorial restraints, general attitudes of the reading public, as well as the author's good taste and interest in accurately representing the way people speak. Brittin cites examples from MacDonald's contemporaries as well as from his own works.

Cleveland, Carol. "Travis McGee, the Feminist's Friend." *The Armchair Detective* 16 (Autumn, 1983): 407-413.
Cleveland notes the charges that MacDonald's Travis McGee stories are filled with sadistic scenes and machismo, and examines the books to determine the accuracy of the criticism. Discusses the characteristics of the women in the McGee series and the nature of the "wounded woman" syndrome that certainly exists. Includes a checklist of the first eighteen Travis McGee titles.

Cook, Wister. "John D. MacDonald: A Little Ecology Goes a Long Way." *Clues: A Journal of Detection* 1 (Spring, 1980): 57-62.
Cook discusses the ways in which MacDonald allows the reader to identify with Travis McGee, the hero of seventeen novels. Depicted as a consumer with concerns about the ecology, McGee is as helpless in the face of insurmountable odds as any reader; as such, he represents universal concerns of the mid-twentieth century.

Geherin, David. *John D. MacDonald.* New York: Frederick Ungar, 1982.
The first book-length critical study of the crime novels of John D. MacDonald. Geherin emphasizes MacDonald's publications before he created Travis McGee, but includes four chapters of plot summaries and commentary on the McGee books published to 1982. Geherin considers that MacDonald belongs to the category of the serious American novelist but contends that McGee is only a fantasy figure. Summing-up chapter on MacDonald's style. Includes primary and secondary bibliographies. Index.

Grimes, Larry E. "The Reluctant Hero: Reflections on Vocations and Heroism in the Travis McGee Novels of John D. MacDonald." *Clues: A Journal of Detection* 1 (Spring, 1980): 103-108.
Discusses the vocation of McGee as a hero whose goal in life is to retire to live like a beach bum and how that goal turns into another kind of vocation. Grimes considers it ironic that life as a hero for McGee then becomes more satisfying than the lazy life to which he aspires.

Hirschberg, Edgar W. *John D. MacDonald*. Boston: Twayne, 1985.
Hirschberg evaluates MacDonald's work within the context of American literature, not as mystery or suspense fiction. Examines his development and technique as a writer, the underlying themes of his fiction, and considers the
morality in his writing and his work as a social critic. Does not confine himself
to the Travis McGee series. Selected bibliography of novels and collections of
short stories, articles on writing, and environmental concerns. Also lists secondary sources. Index.

_____ . "John D. MacDonald as Social Critic." *Clues: A Journal of Detection* 1 (Spring, 1980): 129-134.
A distinguishing feature of all of John D. MacDonald's fiction is its strong
social consciousness. Hirschberg finds Travis McGee's vocation as a "salvage
expert" (helping people to put social wrongs right) a fitting example of this
and discusses MacDonald's novels *A Flash of Green* (1962), *A Deadly Shade of
Gold* (1965), and *Dress Her in Indigo* (1969), *The Dreadful Lemon Sky* (1975),
Condominium (1977), to prove his thesis.

Holtsmark, Erling B. "Travis McGee as Traditional Hero." *Clues: A Journal of
Detection* 1 (Spring, 1980): 99-102.
Draws comparisons between Travis McGee and his friend Meyer and such
traditional literary heroes with companions as Achilles and Patroklos, Aeneas
and Achates, Don Quixote and Sancho Panza. Holtsmark also equates McGee
with such "loner" heroes as Odysseus, Herakles, Philoctetes, and Ajax and
compares their roles as monster slayers to explain the appeal of McGee today.

Hoyt, Charles Alva. "*The Damned*: Good Intentions, the Tough Guy as Hero and
Villain." In *Tough Guy Writers of the Thirties*, edited by David Madden.
Carbondale: Southern Illinois University Press, 1968.
Describes John D. MacDonald's 1952 novel, *The Damned*, as imitation Hem-
ingway, but a rare example of having the successful tough guy and the unsuc-
cessful tough guy confront each other in the same story. Hoyt discusses the
arrangement of characters that contribute both to success and to failure in
MacDonald's story.

Kaler, Anne K. "Cats, Colors, and Calendars: The Mythic Basis of the Love Story
of Travis McGee." *Clues: A Journal of Detection* 7 (Fall/Winter, 1986): 147-157.
Discusses the novels *Pale Grey for Guilt* (1968) and *The Lonely Silver Rain*
(1985) in terms of mythic themes: "a triad of goddesses, a daughter avenger,
and a partial resolution for a confused and mythical father/hero." Compares
and contrasts Travis McGee with Odysseus and notes the elements that contribute to mythic context: cats, colors as a code, and the use of an ancient solar-
calendar tradition.

Kelly, R. Gordon. "The Precarious World of John D. MacDonald." In *Dimensions of Detective Fiction*, edited by Larry N. Landrum, Pat Browne, and Ray B. Browne. Bowling Green, Ohio: Bowling Green University Popular Press, 1976.
Kelly examines John D. MacDonald's *The Executioners* (1957) in detail to demonstrate how it represents the sense of the precariousness and vulnerability of life in American society. Compares MacDonald's concept with Dashiell Hammett's version of the same theme in the Flitcraft episode of *The Maltese Falcon* (1929).

Kennedy, Veronica M. S. "The Prophet Before the Fact: A Note on John D. MacDonald's *The End of the Night*." *The Armchair Detective* 7 (November, 1973): 41.
In the light of the growing serious attention devoted to writers of crime fiction, such as Ellery Queen and Georges Simenon, Kennedy believes that it is appropriate to examine MacDonald's *The End of the Night* (1960) as an example of the serious themes possible in crime fiction and draws parallels between the events in the novel and the real-life murders of Charles Manson.

Marotta, Joseph. "The Disorderly World of John D. MacDonald: Or, Travis McGee Meets Thomas Pynchon." *Clues: A Journal of Detection* 3 (Spring/Summer, 1982): 105-110.
Examines John D. MacDonald's *The Green Ripper* (1979) for its representation of the concerns of modern American literature, the attempt to find order amid apparent disorder and meaning in a world apparently without purpose. Marotta makes brief comparisons with the concept of order in Thomas Pynchon's *The Crying of Lot 49* (1966).

Moran, Peggy. "McGee's Girls." *Clues: A Journal of Detection* 1 (Spring, 1980): 82-88.
Moran claims to have counted "some 130 female characters" who have either speaking or functional parts in seventeen of John D. MacDonald's novels about Travis McGee. Comments on the relationship McGee has with a number of them, categorizing most of them as victims, and notes McGee's attitudes toward them and how this varies through the series. (See MacDonald's own comments on this article in the same issue of *Clues*.)

Nevins, Francis M., Jr. Introduction to *The Good Old Stuff: Thirteen Early Stories*, by John D. MacDonald, edited by Martin H. Greenberg, Francis M. Nevins, Jr., Walter Shine, and Jean Shine. New York: Harper & Row, 1982.
To introduce a collection of MacDonald's short stories from the pulps (1947-1952) Nevins provides a biographical sketch, a succinct history of the early publications, and a concise analysis of MacDonald's method of storytelling to explain how he can call him "the consummate storyteller of our time." Quotes a statement of MacDonald on the values he admires in fiction.

_____ . "The Making of a Tale-Spinner: J. D. M.'s Early Pulp Mystery Stories." *Clues: A Journal of Detection* 1 (Spring, 1980): 89-95.

The last of the great American mystery writers to gain experience in storytelling in the pulps, MacDonald can be used as a model for the study of the development of fiction-writing techniques. Nevins categorizes MacDonald's output and identifies notable characters, themes, and plots. Argues that the best of these stories should be collected in book form.

Peek, George S. "Beast Imagery and Stereotypes in the Novels of John D. MacDonald." *Clues: A Journal of Detection* 2 (Spring/Summer, 1981): 91-97.

Peek examines the reasons for the popularity of John D. MacDonald's novels, how he comments on human relationships and attitudes through his use of stereotypes. As examples of these, Peek points out the use of images of animals which reflect the personalities of characters in *The Turquoise Lament* (1973) and *The Quick Red Fox* (1964).

_____ . "Conquering the Stereotypes: On Reading the Novels of John D. MacDonald." *The Armchair Detective* 13 (Spring, 1980): 90-93.

Peek discusses stereotypical treatments of women in three of the Travis McGee novels (*A Purple Place for Dying*, 1964; *Bright Orange for the Shroud*, 1965; and *The Dreadful Lemon Sky*, 1975) to indicate how MacDonald employs them so the reader can make judgments on the nature of the use of stereotyping itself in characterization.

Pratt, Allan D. "The Chronology of the Travis McGee Novels." *The Armchair Detective* 13 (Spring, 1980): 83-89.

Pratt speculates on the place of John D. MacDonald's Travis McGee in the real world. Pratt lists the seventeen titles in the series to date (up to *The Empty Copper Sea*, 1978) and assigns each an internal date (when events in the story occur) with arguments to support his theory. Summarizes his findings and makes some deductions about McGee's life before the events of the first book (*The Deep Blue Good-by*, 1964). Illustrated. Includes a list of the published order of the series and a chart summarizing the internal order.

Tolley, Michael J. "Color Him Quixote: MacDonald's Strategy in the Early McGee Novels." *The Armchair Detective* 10 (January, 1977): 6-13.

Tolley defines the "Quixote" as a romantic hero in a cynical age. According to this definition, Travis McGee is such a hero and Tolley cites examples of this from MacDonald's works. He considers that this is not due to accident but to careful planning on the part of the author.

ROSS MACDONALD
(Kenneth Millar)

Biography

Bruccoli, Matthew J. *Ross Macdonald*. New York: Harcourt Brace Jovanovich, 1984.
A brief but lavishly illustrated critical biography of Kenneth Millar, better known under his pseudonym of Ross Macdonald. Bruccoli traces Millar's popular and critical reputation as a writer with commentary on the major fiction and liberal references from the critical reviews. The appendix includes an abstract of Millar's doctoral dissertation on Samuel Taylor Coleridge, notes, and a bibliography. Illustrations of Millar and his wife, pages from the notebooks in which he wrote his novels, and covers from various editions of his books. Index.

Cooper-Clark, Diana. "Interview with Ross Macdonald." In her *Designs of Darkness: Interviews with Detective Novelists*. Bowling Green, Ohio: Bowling Green State University Popular Press, 1983.
Macdonald comments on Canadian and American culture, the elements of biography in his novels, his use of family relationships, the background of Greek myth one finds there, morality in his books, and the difficulty critics may find in assessing his work accurately and universally.

Grogg, Sam L., Jr. "Interview with Ross Macdonald." In *Dimensions of Detective Fiction*, edited by Larry N. Landrum, Pat Browne, and Ray B. Browne. Bowling Green, Ohio: Bowling Green University Popular Press, 1976.
Macdonald is asked about his response to the critical attention given his work, the influence of the hard-boiled tradition on his work, his interest in Southern California as a setting, the importance of nature and ecology, the process of writing a novel, and his own concept of Lew Archer.

Lynds, Dennis. "In Memorium." *The Armchair Detective* 16 (Summer, 1983): 227.
A brief memorial statement on the occasion of the death of Ross Macdonald (1915-1983), written by a colleague among suspense-fiction writers. A moving tribute to Macdonald's work, his achievements, and his influence on other writers. Lynds considers that Macdonald left the crime-fiction field better than he found it.

Macdonald, Ross. *Self-Portrait: Ceaselessly into the Past*. Santa Barbara, Calif.: Capra Press, 1981.
A collection of occasional essays, introductions, and prefaces to Ross Macdonald's own fiction and that of other writers, which serves as a basic auto-

biography. Macdonald talks about his childhood, the influences on him and on his writing, as well as his concepts of detective fiction and the detective hero. Introduction by Eudora Welty, list of sources for the essays in this collection, and a checklist of Macdonald's books.

Commentary

Chandler, Raymond. "Letter to James Sandoe, April 14, 1959." In *Raymond Chandler Speaking*, edited by Dorothy Gardiner and Katherine Sorley Walker. Boston: Little, Brown, 1962.

Raymond Chandler's letter is brief, but interesting in its assessment of Macdonald's first detective novel about Lew Archer, *The Moving Target* (1949). Chandler has praise for the way scenes are handled and for Macdonald's obvious experience, but he is critical of the use of some of his similes and phrases that evoke inappropriate images.

Combs, William W. "The Detective as Both Tortoise and Achilles: Archer Gets the Feel of the Case in *The Chill.*" *Clues: A Journal of Detection* 2 (Spring/Summer, 1981): 98-105.

Compares the contradictions of feelings and information that Lew Archer encounters in *The Chill* (1964) with the topics for discussion that helped the early Greek philosophers develop their ways of thinking. Combs examines Zeno's paradoxes about Achilles' attempt to catch up with a tortoise and the arrow which cannot reach its target and applies these to Archer's situation in the novel.

Delaney, Bill. "Ross Macdonald's Literary Offenses." *The Armchair Detective* 19 (Summer, 1986): 246-248, 250, 252, 254-258.

Delaney argues with the received opinion that Ross Macdonald was a skillful craftsman in the tradition of Dashiell Hammett and Raymond Chandler. Detailed acerbic analysis of *The Moving Target* (1949), the first Lew Archer novel, to demonstrate how Macdonald failed to make a significant contribution to the hard-boiled detective story.

Dorinson, Zahava K. "Ross Macdonald: The Personal Paradigm and Popular Fiction." *The Armchair Detective* 10 (January, 1977): 43-45, 87.

Dorinson draws distinctions between serious literature and popular literature, noting how Ross Macdonald's novels remain variations on the formula of the detective story. Considers whether Macdonald is sufficiently inventive to be distinguished from his contemporaries. Macdonald's "personal paradigm" is the use of a disappearance followed by a murder with the solution buried in the past that involves a question of identity and relationship. Discusses Macdonald's skill in using this paradigm.

Finch, G. A. "The Case of the Underground Man: Evolution or Devolution." *The Armchair Detective* 6 (August, 1973): 210-212.

Reviews Macdonald's *The Underground Man* (1971) against a background of the critical attention his novels had recently received in *The New York Times Book Review* and the idea that there is a distinction between the current Lew Archer novel and some of its predecessors to question whether the novel is the masterpiece that critics claim.

Fishman, Charles. "Another Heraldic Cry: Heraldic Birds in Five Lew Archer Novels." *Clues: A Journal of Detection* 2 (Spring/Summer, 1981): 106-115.

Fishman examines the Lew Archer stories of Ross Macdonald for images that demonstrate the allegorical nature of his work. In the books, birds are referred to frequently, and Fishman categorizes them as sentinels, predators, scavengers, and dead birds, identifying their significance in Macdonald's works.

Geherin, David. "Archer in Hollywood: The 'Barbarous Coast' of Ross Macdonald." *The Armchair Detective* 9 (November, 1975): 55-58.

Geherin discusses Ross Macdonald as an example of a writer using Hollywood as a setting in his fiction in the manner of F. Scott Fitzgerald or Nathaniel West. Examines the entire Lew Archer series for its changing portrait of the city that "reflects changes in Macdonald's artistry, his attitude toward Hollywood, and the nature of Hollywood itself."

Goldman, William. "*The Goodbye Look.*" *The New York Times Book Review* 74 (June 1, 1969): 1-2.

Goldman has been given credit for writing the first serious critical essay on Ross Macdonald's work in this review of the fifteenth novel *The Goodbye Look* (1969). Discusses the overall structure of later novels in the series and speculates on what Lew Archer does that gives the novels an irresistible narrative attraction. Considers Macdonald to be an unpretentious artist.

Grella, George. "Evil Plots: Ross Macdonald." *The New Republic* 173 (July 26, 1975): 24-26.

Grella discusses Ross Macdonald's work in terms of epic literature or mythic categories. Notes that his plots are so complex they are difficult to discuss, but breaks them into four types: the quest of the Archer, the search for the past, the metamorphic pattern, and the mythic plot. Defines each and shows how it fits into Macdonald's work. Uses *The Chill* (1964), *The Instant Enemy* (1968), and *The Goodbye Look* (1969) as examples.

Leonard, John. "I Care Who Killed Roger Ackroyd." *Esquire* 84 (August, 1975): 60-61, 120.

Leonard, once editor of *The New York Times Book Review*, explains the circumstances that put a review of Ross Macdonald's *The Goodbye Look* (1969)
on the front page of *The New York Times Book Review* in 1969, accompanied by
an interview with Macdonald, how Eudora Welty was asked to review *The
Underground Man* (1971), and how Raymond Sokolov placed a cover story on
Macdonald with *Newsweek*.

Macdonald, Ross. "Lew Archer." In *The Great Detectives*, edited by Otto Penzler.
Boston: Little, Brown, 1978.
Macdonald discusses his own reading of detective fiction and his view of the
typical detective hero, what makes a private detective, the significance of the
detective in fiction, the influence of the Lew Archer stories on at least one
real-life detective, and the thin line that exists between the detective and the
potential criminal.

Pry, Elmer. "Lew Archer's 'Moral Landscape.' " In *Dimensions of Detective Fiction*, edited by Larry N. Landrum, Pat Browne, and Ray B. Browne. Bowling
Green, Ohio: Bowling Green University Popular Press, 1976.
Discusses the use of descriptions of landscapes and the naming of characters in
Ross Macdonald's Lew Archer stories to represent California as a kind of
"paradise lost." Pry considers the way Archer serves as a moral agent and
cites specific examples from several novels.

Sokolov, Raymond A. "The Art of Murder." *Newsweek* 77 (March 22, 1971):
101-102, 104, 106, 108.
On the occasion of the publication of *The Underground Man* (1971), Ross
Macdonald becomes the subject of a cover story that surveys his life and
literary career. Sokolov discusses the characteristics of his books and his style,
describes the area of California referred to as "Archer country," and the nature
of Archer as therapist. Finds a significance in Macdonald's concern for ecology and the environment.

Speir, Jerry. *Ross Macdonald*. New York: Frederick Ungar, 1978.
Speir begins with a biographical chapter followed by discussions and plot
synopses of Macdonald's books. Devotes a chapter to Lew Archer, another to
themes, another to Macdonald's style, and finally one summing up his overall
achievement and the significance of his using California as a setting. Includes
bibliography of books and articles by and about Macdonald. Index.

Wolfe, Peter. *Dreamers Who Live Their Dreams: The World of Ross Macdonald's
Novels*. Bowling Green, Ohio: Bowling Green University Popular Press, 1976.
The first book to deal entirely with Ross Macdonald. Wolfe considers Mac-
donald to be a serious writer who knows how to say things that are worth

hearing. Chapters deal with the character of Lew Archer, contain summaries of all the novels in great detail through *The Sleeping Beauty* (1973). Bibliographic notes. Index.

190

NGAIO MARSH

Biography

Mann, Jessica. "Ngaio Marsh." In *Deadler Than the Male: Why Are So Many Respectable English Women So Good at Murder?* New York: Macmillan, 1981.
A biographical sketch of Ngaio Marsh, who remained a very private person all of her life. Mann discusses her childhood in New Zealand as well as her schooldays, her experiences in the theater, her move to England, and her beginnings as a writer of detective stories. Comments on the critical reception her work has received and the changing character of Roderick Alleyn.

Marsh, Ngaio. *Black Beech and Honeydew: An Autobiography.* Boston: Little, Brown, 1965. Rev. ed. London: Collins, 1981.
An autobiography that concentrates less on Ngaio Marsh the writer of detective fiction than the New Zealand born producer and director of stage plays. Marsh paints humorous portraits of her family, friends, and the theater people who touched her life. Includes eight pages of photographs. No index or checklist of her publications. (Revised edition contains more extensive comments on her detective fiction and additional photographs.)

"Ngaio Marsh." In *Contemporary Authors*, edited by Ann Evory, vol. 6. Detroit: Gale Research, 1982.
An account of personal details in Marsh's life, followed by a survey of some facts in her career as actress, dramatist, and director. Notes the awards and honors she won. Contains a list of all novels from 1934 to 1980, as well as nonfiction titles, plays, and contributions to anthologies. Excerpts from selected reviews of her books. List of biographical and critical sources in books and magazines from 1940 to 1980. Obituaries from United States newspapers.

Commentary

Bargainnier, Earl F. "Ngaio Marsh." In *Ten Women of Mystery*, edited by Earl F. Bargainnier. Bowling Green, Ohio: Bowling Green University Popular Press, 1981.
A chronology of significant dates in Ngaio Marsh's life is followed by a survey of her Roderick Alleyn stories, in which Bargainnier stresses her variety of structure and detail within the conventions of the classic detective story. Notes much of the negative criticism her work has received but finds reasons for Marsh's having written as she did. (Similar, but not identical, to an article Bargainnier published in *The Armchair Detective*, April 1977.)

_____ . "Ngaio Marsh's 'Theatrical Murders.' " *The Armchair Detective* 10 (April, 1977): 175-181.
Discusses the way that Ngaio Marsh's career as director and producer of stage drama combines with her career as detective novelist. Bargainnier briefly surveys her involvement with the theater and examines *Enter a Murderer* (1935), *Vintage Murder* (1937), *Overture to Death* (1939), *Colour Scheme* (1943), *Final Curtain* (1947), *Night at the Vulcan* (1951), *False Scent* (1960), and *Killer Dolphin* (1966) against a background of her own autobiography, *Black Beech and Honeydew* (1965).

_____ . "Roderick Alleyn: Ngaio Marsh's Oxonian Superintendent." *The Armchair Detective* 11 (January, 1978): 63-71.
Discusses Roderick Alleyn as an example of the gentleman-policeman who makes the transition to the hero of the police procedural. Bargainnier comments on the personal characteristics of Alleyn as well as on the effect that his background has on his career as a detective. Includes a chronology that begins with his presumed date of birth (1896) and concludes with the events in spring, 1973, of *Black as He's Painted* (1974). Contains a checklist of the Alleyn novels.

Marsh, Ngaio. "Roderick Alleyn." In *The Great Detectives*, edited by Otto Penzler. Boston: Little, Brown, 1978.
A brief, editorial background essay on Ngaio Marsh is followed by Marsh's own account of creating Roderick Alleyn one rainy day after reading a detective story by Agatha Christie or Dorothy L. Sayers. Marsh explains how she planned his character to differ from the then-currently fashionable detective hero types and quickly surveys his career. Comments on the origin of his name.

Panek, LeRoy L. "Ngaio Marsh." In his *Watteau's Shepherds: The Detective Novel in Britain, 1914-1940.* Bowling Green, Ohio: Bowling Green University Popular Press, 1979.
Surveys Marsh's detective stories thematically, discussing the major recurring characters and the roles they play. Panek comments on the ways in which Roderick Alleyn's character develops through the series from adventure hero to aristocratic policeman. Discusses the problems involved in making the classic puzzle story realistic and draws comparisons with Dorothy L. Sayers.

Routley, Erik. "Quartet of Muses: Second Pair." In *The Puritan Pleasures of Detective Fiction*. London: Victor Gollancz, 1972.
A survey of Ngaio Marsh's career. Routley considers Marsh an excellent craftsperson and creator of the "last romantic hero" in detective fiction. A writer of police novels and not thrillers, Marsh produced a series of entertaining stories

that seldom disturb the reader. Notes the prevailing theme of theatrical backgrounds in her books.

White, Jean. "Murder Most Tidy: Ngaio Marsh." *The New Republic* 177 (July 30, 1977): 36-38.

A general overview of Ngaio Marsh's position in detective fiction. White sees the key to her success in the characters who populate her books, especially Roderick Alleyn, but also discusses her impeccable style and the trappings of the "Golden Thirties" in the detective story (country houses and vicars) that she has brought into the modern scene, and her ingenuity with murder weapons.

MARGARET MILLAR

Biography

Bruccoli, Matthew J. *Ross Macdonald*. San Diego: Harcourt Brace Jovanovich, 1984.
Brief references to the life, career, and work of Margaret Millar, who began writing mysteries about two years after her marriage to Kenneth Millar, who wrote mysteries under the pen name Ross Macdonald. Includes a checklist of Margaret Millar's books from 1941 to 1979. Comments on her work as screenwriter at Warner Bros. studio. Lavishly illustrated with photographs of Kenneth Millar at work and at home with examples of his handwriting and the cover designs of his books. Some illustrations include Maragart Millar.

Cooper-Clark, Diana. "Interview with Margaret Millar." In her *Designs of Darkness: Interviews with Detective Novelists*. Bowling Green, Ohio: Bowling Green University Popular Press, 1983.
Millar discusses the lack of a detective-novel tradition in her native Canada, the critical attention paid to detective fiction, why she cannot write criticism, her theories on plotting and creating characters, on not using a series character, mysteries with roots in the past, and her difficulties writing while she is legally blind.

Hoch, Edward D. "Margaret Millar." In *Twentieth Century Crime and Mystery Writers*, edited by John M. Reilly. New York: St. Martin's Press, 1980.
A brief list of the personal details of the life of Margaret Millar, along with some facts about her literary career. Lists her publications in chronological order and by category. About 750 words of commentary assessing her achievement as a writer.

Schelde, Per. "Margaret Millar." In *Critical Survey of Mystery and Detective Fiction*, edited by Frank M. Magill, vol. 3. Pasadena, Calif.: Salem Press, 1988.
Describes Margaret Millar's principal series characters (Dr. Paul Prye, Inspector Sands, and Tom Aragon) and notes the themes of the inner life of the individual and distortions of reality that her books portray. A short biographical sketch is followed by an extended analysis of *The Iron Gates* (1945), *Beast in View* (1955), *How like an Angel* (1962), and *The Fiend* (1964) as examples of her significant contributions to the genre. Selected list of her mystery novels and other works, with a bibliography of secondary sources.

Wiloch, Thomas. "Margaret Millar." In *Contemporary Authors*, edited by Linda Metzger and Deborah A. Straub, vol. 16. Detroit: Gale Research, 1986.

A brief list of facts in the personal life of Margaret Ellis Sturm, who married Kenneth Millar on June 2, 1938, along with details of her literary career. Contains a list of publications in chronological order and arranged by categories. Surveys critical response to her work and assesses her achievement as a writer. Lists biographical and critical sources in books, magazines, and newspapers.

Commentary

Lachman, Marvin. "Margaret Millar: The Checklist of an 'Unknown' Mystery Writer." *The Armchair Detective* 3 (January, 1970): 85-88.
An annotated checklist of fifteen mystery and detective novels by Margaret Millar is prefaced by a biographical sketch. Lachman lists the novels in the order of publication, giving names of publishers of hardcover and paperback editions. Indicates critical reception, film or television adaptations, original magazine appearances, and evaluative comments.

Reilly, John M. "Margaret Millar." In *Ten Women of Mystery*, edited by Earl F. Bargainnier. Bowling Green, Ohio: Bowling Green University Popular Press, 1981.
Discusses the lack of critical attention to Margaret Millar's books and how difficult it is to fit her work into any standard generic categories: gothic, suspense, or detective. Reilly considers that there exists a tension between the expected patterns produced by the conventional formulas and Millar's innovations that adds to the interest and success of her writing. Compares examples from early and late works to indicate her development.

Sandoe, James. "Dagger of the Mind." In *The Art of the Mystery Story*, edited by Howard Haycraft. New York: Simon & Schuster, 1947. Reprint. Grossett & Dunlap, 1961.
Analyzes and discusses the modern tale of terror known as the "psychological thriller," relating it by definition and heritage to the horror story. Uses Margaret Millar's novels *Wall of Eyes* (1943) and *The Iron Gates* (1945) as examples in his discussion. Also discusses Freeman Wills Croft's *Wilful and Premeditated* (1934), Patrick Hamilton's *Hangover Square: Or, The Man with Two Minds, A Story of Darkest Earl's Court in the Year 1939* (1941), and the works of Graham Greene, Eric Ambler, and Cornell Woolrich.

E. PHILLIPS OPPENHEIM

Biography

Oppenheim, E. Phillips. "My Religion." In *My Religion*, by Arnold Bennett, et al. London: Hutchinson, 1925.

Oppenheim comments in general terms on the importance of having a faith in God, how difficult it is for most people to discuss the topic of the Hereafter. Argues the value of such belief and discusses the best preparation for the "inevitable end." (Individual essays in this collection have no distinctive titles.)

——————— . *The Pool of Memory*. Boston: Little, Brown, 1942.

Oppenheim's autobiography contains anecdotes of his external life and something of his philosophy. Notes which of his books were most favored by his public and describes the life of gracious living that being a best-selling author made possible. Little about the actual work of writing or the source of his ideas other than his preference for those drawn from his imagination over those drawn from observation. Includes a checklist of Oppenheim's books arranged by novels, collections of short stories, omnibus volumes, and miscellaneous (travel and autobiography) through 1941. Illustrated with eleven photographs. No index in the U.S. edition.

Standish, Robert. *The Prince of Story-Tellers: The Life of E. Phillips Oppenheim*. London: Peter Davies, 1957.

Standish describes the process by which he wrote this biography of the famous writer: partly by interviews with people who knew him, partly by studying Oppenheim's papers while living in Oppenheim's own house after the author's death, partly from a study of his work. Includes much factual data based on royalty statements and Oppenheim's notes on how long he had worked on specific books and how much money they had earned for him. Complete checklist of Oppenheim's books and short-story collections. Frontispiece. No index.

Commentary

Murray, Will. "E. Phillips Oppenheim." In *Dictionary of Literary Biography*, edited by Bernard Benstock and Thomas F. Staley, vol. 70. Detroit: Gale Research, 1988.

Seven pages of bibliography of Oppenheim's work, arranged by publication date with both U.S. and British titles indicated, is followed by Murray's survey of Oppenheim's contributions to mystery fiction. Rates *The Great Impersonation* (1920) as Oppenheim's most successful novel and notes his skill in writing novels that predicted future political situations. Discusses possible influences of Baroness Orczy on his work and indicates some of Oppenheim's own political beliefs. Illustrated with photographs of Oppenheim, and illustrations from his works, book jackets, and scenes from the film version of *The Great Impersonation*.

Overton, Grant. "A Great Impersonation by E. Phillips Oppenheim." In *Cargoes for Crusoes*. Boston: Little, Brown, 1924.

Overton divides his essay into four parts, some of it taken from an interview with Oppenheim: a bit of whimsy about how prolific Oppenheim is as a writer, Oppenheim's methods of plotting and writing a story, a very brief biography, and an assessment of his achievement using *The Way of These Women* (1913) as an example. Includes a checklist of Oppenheim's works (1887-1924) and references to secondary sources.

Panek, LeRoy L. "E. Phillips Oppenheim." In his *The Special Branch: The British Spy Novel, 1890-1980*. Bowling Green, Ohio: Bowling Green University Popular Press, 1981.

Panek's generally negative assessment of Oppenheim's novels and his position in the early history of the spy novel centers on three representative books from the beginning, middle, and end of his career. Discusses *The Mysterious Mr. Sabin* (1898) *The Pawns Count* (1918), and *Up the Ladder of Gold* (1931) while referring to some of his other titles in passing. Considers Oppenheim's primary contribution to be in writing novels that centered on secret and clandestine diplomacy.

BARONESS ORCZY

Biography

"Baroness Orczy." In *Twentieth Century Authors*, edited by Stanley J. Kunitz and Howard Haycraft. New York: H. W. Wilson, 1942.

A brief account of the life and artistic career of Baroness Orczy. Discussion of her work is evenly divided between the Scarlet Pimpernel and the stories of the Old Man in the Corner. Offers a brief assessment of her achievement as a writer. Selected bibliography of her books from 1899 to 1940 with references to some secondary sources. Photograph of Baroness Orczy.

"Baroness Orczy." In *Twentieth Century Authors: First Supplement*, edited by Stanley J. Kunitz. New York: H. W. Wilson, 1955.

An obituary notice for Baroness Orczy, who died on November 12, 1947, in London at the age of eighty-two. Comments on some of the activities in her life since the beginning of World War II. Discusses her work in general and assesses her achievement as a writer. Select list of publications from 1942 to 1947. Cites her autobiography and obituary notices for biographical information.

Bleiler, E. F. "Baroness Orczy." In *Twentieth Century Crime and Mystery Writers*, edited by John M. Reilly. New York: St. Martin's Press, 1980.

A very brief list of personal details of the life of Baroness Orczy, followed by an extensive checklist of her publications in chronological order and arranged by category. About 250 words of commentary assessing her achievement in crime fiction, particularly the Old Man in the Corner stories, the stories of Lady Molly and Patrick Mulligan, as well as the combined historical and mystery-adventure in *The Man in Grey, Being Episodes of the Chouan Conspiracies in Normandy During the First Empire* (1918) and *Castles in the Air* (1921).

Orczy, Baroness. *Links in the Chain of Life: The Autobiography of Baroness Orczy*. London: Hutchinson, 1945.

Orczy divides her autobiography into five sections: childhood, musical life, artistic career, early married life, and the Scarlet Pimpernel. The last section covers more than half of her book and serves as an outline of her writing career. Briefly discusses the concept behind the Old Man in the Corner stories but devotes most of her discussion to *The Scarlet Pimpernel* (1905; as book, play, film, and phenomenon) and her other historical novels. Closes with an account of her memories of World War II. Illustrated with photographs. Index.

Commentary

Bleiler, E. F. Introduction to *The Old Man in the Corner: Twelve Mysteries*, by Baroness Orczy. New York: Dover, 1980.

Bleiler provides a concise biographical sketch of Emmuska, Baroness Orczy, how she began her career as a writer at the turn of the century, and how she is remembered as a person. Discusses the significance of the stories about the Old Man in the Corner and their publishing history, with brief references to other detective fiction by Orczy. (This collection of the early stories is taken from the original magazine appearances and does not duplicate the collection known as *The Old Man in the Corner*.)

Dueren, Fred. "Was the Old Man in the Corner an Armchair Detective?" *The Armchair Detective* 14 (Summer, 1981): 232-233.

A survey of the literature on Orczy's character from the Old Man in the Corner stories that identifies him as an armchair detective. Dueren examines the texts of a dozen of the stories to support his argument that the Old Man is a more active figure than is popularly supposed.

Staples, Katherine. "Emma, Baroness Orczy." In *Dictionary of Literary Biography*, edited by Bernard Benstock and Thomas F. Staley, vol. 70. Detroit: Gale Research, 1988.

A survey of Orczy's life and contributions to the detective story. Staples discusses the characteristics of the Old Man in the Corner as a character and the series of stories about him, using "The Fenchurch Street Mystery" as an example of her plot outlines. Briefly comments on *Lady Molly of Scotland Yard* (1910), *Skin o' My Tooth* (1928), the Scarlet Pimpernel series, and the mystery elements in her adventure stories. Illustrated. Extensive bibliography of Orczy's work.

Starrett, Vincent. Introduction to *The Old Man in the Corner*, by Baroness Orczy. New York: W. W. Norton, 1966.

Describes the creation of the Old Man in the Corner, drawing on Orczy's autobiography for details. Starrett provides concise biographical information, and some comments on the Scarlet Pimpernel. Concludes with a character sketch of Orczy, suggesting the scope of her contribution to popular culture.

ROBERT B. PARKER

Biography

Carr, John C. "Robert B. Parker." In his *The Craft of Crime: Conversations with Crime Writers*. Boston: Houghton Mifflin, 1983.
A survey of Parker's general achievements with the detective story precedes the actual interview that covers why people read detective stories; Parker's experiences before becoming a novelist, especially in the academic world; his opinions on writing and writers; why character interests him more than plot; comments on some of his own works; and detective fiction in the context of American literature.

Herbert, Rosemary. "Mortal Steaks: A Dinner with Robert B. Parker." *The Armchair Detective* 18 (Winter, 1984): 71-73.
Describes the "First Spenser Supper" sponsored by Kate Mattes' Mystery Books /Murder Under Cover bookstore in Cambridge, Massachusetts, to celebrate its first anniversary and to honor Robert B. Parker for putting Boston back on the map for mystery readers. Photographs of Parker with local celebrities.

Parker, Robert B., and Anne Ponder. "What I Know About Writing Spenser Novels." In *Colloquium on Crime: Eleven Renowned Mystery Writers Discuss Their Work*, edited by Robin W. Winks. New York: Charles Scribner's Sons, 1986.
Parker has expanded and rewritten the dialogue he had with Anne Ponder, published in *The Armchair Detective*, 1984. Describes his writing methods, his opinions of other writers, his experiences in publishing, his first detective novel, his characters, and his pride in the work he does.

Ponder, Anne. "A Dialogue with Robert B. Parker." *The Armchair Detective* 17 (Fall, 1984): 341-348.
Ponder interviews Parker, December 15, 1983, at the National Humanities Center in North Carolina. Topics: why Parker writes what he does, what he has learned from Spenser, the characteristics he has assigned Spenser, the role of dialogue in fiction, influences on his writing style, his opinions of William Faulkner, Ernest Hemingway, Raymond Chandler, and Dashiell Hammett, and his female characters.

Commentary

Carter, Steven R. "Spenserian Ethics: The Unconventional Morality of Robert B. Parker's Traditional American Hero." *Clues: A Journal of Detection* 1 (Fall/ Winter, 1980): 109- 118.

The characteristics that Parker assigned to Spenser were intended to give a "ritualistic overtone" to the stories and remind readers of Spencer's origins in the hard-boiled tradition. Carter compares Spenser to other traditional American heroes: the sports superstar, the Western hero, and the tough-guy movie hero, to show how he blends traditions and yet departs from them by being a loner. Titles discussed: *Mortal Stakes* (1975), *Promised Land* (1976), *The Judas Goat* (1978), and *Looking for Rachel Wallace* (1980).

Evans, T. Jeff. "Robert B. Parker and the Hard-Boiled Tradition of American Detective Fiction." *Clues: A Journal of Detection* 1 (Fall/Winter, 1980): 100-108.
Describes the world of the tough private detective of fiction, contrasting it with the tradition of Arthur Conan Doyle, Jacques Futrelle, and Rex Stout. Evans discusses Parker's work to 1980 (six novels "self-consciously in the . . . tradition of Hammett, Chandler, and Macdonald") to demonstrate how Spenser, the detective, fits their examples.

Geherin, David. *Sons of Sam Spade: The Private Eye Novel in the 70's*. New York: Frederick Ungar, 1980.
One half of this book is devoted to Robert B. Parker, with a biographical sketch and detailed discussions of *The Godwulf Manuscript* (1974), *God Save the Child* (1974), *Mortal Stakes* (1975), *Promised Land* (1976), and *The Judas Goat* (1978), tracing Parker's development as a writer, beginning as a follower of Raymond Chandler, then developing his own themes, characters and style. Includes notes and a bibliography of Parker's works (other works as well as detective novels) and selected book reviews.

Gray, W. Russell. "The 'Eyes' Have It: Reflections on the Private Detective as Hero." *Clues: A Journal of Detection* 6 (Fall/Winter, 1985): 27-39.
Discusses the rise of the hero in popular culture, the development of the private investigator in fiction, from the operatives in the books of Allan Pinkerton to the present day. In a brief survey contrasts real and fictional private detectives, using Parker's Spenser, Stephen Greenleaf's John Tanner, MacDonald's Travis McGee, and Jonathan Valin's Harry Stoner as examples.

——————— . "Reflections in a Private Eye: Robert B. Parker's Spenser." *Clues: A Journal of Detection* 5 (Spring/Summer, 1984): 1-13.
Traces the evolution of the private detective in fiction from the pulps of the 1920's and 1930's through the refining of Dashiell Hammett, Raymond Chandler, and Ross Macdonald to Parker's "state-of-the-art" detective Spenser. Gray describes the characteristics of Spenser as hero, contrasting them with those of his predecessors. Speculates on the reasons that readers keep coming back to the Spenser stories.

Hoffman, Carl. "Spenser: The Illusion of Knighthood." *The Armchair Detective* 16 (Spring, 1983): 131-138.

Discusses the themes of Parker's first six novels about Spenser to demonstrate the patterns the author uses to solve the problem of bringing the private detective of the 1930's and 1940's up-to-date for the 1970's and 1980's. Hoffman analyzes each book in turn, noting the critical response. Includes a bibliography of Parker's novels and sources for reviews.

Saylor, V. Louise. "The Private Eye and His Victuals." *Clues: A Journal of Detection* 5 (Fall/Winter, 1984): 111-118.

Cites examples in which descriptions of food and eating are significant episodes in detective novels by Raymond Chandler, Ross Macdonald, Michael Z. Lewin, and Richard Hoyt and discusses the example of excessive eating found in Robert B. Parker's Spenser series. Quotes examples from three Parker novels, one of which is a recipe for lamb cutlets.

Zalewski, James W., and Lawrence B. Rosenfeld. "Rules for the Game of Life: The Mysteries of Robert B. Parker and Dick Francis." *Clues: A Journal of Detection* 5 (Fall/Winter, 1984): 72-81.

Compares the depiction of life as a game with rules to be followed in Robert B. Parker and Dick Francis, using a moral code founded either on the concept of honor as an example or as a model. Discusses the themes of missing children, missing spouses, death, or corruption of a family unit.

EDGAR ALLAN POE

Biography

Allen, Hervey. *Israfel: The Life and Times of Edgar Allan Poe*. Rev. ed. New York: Farrar & Rinehart, 1934.
Originally published in 1926 in two volumes, this biography clarified many aspects of Poe's life for the first time. An early attempt to portray Poe's human side. Explores Poe's physical and mental condition. Illustrated. Appendixes on ancestry and legal documents.

Hammond, J. R. *An Edgar Allan Poe Companion*. Totowa, N.J.: Barnes & Noble Books, 1981.
Part 1 examines Poe's life and literary accomplishments. Includes an alphabetical listing of all stories, essays, and poems that Poe collected into books, along with the earlier periodical appearances. Separate chapters on stories, romances, essays, and poetry. Discusses the autobiographical thread in his poems.

Quinn, Arthur Hobson. *Edgar Allan Poe: A Critical Biography*. New York: D. Appleton-Century, 1941.
Based on extensive research into Poe's correspondence, this is the best and most comprehensive biography of Poe. Contains critical analysis of his works, which is, however, somewhat dated.

Symons, Julian. *The Tell-Tale Heart: The Life and Works of Edgar Allan Poe*. New York: Harper & Row, 1978.
Symons divides this book into two unequal parts: Two-thirds deals with Poe's life; the remainder is criticism showing Poe's relationship to American literature, his qualities as critic and poet. Poe's fiction is discussed under headings of humor, horror, reality and super-reality, and the tales of detection. Symons devotes a chapter each to the psychoanalytical approach to his work, a survey of published literary theories about Poe, and the question of why he wrote what he did. Selected annotated bibliography of material published about Poe. Index.

Thomas, Dwight, and David K. Jackson. *The Poe Log: A Documentary Life of Edgar Allan Poe, 1809-1849*. Boston: G. K. Hall, 1987.
A presentation of events in Poe's life as revealed in various excerpts from contemporary documents. Contains letters, newspaper reports, periodical articles, legal records, and reminiscences. Also includes biographical notes on persons mentioned, a list of sources, and a comprehensive index. This is the raw data, rather than interpretive material.

Commentary

Cawelti, John G. "The Formula of the Classical Detective Story." In his *Adventure, Mystery, and Romance: Formula Stories as Art and Popular Culture*. Chicago: University of Chicago Press, 1976.
Explains the four aspects of the detective-story formula that Poe defined: situation, pattern of action, characters and relationships, and setting, with comments on the cultural background of the formula. Cawelti discusses some of the writers who have made use of Poe's conventions.

Christopher, Joe R. "Poe and the Tradition of the Detective Story." In *The Mystery Writer's Art*, edited by Francis M. Nevins, Jr. Bowling Green, Ohio: Bowling Green University Popular Press, 1970.
A consideration of Poe's contributions to the tradition of the detective story and how they have been followed up by later writers. Summarizes critical comment on Poe's fiction and includes discussion of "Thou Art the Man" and "The Gold Bug." Selective annotated bibliography of criticism on Poe and the detective story.

Daniel, Robert. "Poe's Detective God." In *Twentieth Century Interpretations of Poe's Tales*, edited by William L. Howarth. Engelwood Cliffs, N.J.: Prentice-Hall, 1971.
Discusses C. Auguste Dupin as a character and compares him to Roderick Usher of "The Fall of the House of Usher" and to Poe himself. Daniel considers Poe's detective stories to be stories of the supernatural and discusses the language of the stories as well as the plot construction and setting.

Davidson, Edward H. "The Tale as Allegory." In his *Poe: A Critical Study*. Cambridge, Mass.: Harvard University Press, 1957.
Davidson discusses Poe's detective stories and the character of C. Auguste Dupin as part of the American Dream. Comments on their autobiographical, moral, and philosophical content and compares Dupin to other figures in American literature and culture, contrasting him with other heroes in Poe's own fiction.

Engel, Leonard W. "Truth and Detection: Poe's Tales of Ratiocination and His Use of the Enclosure." *Clues: A Journal of Detection* 3 (Fall/Winter, 1982): 83-86.
Engel discusses the significance of the artistic and imaginative use of the key element of a physical enclosure in Poe's detective fiction. Compares the plot of "The Murders in the Rue Morgue" with Joseph Sheridan Le Fanu's story "Passage in the Secret History of an Irish Countess" (1838).

Gavrell, Kenneth. "The Problem of Poe's 'Purloined Letter.' " *The Armchair Detective* 15 no. 4 (1982): 381-382.

Gavrell discusses the most significant flaw in Edgar Allan Poe's third story about C. Auguste Dupin, the construction of the letter so that the seal and the address could not have been visible at the same time, then goes on to indicate other problems related to the form of the letter and to suggest a possible solution.

Goldhurst, William. "Misled by a Box: Variations on a Theme from Poe." *Clues: A Journal of Detection* 3 (Spring/Summer, 1982): 31-37.
Goldhurst notes how Poe may have based his short story "The Oblong Box" on a real-life murder case from 1841. Compares the characters in that story to those in some of Poe's other stories, including "The Fall of the House of Usher." Compares the Poe story to Arthur Conan Doyle's "That Little Square Box" (1881) and Eugene O'Neill's one-act play "In the Zone" (1917).

Haycraft, Howard. "Time: 1841 — Place: America." In *Murder for Pleasure: The Life and Times of the Detective Story*. New York: D. Appleton-Century, 1941.
Haycraft discusses Poe's contributions to the detective story in the context of the times and of his predecessors in social and literary history. Examines all three Dupin stories, discusses the origin of the name of the detective, and speculates on the reasons that Poe wrote only three tales of ratiocination. Illustrations of Poe's home, the possible model for Dupin, and the opening manuscript page of "The Murders in the Rue Morgue."

Hoffman, Daniel. *PoePoePoePoePoePoePoe*. Garden City, N.Y.: Doubleday, 1972.
A very personal account of Hoffman's fascination with Poe and his works. Discusses "The Gold Bug" and "Thou Art the Man," along with the three Dupin short stories. Notes how carefully Poe constructed these tales, how C. Auguste Dupin's mind works by association. Considers Dupin one of Poe's finest creations and examines the duality of character that Poe presents. (Chapter 4, "Disentanglements," covers the detective stories.) Index.

Lowndes, R. A. W. "The Contributions of Edgar Allan Poe." In *The Mystery Writer's Art*, edited by Francis M. Nevins, Jr. Bowling Green, Ohio: Bowling Green University Popular Press, 1970.
Lowndes examines Poe's short stories of ratiocination and compiles a listing, story-by-story, of thirty-two specific contributions made by Poe. There are twenty in "The Murders in the Rue Morgue," an additional seven in "The Mystery of Marie Roget," and five in "The Purloined Letter." Considers no later writer to have contributed half as much.

Matthews, J. Brander. "Poe and the Detective Story." In *The Recognition of Edgar Allan Poe: Selected Criticism Since 1829*, edited by Eric W. Carlson. Ann Arbor: University of Michigan Press, 1966.

Surveys the field of the gothic mystery; places Poe's works in context; and explains what is significant about Poe's achievement in creating the detective story. Matthews discusses "The Murders in the Rue Morgue," compares it to "The Gold Bug," Voltaire's *Zadig: Or, The Book of Fate* (1749), and other early stories.

Moskowitz, Sam. "Poe on Trial." *The Armchair Detective* 4 (October, 1970): 10-11.
Moskowitz presents the suggestion that E. T. A. Hoffmann's "Das Freulein von Scuder" was influential on Poe's creation of "The Murders in the Rue Morgue" and then, systematically and carefully, demonstrates that the pattern developed by Poe was indeed an original. Compares the Hoffmann story with Poe's trilogy and notes biographical facts about Poe that support his argument.

Murch, Alma Elizabeth. "The Short Detective Story: Edgar Allan Poe." In her *The Development of the Detective Novel*. New York: Philosophical Library, 1958. Reprint. Port Washington, N.Y.: The Kennikat Press, 1968.
Murch enumerates Poe's contributions to the detective story in his tales of C. Auguste Dupin, discusses his use of a French background for his detective, compares and contrasts the character with François-Eugène Vidocq, and describes the influence of Poe as a writer and his popularity in Europe.

Paul, Raymond. *Who Murdered Mary Rogers?* Englewood Cliffs, N.J.: Prentice-Hall, 1971.
Drawing on contemporary newspaper accounts, Paul reconstructs the circumstances surrounding the murder in 1841 of Mary Cecilia Rogers, presents the various theories advanced at the time, and suggests a solution to the case. Appendix identifies all characters in the story, sources for Paul's research, other treatments of the case, and the text of Poe's "The Mystery of Marie Rôget," which was based on the real case, with notes. Bibliography of secondary materials. Illustrated with line drawings. Index.

Symons, Julian. "The Two Strands: Godwin, Vidocq, Poe." In his *Bloody Murder: From the Detective Story to the Crime Novel, a History*. Rev. ed. New York: Viking Press, 1985.
Symons praises Poe's imaginative powers in writing detective stories that are not based on actual police methods and notes Poe's debt to François-Eugène Vidocq. Briefly summarizes Poe's contributions to creating the themes and traditions of the detective story, admits that there are flaws in some of the reasoning in his stories, considers Poe's fatherhood of the genre accidental.

Thomson, H. Douglas. "Edgar Allan Poe." In his *Masters of Mystery: A Study of the Detective Story*. London: Collins, 1931. Reprint with notes. New York: Dover, 1978.

Compares the merits of the short detective-story with those of the novel. Thomson discusses each of Poe's Dupin stories, noting the elements that have become conventions in detective fiction. Examines the character of C. Auguste Dupin and comments on the role of the police. Brief consideration given to "The Gold Bug" to explain why it cannot be considered a detective story.

Walsh, John Evangelist. *Poe the Detective: The Curious Circumstances Behind "The Mystery of Marie Rôget."* New Brunswick, N.J.: Rutgers University Press, 1968.

An account of the way Poe constructed the story "The Mystery of Marie Rôget" from the facts of the real-life murder of Mary Cecilia Rogers near Weehawken, New Jersey. Includes the text of Poe's story and contemporary illustrations from newspapers and magazines. Selected bibliography on Poe and the short story itself. Index.

MELVILLE DAVISSON POST

Biography

"Melville Davisson Post." In *Twentieth Century Authors*, edited by Stanley J. Kunitz and Howard Haycraft. New York: H. W. Wilson, 1942.
A brief account of the personal details of the life of Melville Davisson Post, along with a discussion of the Randolph Mason and Uncle Abner stories with an assessment of his contributions to detective literature. Selected checklist of his works from 1896-1930 with some references to secondary sources. Includes a photograph of Post.

Norton, Charles A. *Melville Davisson Post: Man of Many Mysteries.* Bowling Green, Ohio: Bowling Freen University Popular Press, 1973.
This is the only full-length study of Melville Davisson Post. One quarter of it is devoted to biography; the rest is a critical study of his work in the order in which he wrote it. Norton devotes a chapter each to the Randolph Mason stories and to the Uncle Abner books. Includes notes, an extensive bibliography of Post's books, the appearance of his fiction and nonfiction in magazines. Illustrated with five pages of photographs. Index of titles.

Yates, Donald A. "Melville Davisson Post." In *Twentieth Century Crime and Mystery Writers*, edited by John M. Reilly. New York: St. Martin's Press, 1980.
A brief account of the personal details in the life of Melville Davisson Post, along with some facts of his career as a lawyer. Contains a checklist of books and uncollected short stories and articles in chronological order and arranged by categories. Includes 250 works of commentary assessing Post's achievement as a writer.

Commentary

Boucher, Anthony. "Boucher on Post." In *The Complete Uncle Abner*, by Melville Davisson Post. Del Mar, Calif.: Publisher's Inc., 1977.
A survey of Post's contributions to detective fiction with comments on the Randolph Mason stories. Contains a more detailed appreciation of the Uncle Abner series with reasoned evaluations of their significance. Boucher cites Ellery Queen and Howard Haycraft's comments on the Abner stories and the influence they had on William Faulkner's *Knight's Gambit* (1949).

Hubin, Allen J. Introduction to *The Complete Uncle Abner*, by Melville Davisson Post. Del Mar, Calif.: Publisher's Inc., 1977.

Hubin comments on the fact that Post's Uncle Abner stories are so "peculiarly American," which may explain why they are so little known elsewhere. Provides biographical data on Post, a discussion of the character of Abner and (included in this edition) an annotated bibliography of Post's collected writings, noting original magazine appearances for some of the short stories.

Overton, Grant. "The Art of Melville Davisson Post." In *Cargoes for Crusoes*. Boston: Little, Brown, 1924.
Discusses Post's theories of writing, including the importance of plot over character. Overton draws comparisons between Post's detective stories and those of other writers, including Edgar Allan Poe. Some biographical details and an account of the critical response to Post's stories are included. Checklist of books by Post (1896-1924) and a survey of other sources on his work. Includes some statements by Post on detective fiction.

Williams, Blanche Colton. "Melville Davisson Post." In *Our Short Story Writers*. New York: Dodd, Mead, 1920.
A general survey of Post's contributions to detective fiction. Concentrates on the manner by which Post may be considered to have improved upon Poe's model. Discusses the stories about Randolph Mason, Post's own statements on fiction, the Uncle Abner stories, and *The Mystery at the Blue Villa* (1919) with references to some of Post's other work. Includes short list of Post's books through 1920.

ELLERY QUEEN

Biography

Gaiter, Dorothy J. "Frederic Dannay, 76, Co-Author of Ellery Queen Mysteries, Dies." *The New York Times*, September 5, 1982: 36.

An obituary that surveys the highlights of the Ellery Queen collaboration, quoting Frederic Dannay's views on detective fiction and his attitudes toward writers of detective fiction. Describes Ellery Queen the detective and Dannay's work as editor of *Ellery Queen's Mystery Magazine*. Few specific biographical details. List of survivors.

Hubin, Allen J. "Frederic Dannay: Doctor of Humane Letters." *The Armchair Detective* 12 (Summer, 1979): 236-237.

An account of the awarding of an honorary doctorate of humane letters to Frederic Dannay, April 17, 1979, at Carroll College, Waukesha, Wisconsin. Dannay declined to give an address but submitted to questions by a panel of experts in the field of detective fiction. Illustrated with photographs of the ceremony and the participants.

Nathan, Daniel. *The Golden Summer*. Boston: Little, Brown, 1953.

An autobiographical novel by the man who called himself Frederic Dannay, and who, with his cousin Manford Lepofsy, also known as Manfred B. Lee, created Ellery Queen. Nostalgically describes the events of the summer of 1915 in a small town in upstate New York. Nathan's experiences as a boy explain much of the attitude and personality of the man who became Ellery Queen.

Queen, Ellery (Frederic Dannay). "Who Shall Ever Forget?" In *The Mystery Writer's Art*, edited by Francis M. Nevins, Jr. Bowling Green, Ohio: Bowling Green University Popular Press, 1970.

A nostalgic reminiscence by one of the creators of Ellery Queen of his boyhood discovery of the Sherlock Holmes stories. Dannay comments on the books he read as a child, speculates on the lack of crime fiction as reading matter, and notes the impact that reading *The Adventures of Sherlock Holmes* (1892) had on him.

Shenker, Israel. "Ellery Queen Won't Tell How It's Done." *The New York Times*, February 22, 1969: 36.

On the fortieth anniversary of the publication of *The Roman Hat Mystery* (1929), Frederic Dannay and Manfred B. Lee are interviewed about their contribution to detective fiction. Surveys the creation and development of the Ellery Queen series with comments on the authors' attitudes toward violence, writing, and their place in literature. Photographs of Dannay and Lee at home.

Sullivan, Eleanor. "Fred Dannay and *EQMM*." *The Armchair Detective* 12 (Summer, 1979): 201-202.

The managing editor of *Ellery Queen's Mystery Magazine* describes her experiences in applying for the position and summarizes what she learned in working for Frederic Dannay after she had accepted the responsibility. Discusses what Dannay considered irritating and challenging in editing the magazine he founded and how he made the magazine one of his lasting and unique contributions to the genre.

Commentary

Bainbridge, John. "Ellery Queen: Crime Made Him Famous and His Authors Rich." *Life* 15 (November 22, 1943): 70-76.

An extensive and informal profile of Manfred B. Lee and Frederic Dannay and their collaboration as Ellery Queen. Describes the marketing of mystery novels in general, the creation of Ellery Queen as a character, hints at how they plot their stories, their sources for ideas, and the development of the series. Illustrated with photographs of the two authors at work and of a brownstone house on 87th Street like detective Ellery Queen inhabits.

Biederstadt, Lynn. "To the Very Last: The Dying Message." *The Armchair Detective* 12 (Summer, 1979): 209-210.

Discusses the use of the dying message as a clue in the Ellery Queen stories and why the character of Ellery Queen should be particularly appropriate as a solver of such riddles. Biederstadt explains how successful this is as a device in some of the stories yet produces too ambiguous a solution in others.

Boucher, Anthony. "There Was No Mystery in What the Crime Editor Was After." *The New York Times Book Review* 66 (February 26, 1961): 4-5, 50.

An appreciation of *Ellery Queen's Mystery Magazine* and the part the editor has had in preserving crime short-fiction of the past while encouraging new writers. Boucher notes some of the frequent contributors by name. This article was reprinted in *Ellery Queen's Mystery Magazine* (June, 1961) and appears slightly revised as the introduction to *The Quintessence of Queen* (1962), selected by Anthony Boucher.

"A Case of Double Identity." In *The Tragedy of X*, by Ellery Queen. Del Mar, Calif.: Publisher's Inc., 1978.

A profile of Ellery Queen that discusses the two authors (Frederic Dannay and Manfred B. Lee), their collaboration, with anecdotes of the origins of some of their plots, the developing character of detective Ellery Queen, and a summary of their achievement. Discusses the role that Ellery Queen played in developing a radio audience for detective fiction and in founding *Ellery Queen's Mystery Magazine*.

"A Century of Thrills and Chills: Ellery Queen Meets the Critics." *Wilson Library Bulletin* 16 (April, 1942): 638-644, 661.
A transcript of a radio broadcast in the "Speaking of Books" series broadcast on November 28, 1941, over WGY, Schenectady, New York. Granville Hicks, Basil Davenport, and Howard Haycraft discuss the detective story and two publications, Haycraft's *Murder for Pleasure: The Life and Times of the Detective Story* (1941) and Ellery Queen's anthology *101 Years' Entertainment: The Great Detective Stories, 1841-1941* (1941, revised 1946). Frederic Dannay and Manfred B. Lee are interviewed.

Christopher, Joe R. "Cross-Trumps: A Conjectural Note on Rex Stout and Ellery Queen." *The Armchair Detective* 1 (October, 1967): 9.
Compares the work of Rex Stout and Ellery Queen with regard to the use of similar titles and themes based on the rules of poker, setting stories in foreign lands, chess gambits, and the annual cycle of national holidays, both secular and religious. Compares the structures of Queen's *Calendar of Crime* (1952) with Stout's *And Four to Go* (1958).

—————— . "Last, but Not Least." *The Armchair Detective* 4 (October, 1970): 11.
A brief note about the device of ending a detective story with the name of the murderer. Christopher cites *The French Powder Mystery* (1930), two stories in *The Adventures of Ellery Queen* (1934), two stories in *The New Adventures of Ellery Queen* (1940), one each in *Calendar of Crime* (1952), and *QED: Queen's Experiments in Detection* (1968), and three in *QBI: Queen's Bureau of Investigation* (1954).

—————— . "The Mystery of Social Reaction: Two Novels by Ellery Queen." *The Armchair Detective* 6 (October, 1972): 28-32.
An analysis of *The Glass Village* (1954) and *Cop Out* (1969), two crime novels by Ellery Queen that do not include Queen as the detective protagonist. Christopher discusses these in the context of the times they were written—not as puzzle-centered detective novels but as novels of social comment. The first concerns the question of justice, the second, simple cooperation and mutual concern.

—————— . "The Re-Shattered Raven." *The Armchair Detective* 3 (January, 1970): 133.
Discusses Edward D. Hoch's *The Shattered Raven* (1969) as a fair-play detective novel that uses the dying-message motif to suggest that the tradition

established by Ellery Queen has been continued in this detective novel. Explains the "symbolically fitting touch" of suggesting that Frederic Dannay is present among the guests at the Mystery Writers of America dinner.

"Ellery Queen Builds Collection of Rare Detective Short Stories." *Publishers Weekly* 144 (November 20, 1943): 1946-1949.
Describes the collection of detective short stories put together by Frederic Dannay that consists of about twelve hundred volumes and is considered one of the finest in existence. Illustrated with photographs of some of the key titles in the collection (including five in dime-novel formats) and Dannay at his desk. Throughout the article, Dannay is referred to only as "Ellery Queen."

Godfrey, Thomas. "*The Lamp of God*." *The Armchair Detective* 12 (Summer, 1979): 212-213.
Godfrey discusses Ellery Queen's 1940 novelette *The Lamp of God* in detail to demonstrate how the story succeeds as a detective story and holds up on repeated readings. Using five categories, he covers fair play, atmosphere, the skillful use of clues, and how *The Lamp of God* can be called great fiction as well as a great mystery story.

Nevins, Francis M., Jr. "Ellery Queen on the Small Screen." *The Armchair Detective* 12 (Summer, 1979): 216-223.
A survey of the television appearances of Ellery Queen from 1955 to 1976. Nevins notes the cast, director, and scriptwriter wherever possible and notes which television scripts were based on Ellery Queen novels and which on novels by other writers, giving listings by date of all episodes with plot synopses. Includes a made-for-television film starring Peter Lawford and the 1975-1976 series with Jim Hutton and David Wayne. Illustrated with photographs of Hutton, Wayne, and Lee Phillips.

_____ . "From the Dawn of Television: The Live Television of Ellery Queen." *The Armchair Detective* 17 (Fall, 1984): 411-417.
Describes the translation of detective Ellery Queen to the television screen in the 1950's. Discusses the actors, notes the critical response, and supplies an annotated episode guide to the programs broadcast from October 19, 1950 to November 26, 1952.

_____ . Introduction to *The Tragedy of X*, by Ellery Queen. Del Mar, Calif.: Publisher's Inc., 1978.
The story of the publication of the first Ellery Queen novel is told and followed up by a discussion of this first Drury Lane novel and its sequels, with comments on recurring themes in the Queen stories and the real reason that Dannay and Lee decided not to continue the Drury Lane series.

_____ . *Royal Bloodline: Ellery Queen, Author and Detective*. Bowling Green, Ohio: Bowling Green University Popular Press, 1974.

A critical survey of the work of Ellery Queen with brief, biographical details as background. Discusses the books about detective Ellery Queen in the order of publication and divided into four categories to demonstrate the development of the character. Separate chapters cover the radio series, the work of Queen as editor, and the Drury Lane books. Extensive checklist of Queen's publications, selectively annotated. Illustrated with ten pages of photographs. Index.

Nevins, Francis M., Jr., and Ray Stanich. *The Sound of Detection: Ellery Queen's Adventures in Radio*. Madison, Ind.: Brownstone Books, 1983.

A critical survey of the Ellery Queen radio program (1939-1948) describing the history of the series and discussing specific broadcasts, actors, and screenwriters. Comments on the radio program in the context of the other work that Dannay and Lee were producing at the time. Photographs of writers and actors. Chronology and episode guide.

Queen, Ellery (Frederic Dannay). Introduction to *The Roman Hat Mystery*, by Ellery Queen. New York: Mysterious Press, 1979.

Dannay re-creates his literary childhood by discussing the books and magazines he read that had an influence on his choice of profession as a mystery writer. Describes how he and his cousin, Manfred Lee, plotted a detective story in their youth, and some of the circumstances behind the writing of the first Ellery Queen novel.

RUTH RENDELL
(Ruth Grasemann)

Biography

Carr, John C. "Ruth Rendell." In *The Craft of Crime: Conversations with Crime Writers*. Boston: Houghton Mifflin, 1983.

A brief survey of Rendell's achievement as a writer is followed by an extensive interview with her about her work, the settings for her novels, and her opinions about police science and the need for research in writing crime novels. Other subjects covered are some of the differences between English and American society, psychology, determinism, psychopathic sex, and other themes in her novels.

Cooper-Clark, Diana. "Interview with Ruth Rendell." In her *Designs of Darkness: Interviews with Detective Novelists*. Bowling Green, Ohio: Bowling Green University Popular Press, 1983.

Ruth Rendell was interviewed in 1982 on such topics as her use of quotations from classic literature, on William Shakespeare, on the choice of titles for her books, the way modern detective fiction reflects the world as it is, the characteristics of the victims in her novels, and her preference for writing the non-series books.

"Ruth Rendell." In *Contemporary Authors*, edited by Hal May, vol. 109. Detroit: Gale Research, 1983.

A brief list of personal details of Rendell's life, followed by some facts of her literary career. Contains a checklist of her crime novels from 1964 to 1982, arranged in order of publication and followed by a list of short story collections with contents. Surveys the critical reception of her work and includes excerpts from selected reviews. List of biographical and critical sources in newspapers and magazines form 1967 to 1982.

Commentary

Bakerman, Jane S. "Explorations of Love: An Examination of Some Novels by Ruth Rendell." *The Armchair Detective* 11 (April, 1978): 139-144.

Discusses six novels by Ruth Rendell (*From Doon with Death*, 1964; *The Best Man to Die*, 1969; *A Guilty Thing Surprised*, 1970; *No More Dying Then*, 1971; *Murder Being Once Done*, 1972; *Some Lie and Some Die*, 1973) as they express three types of love: friendship, familial love, and sexual love. Her novels are considered to be more than detective puzzles.

_____ . "Ruth Rendell." In *Ten Women of Mystery*, edited by Earl F. Bargainnier. Bowling Green, Ohio: Bowling Green University Popular Press, 1981.
Bakerman claims that the combination of irony and theme is prominent in Rendell's works. She identifies the basic themes; then discusses the nonseries books, where characterization is dominant; and the Inspector Wexford stories in terms of personal and professional "families." Summary of Rendell's achievements precedes the checklist of titles of her work (including short stories) from 1964 to 1979.

Barnard, Robert. "A Talent to Disturb: An Appreciation of Ruth Rendell." *The Armchair Detective* 16 (Spring, 1983): 146-152.
Barnard surveys Ruth Rendell's novels, contrasting them with the writers with whom she is most often compared, Agatha Christie and Margery Allingham. He prefers her more realistic nonseries novels to her Inspector Wexford stories, which seem to be more predictable. Discusses several novels at length, noting only four that fit the "chiller-killer" description one critic has applied to Rendell's non-Wexford stories. Checklist of her books through 1983.

Vicarel, Jo Ann Genaro. "A Rendell Dozen Plus One." *The Armchair Detective* 9 (June, 1976): 198-200, 235.
This is basically an annotated checklist of Ruth Rendell's crime novels published between 1964 (*From Doon with Death*) and 1974 (*The Face of Trespass*), followed by a discussion of her work according to theme. Vicarel prefers the Inspector Wexford stories to the nonseries or suspense novels that deal with obsessions.

CRAIG RICE
(Georgianna Ann Randolph)

Bibliography

Cox, J. Randolph. "Craig Rice." In *Critical Survey of Mystery and Detective Fiction*, edited by Frank N. Magill, vol. 4. Pasadena, Calif.: Salem Press, 1988.

A catalog and description of the principal series characters in Rice's fiction, followed by an assessment of her contribution to the detective story in combining humor and homicide. The recorded facts of her life are few and sketched accordingly. An extended analysis of her work concentrates on *The Fourth Postman* (1948) as an example of her originality of plot and style. Lists her principal novels and other major works with a bibliography of secondary sources.

——————— . "Craig Rice." In *Twentieth Century Crime and Mystery Writers*, edited by John M. Reilly. New York: St. Martin's Press, 1980.

A brief list of some personal details in the life of Georgianna Ann Randolph, who wrote as Craig Rice, along with some of the more reliable facts of her literary career. Includes a checklist of her books, uncollected short stories, and related crime publications in chronological order and by category. About 750 words of commentary assessing her achievement as a crime writer.

Commentary

Dueren, Fred. "John J. Malone (and Cohorts)." *The Armchair Detective* 8 (November, 1974): 44-47.

Dueren surveys the John J. Malone series by Craig Rice to profile the leading character and his associates, Jake and Helene Justus, Max the Hook, Captain Daniel von Flanagan, and Joseph Di Angelo of Joe the Angel's City Hall Bar. Speculates on John J. Malone's age and early life, refers to specific Rice novels for a description of Malone and his methods as lawyer and solver of mysteries.

Grochowski, Mary Ann. "Craig Rice: Merry Mistress of Mystery and Mayhem." *The Armchair Detective* 13 (Summer, 1980): 265-267.

Grochowski's lighthearted article matches the style of Craig Rice's detective novels. A biographical sketch is followed by a survey of her work with references to two of her John J. Malone stories and all three of her Bingo Riggs titles. Comments on titles ghosted by her for George Sanders and Gypsy Rose Lee. Checklist of her books.

Jasen, David A. "The Mysterious Craig Rice." *The Armchair Detective* 5 (October, 1971): 25-27, 34.

A survey of the career of Craig Rice with brief comments on individual books and information about her short fiction and true-crime articles. Contains a bibliography of her twenty-eight books in the order of date of publication with specific dates of release. List of short stories with titles and dates of magazine appearances, short stories in anthologies, and articles on mystery writing.

Moran, Peggy. "Craig Rice." In *And Then There Were Nine . . . More Women of Mystery*, edited by Jane S. Bakerman. Bowling Green, Ohio: Bowling Green University Popular Press, 1985.

No matter what their chronological ages, Craig Rice's characters are optimistic children. Discusses the stories of John J. Malone, Helene and Jake Justus, and the novels about Bingo Riggs and Melville Fairr. Notes themes that appear to have been based on situations in Rice's own life. Warning: Solutions are revealed for several of her mysteries.

"Mulled Murder with Spice." *Time* 47 (January 28, 1946): 84, 86, 88, 90.

A profile of Georgianna Ann Randolph, who wrote crime fiction under the name Craig Rice. Discusses her background and some biographical details. Compares her popularity to that of other crime writers. This was the first occasion on which a female crime writer appeared on the cover of *Time* magazine. Illustrated with photographs of Rice as child and adult, with her children, her mother, her most recent husband, and in costume as "Michael Venning," one of her pseudonyms.

MARY ROBERTS RINEHART

Biography

Breit, Harvey. "Mary Roberts Rinehart." *The New York Times Book Review* 57 (February 3, 1952): 18. Reprint. In *The Writer Observed*, by Harvey Breit. Cleveland: World Publishing, 1956.

Interviewed on the occasion of the publication of a new book (her sixty-first) and passing the age of seventy-five, Mary Roberts Rinehart comments on her mail from readers, her interest in people and their motivations, her reading, and the current situation for writers.

Cohn, Jan. *Improbable Fiction: The Life of Mary Roberts Rinehart*. Pittsburgh: University of Pittsburgh Press, 1980.

A thematic yet chronologically arranged biography of Rinehart based on correspondence, diaries, an unpublished version of her autobiography, as well as Rinehart's own publication records. Interviews with members of the Rinehart family fill out the record. Illustrated with more than twenty-five photographs. Contains a chronological bibliography of Rinehart's work with the prices she was paid for articles, stories, and serials.

Rinehart, Mary Roberts. *My Story*. New York: Farrar and Rinehart, 1931. Rev. ed. New York: Rinehart, 1948.

The autobiography of Mary Roberts Rinehart, "shaped and altered . . . through conscious acts of tact and unconscious defenses of memory," is structured much like an autobiographical novel. Rinehart writes of her family and friends, her experiences on travels, and her methods in writing her mystery stories and other fiction. The revised edition covers seventeen additional years and more than 150 additional pages. Illustrated with photographs. No index.

Van Gelder, Robert. "An Interview with Mary Roberts Rinehart." In his *Writers and Writing*. New York: Charles Scribner's Sons, 1946.

Interviewed on December 15, 1940, in her Park Avenue apartment, Mary Roberts Rinehart talks about her work and her health. Discusses storytelling and discipline in writing, her experiences in selling her first stories to *Munsey's*, her later acceptances by *Scribner's* and *The Saturday Evening Post*, and the publication of her first story in the Letitia (Tish) Carberry series.

Commentary

Cohn, Jan. "Mary Roberts Rinehart." In *Ten Women of Mystery*, edited by Earl F. Bargainnier. Bowling Green, Ohio: Bowling Green University Popular Press, 1981.

A concise yet comprehensive survey of Rinehart's crime fiction from 1906 to 1953. Cohn includes plot summaries as well as critical analysis and provides a set of charts for *The Great Mistake* (1940) to demonstrate the relationships between characters and the structure of the novel. Checklist of Rinehart's crime fiction, collections of her short fiction, and omnibus collections of her novels.

Dance, James C. "Spinsters in Jeopardy." *The Armchair Detective* 22 (Winter, 1989): 28-37.
Describes the "spinster heroine" created by Mary Roberts Rinehart and traces her use of the character as a literary convention. Dance discusses Rinehart's mystery stories in a roughly chronological sequence, considers Letitia Carberry (Tish) as a comic exaggeration of Rinehart's other spinsters and questions the extent to which this stock character has become dated.

Hellmann, Geoffrey T. "Mary Roberts Rinehart: For 35 Years She Has Been America's Best-Selling Lady Author." *Life* 20 (February 25, 1946): 55-56, 58, 61-62.
A profile of Mary Roberts Rinehart with statistics to prove the claim that she headed the list of best-selling women writers. Discusses her social life, her home, her attitude toward other writers, her family, some of her working methods, and her acquaintanceship with five American presidents. Includes photographs of her family and illustrations from early editions of her novels. Much of the information has been taken from her autobiography and interviews with her sons.

Overton, Grant. "The Vitality of Mary Roberts Rinehart." In *When Winter Comes to Main Street*. New York: George H. Doran, 1922.
The thoughts of Mary Roberts Rinehart on writing as a profession and on reconciling her public and private lives. Overton discusses Rinehart's early years as a writer and the variety in her work. Novels mentioned include: *The Circular Staircase* (1908), *Long Live the King!* (1917), *The Amazing Interlude* (1918), and *The Breaking Point* (1921). Checklist of Rinehart's books and some sources about her.

Tebbel, John. *George Horace Lorimer and "The Saturday Evening Post."* Garden City, N.Y.: Doubleday, 1948.
Describes the relationship, both professional and social, between George Horace Lorimer, editor of *The Saturday Evening Post*, and Mary Roberts Rinehart, one of the most prominent authors for the magazine. Discusses the popularity of her articles during World War I and mentions some of the serials and short stories she sold to *The Saturday Evening Post*.

Whitney, Phyllis. Introduction to *The Circular Staircase*, by Mary Roberts Rinehart. Del Mar, Calif.: Publisher's Inc., 1977.

Discusses the experiences in Rinehart's life that she brought to her writing, her methods of writing, her choice of light fiction as her genre, and her battle with ill health. Whitney recounts her own feelings on re-reading *The Circular Staircase* (1908) and reflects on Rinehart's lasting contributions to the mystery genre.

SAX ROHMER
(Arthur Henry Sarsfield Ward)

Biography

"Doctor's Blade." *The New Yorker* 23 (November 29, 1947): 36-37.
Sax Rohmer, interviewed at the Ritz-Carlton Hotel, outlines a scheme for securing lasting peace in the world. Discusses the changes in Fu Manchu since 1940 (*President Fu Manchu*, 1936), plans for a new magazine serial and a play about the character, reviews some of the details of his past, tells one version of the origin of his pseudonym, and gives his opinion on ways Chinatown has changed since his earlier visits.

Rohmer, Sax. "Meet Dr. Fu Manchu." In *Meet the Detective*, edited by Cecil Madden. New York: Telegraph Press, 1935.
Rohmer's account of his creation of Dr. Fu Manchu may be the product of his own imagination, but he tells a good story. Describes seeing a tall Chinese, followed by an Arab or Egyptian girl, getting out of a car one night in London. From this he began building the Fu Manchu legend. Rohmer indicates possible sources for Nayland Smith and Dr. Petrie.

Van Ash, Cay, and Elizabeth Sax Rohmer. *Master of Villainy: A Biography of Sax Rohmer*, edited by Robert E. Briney. Bowling Green, Ohio: Bowling Green University Popular Press, 1972.
The only full-length biography and study of Arthur Sarsfield Ward (Sax Rohmer). Basing their research on an unpublished autobiography, Rohmer's widow and a close friend have written a moving biography of a major figure in popular culture. Discusses the sources for much of his fiction. Illustrated with twelve pages of photographs. Chronological checklist of Rohmer's books with a list of his characters in series books. Index.

Commentary

Briney, Robert E. Introduction to *The Wrath of Fu Manchu and Other Stories*, by Sax Rohmer. New York: DAW Books, 1976.
A concise survey of Sax Rohmer's life and work preceding a discussion of the circumstances that accompanied the writing and publication of this collection of short fiction. Briney includes the titles of the original magazines and the publication dates of the stories. Stories in the collection are drawn from all periods of Rohmer's career.

_____ . "Sax Rohmer: An Informal Survey." In *The Mystery Writer's Art*, edited by Francis M. Nevins, Jr. Bowling Green, Ohio: Bowling Green University Popular Press, 1970.
A biographical sketch and critical survey of the works of Sax Rohmer. Briney discusses the Fu Manchu series, the Sumaru books, and the stories about Gaston Max and Paul Harley before discussing the nonseries novels and the short-story collections. Includes a detailed and extensive chronological checklist of Rohmer's books with information about British and American editions and the contents of the books of short fiction.

Chung, Sue Fawn. "From Fu Manchu, Evil Genius, to James Lee Wong, Popular Hero: A Study of the Chinese-American in Popular Periodical Fiction from 1920 to 1940." *Journal of Popular Culture* 10 (Winter, 1976): 534-547.
Chung discusses the stereotypes of Chinese living in America found in stories in *The Saturday Evening Post*, *Collier's Weekly*, and *Sunset* magazines. Considers Sax Rohmer's Fu Manchu, Earl Derr Biggers' Charlie Chan, and Hugh Wiley's James Lee Wong to be the major figures in a sequence of transitional attitudes.

Cooper, Anice Page. "Sax Rohmer and the Art of Making Villains." In *Authors and Others*. Garden City, N.Y.: Doubleday, Page, 1927.
A concise account of Sax Rohmer's early struggles as a writer: his receiving rejection slips for stories and drawings, and his attempts to break into the fields of theater and music composition. According to Cooper, Rohmer's real art was in creating villains in popular fiction. Refers to an early short story inspired by reading Mark Twain and the varied experiences that gave him the ideas for his exotic tales.

Murray, Will. "Sax Rohmer." In *Dictionary of Literary Biography*, edited by Bernard Benstock and Thomas F. Staley, vol. 70. Detroit: Gale Research, 1988.
A concise yet comprehensive survey of Rohmer's works against the background of his life. Murray presents an overview of the Fu Manchu stories then discusses Rohmer's other works that have been overshadowed by the more famous creation in the order of their publication. Covers characters, themes, and publication anecdotes but gives away no solutions. Concludes with a summary of Rohmer's achievements. Includes an extensive bibliography of Rohmer's books and a list of productions of his plays.

Prager, Arthur. "The Mark of Kali." In *Rascals at Large*. Garden City, N.Y.: Doubleday, 1971.
A nostalgic account of Prager's introduction to the Fu Manchu stories when he read *The Insidious Dr. Fu Manchu* (1913) as a boy while recovering from a fever. Surveys Rohmer's life and work, discussing the changes in the general

pattern of the Fu Manchu series over the years, and supplies some information on motion-picture versions and the Columbia Broadcasting System radio series. Discusses the characters of Fu Manchu, Nayland Smith, and Dr. Petrie.

Squire, J. C. *Life and Letters*. Garden City, N. Y.: George H. Doran, 1921.
Squire discusses *The Hand of Fu Manchu* (1917; British title: *The Si-Fan Mysteries*) which he had just read while rereading all Rohmer's books published to date. Notes the flaws in its style but admits that Rohmer used words as a painter used color, to achieve an effect. Provides a catalog of the exotic conventions with which Rohmer left a permanent impression on his readers.

Wu, William F. *The Yellow Peril: Chinese Americans in American Fiction, 1850-1940*. Hamden, Conn.: Archon Books, 1982.
Discusses the characters of Fu Manchu and Charlie Chan as apparent opposites in popular culture but as really representing a racial duality. Surveys the Fu Manchu novels and some of Rohmer's other stories in terms of the image of Asian culture they present. Comments on the film version of *The Mask of Fu Manchu* (1932).

DOROTHY L. SAYERS

Biography

Brabazon, James. *Dorothy L. Sayers: A Biography.* New York: Charles Scribner's Sons, 1981.
This is the first authorized biography of Dorothy L. Sayers, based on letters and papers made available to Brabazon by her family. The emphasis is on the story of her life, without much discussion of her writing. Includes a selective bibliography of her works, including unpublished titles. Illustrated with twelve pages of photographs. Index. (British edition has subtitle: *The Life of a Courageous Woman.*)

Dale, Alzina Stone. *Maker and Craftsman: The Story of Dorothy L. Sayers.* Grand Rapids, Mich.: Wm. B. Eerdmans, 1978.
Written for a juvenile readership, this book treats Dorothy L. Sayers' life as a story and not as the subject for a literary biography or critical study. Dale's account has been criticized for its inaccuracies on matters regarding detective fiction. Eight pages of Illustrations. Endpaper maps of London and England in Sayers' life and fiction. No documentation for any quotations, no bibliography, and no index.

Hitchman, Janet. *Such a Strange Lady: An Introduction to Dorothy L. Sayers.* New York: Harper & Row, 1975.
The first full-length study of Dorothy L. Sayers, Hitchman's biography is based on interviews with friends and colleagues of Sayers and the official files at the British Broadcasting Corporation and Victor Gollancz publications. Not an authorized biography, it has been criticized for attempting too little and raising more questions than it answers. Two-page selected list of Sayers' books. Four pages of photographs. No index.

Hone, Ralph E. *Dorothy L. Sayers: A Literary Biography.* Kent, Ohio: Kent State University Press, 1979.
This is considered the best of the scholarly biographies. Based on extensive research, reading, and interviews with Sayers' friends and colleagues. Approximately one fourth of the discussion of her work is devoted to her detective fiction. Bibliographical notes but no separate bibliography. Eight pages of photographs, many of which are unique to this book. Index.

Mann, Jessica. "Dorothy L. Sayers." In her *Deadlier Than the Male: Why Are Respectable English Women So Good at Murder?* New York: Macmillan, 1981.
A biographical account of Dorothy L. Sayers with commentary on the publish-

ing of her detective fiction and other writings as it fits into the chronology of her life. Discusses the effect of her academic environment, her friendships, and her family on her work. Anecdotes about her family life at Witham and the paradoxes in her personality.

Sayers, Dorothy L. *"Gaudy Night."* In *The Art of the Mystery Story*, edited by Howard Haycraft. New York: Simon & Schuster, 1947. Reprint. New York: Grosset & Dunlap, 1961.
Sayers describes in some detail the planning and writing of her academic detective novel *Gaudy Night* (1935) as her attempt to combine the detective story with the comedy of manners. She discusses several of the other Lord Peter Wimsey novels, speculating on how near she came to that goal in each of them.

Tischler, Nancy M. *Dorothy L. Sayers: A Pilgrim Soul*. Atlanta: John Knox Press, 1980.
A concise account of Dorothy L. Sayers' life from the viewpoint of her work as a Christian apologist and feminist scholar. Tischler discusses her detective fiction but concentrates on her other achievements. Bibliographies of her work in different categories follow the chapters of the discussion of each category. Notes and index.

Commentary

Allen, L. David. "Dorothy L. Sayers, *Whose Body?*" In his *Detective in Fiction*. Lincoln, Nebr.: Cliffs Notes, 1978.
Allen introduces this discussion of the first Lord Peter Wimsey novel by referring to the television productions of some of Sayers' works. His summary of the plot, covering five paragraphs, is followed by discussions of the main detective characters and an analysis of how the murder was committed, the clues that led to the discovery of the murderer, and a general assessment of the book.

Basney, Lionel. *"The Nine Tailors* and the Complexity of Innocence." In *As Her Whimsey Took Her: Critical Essays on the Work of Dorothy L. Sayers*, edited by Margaret P. Hannay. Kent, Ohio: Kent State University Press, 1979.
Basney examines *The Nine Tailors* (1934) in detail to determine why it is considered the most successful of Dorothy L. Sayers' detective novels at integrating detective themes with a serious "criticism of life." Discusses the crime itself, the ambiguities of murder, and the symbolic meaning of the bells, as well as how Sayers' style contributes to her achievement.

Christopher, Joe R. "The Mystery of Robert Eustace." *The Armchair Detective* 13 (Fall, 1980): 365-367.

Christopher discusses Robert Eustace, who collaborated with mystery writer
L. T. Meade as early as 1898 and with Dorothy L. Sayers some thirty years
later on *The Documents in the Case* (1930). Prompted by an essay by Trevor
Hall ("Dorothy Sayers and Robert Eustace" in *Dorothy L. Sayers: Nine Literary Studies*), Christopher considers the extent and nature of their collaboration
and the possible help he gave her in *Have His Carcase* (1932).

Christopher, Joe R., E. R. Gregory, Margaret P. Hannay, and R. Russell Malone,
comps. "Dorothy L. Sayers's Manuscripts and Letters in Public Collections in
the United States." In *As Her Whimsey Took Her: Critical Essays on the Work
of Dorothy L. Sayers*, edited by Margaret P. Hannay. Kent, Ohio: Kent State
University Press, 1979.
A detailed, annotated guide to material by Dorothy L. Sayers in the Wade
collection, Wheaton College; the Humanities Research Center, the University
of Texas at Austin; the University of Michigan; Harvard University; and North-
western University. Each collection is described in general terms, followed by
a bibliography of the items with full physical descriptions and notes on the
contents.

Gaillard, Dawson. *Dorothy L. Sayers*. New York: Frederic Ungar, 1981.
This study of Dorothy L. Sayers concentrates on her detective fiction. Following an introduction containing a concise biography of Sayers, Gaillard discusses the short stories in chapter 1, the novels in order of publication in
chapters 2 through 5, and uses chapter 6 to assess her legacy under the title
"Values and Aesthetics: A Touch of the Eternal in Sayers's Detective Fiction."
Includes a bibliography of works by and about Sayers. Index.

Gregory, E. R. "Wilkie Collins and Dorothy L. Sayers." In *As Her Whimsey Took
Her: Critical Essays on the Work of Dorothy L. Sayers*, edited by Margaret P.
Hannay. Kent, Ohio: Kent State University Press, 1979.
Using documentary evidence found in the Dorothy L. Sayers collection at the
Humanities Research Center, University of Texas at Austin, as well as an
examination of the text of *The Documents in the Case* (1930), Gregory dis-
cusses the extensive influence of Wilkie Collins on Sayers' detective fiction.
Gregory believes that such a comparison demonstrates a unity in her work that
might otherwise not be noticed.

Hannay, Margaret P., ed. *As Her Whimsey Took Her: Critical Essays on the Work of
Dorothy L. Sayers*. Kent, Ohio: Kent State University Press, 1979.
A collection of essays on all aspects of Dorothy L. Sayers' work: detective fiction, drama, translation, and aesthetics. Most of the articles originated as scholarly papers read at the Modern Language Association conventions, and some
are reprinted from *The Sayers Review*. Includes bibliography, notes, and index.

Heilbrun, Carolyn. "Sayers, Lord Peter, and God." In *Lord Peter*, by Dorothy L. Sayers. New York: Harper & Row, 1972.

Heilbrun surveys Sayers's life and work to explain why she remains a literary and social phenomenon years after she died and decades after she wrote her last Lord Peter Wimsey novel. Considers her ability to plot well, and write dialogue in the "best tradition of the comedy of manners" to be part of the answer. Draws some comparisons between her detective fiction and her theological writings.

Heldreth, Lillian M. "Breaking the Rules of the Game: Shattered Patterns in Dorothy L. Sayers' *Gaudy Night.*" *Clues: A Journal of Detection* 3 (Spring/Summer, 1982): 120-127.

Discusses the novel *Gaudy Night* (1935) in philosophical and metaphorical terms to demonstrate to what extent Dorothy L. Sayers broke with established tradition in the detective story to produce a novel that could be both detective story and a major work of fiction with a significant theme. Includes a bibliography of her novels and relevant collections of criticism.

Klein, Kathleen Gregory. "Dorothy L. Sayers." In *Ten Women of Mystery*, edited by Earl F. Bargainnier. Bowling Green, Ohio: Bowling Green University Popular Press, 1981.

A thematic discussion of the detective fiction of Dorothy L. Sayers as examples of the classic form of the Golden Age; a catalog of the variety, the changes, and the development of the genre, and a literary definition of the social order and the future of society. Includes a checklist of Sayers' novels and short stories.

Leavis, Q. D. "The Case of Miss Dorothy Sayers." *Scrutiny* 6 (December, 1937): 334-340. Reprint. In *A Selection from Scrutiny*, compiled by F. R. Leavis, vol 1. Cambridge: Cambridge University Press, 1968.

A review of *Gaudy Night* (1935) and *Busman's Honeymoon* (1937) in which Leavis attempts to account for the elevation of Dorothy L. Sayers from mere detective-story writer to best-selling novelist. Considers the appearance of literariness, the concern with values, the interest in social issues, and an insider's view of certain areas of life to be her strengths as a detective writer.

McDiarmid, John F. "Reality and Romance: Dorothy Sayers's Intention and Accomplishment." *Clues: A Journal of Detection* 6 (Fall/Winter, 1985): 123-134.

Compares Sayers' statements of what the detective ought to be and what she intended hers to be in her introduction to *The Omnibus of Crime* (1928-1934) and her essay on the writing of *Gaudy Night* (1935) with her novels (especially *The Nine Tailors*, 1934; and *Gaudy Night*) to determine just what she achieved and whether her achievement was what she intended.

McFarland, Trudy. "Lord Peter, Bibliophile." *The Armchair Detective* 21 (Fall, 1988): 396-400, 402-404.

Lord Peter Wimsey's most memorable hobby, apart from his interest in amateur detective work, is his collecting of rare first editions. McFarland identifies and describes the actual volumes mentioned in *Whose Body?* (1932), *Clouds of Witness* (1926), *Unnatural Death* (1927), *The Unpleasantness at the Bellona Club* (1928), *Gaudy Night* (1935), and some of the short stories. While Lord Peter collected Dante in the 1920's, Sayers read his poetry for the first time in 1944.

Morris, Virginia B. "Arsenic and Blue Lace: Sayers' Criminal Women." *Modern Fiction Studies* 29 (Autumn, 1983): 485-496.

Discusses the female criminals and female suspects in Dorothy L. Sayers' *Strong Poison* (1930), *The Documents in the Case* (1930), *Unnatural Death* (1927), and *Gaudy Night* (1935) to demonstrate how she used traditional views in literature yet raised some untraditional questions for the time about the role of women in a changing world.

Panek, LeRoy L. "Dorothy Sayers." In his *Watteau's Shepherds: The Detective Novel in Britain, 1914-1940.* Bowling Green, Ohio: Bowling Green University Popular Press, 1979.

Surveys Dorothy L. Sayers' detective novels, including *The Documents in the Case* (1930), tracing the origins of Lord Peter Wimsey to E. C. Bentley, P. G. Wodehouse, and R. Austin Freeman. Considers the key to Wimsey to be his conscience and discusses the development of the character and the series from a simple caricature to a complex structure that has more to do with life than does most other detective fiction. The problems Sayers confronts do not have easy answers.

Reaves, R. B. "Crime and Punishment in the Detective Fiction of Dorothy L. Sayers." In *As Her Whimsey Took Her: Critical Studies on the Work of Dorothy L. Sayers*, edited by Margaret P. Hannay. Kent, Ohio: Kent State University Press, 1979.

Reaves notes that the punishment of crime is not a theme treated regularly in detective fiction as a rule, but that Dorothy L. Sayers was interested enough in it to treat it in various and subtle ways. Discusses all of her detective novels to indicate how she introduces the theme and how it develops in her work from *Whose Body?* (1923) to *Busman's Honeymoon* (1937).

Reynolds, William. "Dorothy L. Sayers' Detective Short Fiction." *The Armchair Detective* 14 (Spring, 1981): 176-181.

The quality of Dorothy L. Sayers' short fiction is uneven. Reynolds begins by discussing the nonseries stories, continues with a consideration of the eleven

Montague Egg stories, and concludes by discussing the twenty-one Lord Peter Wimsey stories that succeed by their wit and erudition more than by their plots. Warning: Some solutions are given, although Reynolds contends that some of her short stories are not really mysteries.

_____ . "Literature, Latin, and Love: Dorothy L. Sayers' *Gaudy Night.*" *Clues: A Journal of Detection* 6 (Spring/Summer, 1985): 67-78.
Discusses *Gaudy Night* (1935) as a "deliberately literary novel" and notes how the elements that make it so are used, especially the literary allusions and the use of language to engage the reader in a kind of intellectual game to establish the reality of the characters and prepare the reader for what is to come.

Sandoe, James. Introduction to *Lord Peter*, by Dorothy L. Sayers. New York: Harper & Row, 1972.
Sandoe gives a concise survey of Dorothy L. Sayers' detective fiction, book by book, in the order of publication date. Limits himself to the highlights of each title and the characters introduced. Comments very briefly on stories in which Lord Peter Wimsey does not appear. Refers to "The Wimsey Papers" in *The Spectator* but calls the publication a newspaper not a magazine. Gives some indication of Sayers' other accomplishments.

Scott, William M. "Lord Peter Wimsey of Piccadilly: *His Lordship's Life and Times.*" Parts 1/2 *The Armchair Detective* 13 (Winter/Summer, 1980): 17-22, 212-218.
A profile of Lord Peter Wimsey; his life story; his detective methods; his opinions on food and drink (with a catalog of his preferences in wine); his reasons for becoming a detective; his personal habits; his aversions to such things as push-bikes, hard work, bad manners, and telephones; and his knowledge of first editions. Based on a close reading of Dorothy L. Sayers' detective stories.

Scott-Giles, C. W. *The Wimsey Family: A Fragmentary History Compiled from Correspondence with Dorothy L. Sayers.* New York: Harper & Row, 1977.
Based on a long and continuing correspondence with Dorothy L. Sayers, Scott-Giles has compiled a history of the Wimsey family from the Norman Conquest to Lord Peter Wimsey. Illustrated with pictures of the heraldic arms of Lord Peter and his ancestors, a portrait of the tenth Duke of Denver, and of Bredon Hall.

GEORGES SIMENON

Biography

Bresler, Fenton. *The Mystery of Georges Simenon: A Biography.* New York: Beaufort Books, 1983.

A candid biography of Georges Simenon that discusses the inconsistencies and contradictions of the man, attempting to reconcile what has been written of him in the past (by himself as well as by others) with the facts derived from interviews and seemingly exhaustive research. No documentation apart from identification of the sources of quotations within the text. Twenty-four pages of photographs. Index.

Collins, Carvel. "Georges Simenon." In *Writers at Work*, edited by Malcolm Cowley. New York: Viking Press, 1958.

Simenon is interviewed at his Lakeville, Connecticut, home. Discusses the advice he once received from Colette, what is involved in revision of his work, the differences between commercial and noncommercial fiction, the development of his views and themes, his relationship with André Gide, the possible influences of Nikolai Gogol and Fyodor Dostoevski on his work, and why he will never write a big novel.

Garis, Leslie. "Simenon's Last Case." *The New York Times Magazine* April 22, 1984: 20-23, 60-62, 64, 66.

A profile of Georges Simenon on the occasion of the publication of *Intimate Memoirs* (1981) in the United States, which he had written in 1980 while attempting to understand the cause of his daughter's suicide. Simenon is interviewed in September, 1983, on his working methods and why he never wrote long novels. Sections of an account of his life alternate with sections of the interview. His second wife, Denise, is quoted, and Simenon comments on his biography by Fenton Bresler.

Gill, Brendan. "Profiles: Out of the Dark." *The New Yorker* 28 (January 24, 1953): 35-36, 38, 40, 42-53.

A profile of Simenon, whose novels are referred to in Europe merely as "simenons." At the time of this article, he was living in a farmhouse in Connecticut. Gill describes Simenon's life and the joy he found in writing when he began. Lists the titles of some of Simenon's pseudonymous pulp novels as well as the pen names he used, and his creation of Maigret. Describes his Connecticut home and his working methods.

Grunwald, Henry Anatole. "World's Most Prolific Novelist." *Life* 45 (November 3, 1958): 95-96, 98, 100, 105-106, 108.

A profile of Georges Simenon, the "world's most prolific serious novelist," with perhaps four hundred novels to his credit. Grunwald cites the statistics on the number of editions of Simenon titles published each year worldwide. Discusses his working methods (as he charts his progress on a calendar) and his astonishing variety of characters and plots, and describes the planning of his 1958 novel *The President*. Concludes with a survey of Simenon's life. Illustrations include a scene from a Maigret film starring Jean Gabin.

Mok, Michael. "Close Up: Georges Simenon. Excuse Me, I Think I'm About to Have a Novel." *Life* 66 (May 9, 1969): 43-44, 46, 48-49.
Profile of Simenon: on a tour of the Palais de Justice in Paris, the mysterious process of writing a novel, the meticulous arrangement of his house for his comfort, his working methods, a trip to Paris to visit his son, and his concern over the changes that have been made in the city about which he has written so much.

Simenon, Georges. *Intimate Memoirs*. San Diego: Harcourt Brace Jovanovich, 1984.
Originally published in 1981 in France, this autobiography of Georges Simenon was written between February and November, 1980. A view of the author's life, work, and relationships with his family covering nearly eighty years, ending with an account of his daughter Marie-Jo's suicide in 1978. No illustrations or index. Pages 1-659 comprise the memoirs, pages 661-815 are letters, stories, verse, and a transcribed cassette-recorded commentary of Marie-Jo Simenon.

_____ . *When I Was Old*. New York: Harcourt Brace Jovanovich, 1971.
The journals Simenon kept from June 25, 1960, to February 15, 1963, describing events of the day; the relationship with his wife and children; his opinions on education, sex, marriage, and friendship; and his working methods. According to Simenon, he began the journals at a time when he had begun to feel old and had stopped writing them when he realized that he had not felt old for some time. Illustrated with eight pages of photographs. (The British edition has no photographs.)

Commentary

Becker, Lucille F. *Georges Simenon*. Boston: Twayne, 1977.
A survey of Simenon's works. Draws on those works as much as possible to present the man in his own words. Becker traces the origin of Simenon's major themes and characters in discussing the autobiographical *Pedigree* (1948), devotes a chapter to Maigret, and considers the basic themes in his novels, the principal one being escape. Concludes with an analysis of Simenon's theories of the art of the novel and the role of the novelist. Discusses Simenon's style.

Includes detailed chronology and a selected bibliography of works by and about Simenon.

Bishop, John Peale. "Georges Simenon." *The New Republic* 104 (March 10, 1941): 345-346.
An early appreciation of Simenon in this review of the collection of two novellas, *The Flemish Shop* and *The "Guingette" by the Seine*, originally published in 1932 and later published together as *Maigret to the Rescue* (1940). Bishop compares Simenon to Guy de Maupassant, discussing the representation of France Simenon provides, what it is that makes Maigret seem so satisfying as a detective, and what is the secret of Simenon's originality.

Blochman, Lawrence. "Letter." *The Armchair Detective* 7 (November, 1973): 71-72.
The man responsible for translating some of Simenon's works into English discusses the role of the translator and the problems that an inferior translation can cause. Discusses the translation of the title of *Trois Chambres à Manhattan* (1947) and explains why Maigret is not really an inspector, in spite of the translations of his title.

Boucher, Anthony. "On the Brink of Life was Death." *The New York Times Book Review* 69 (April 5, 1964): 1.
A review-essay of Simenon's *The Bells of Bicêtre* (1963) as a "pure" novel that Boucher considers to be the best work the Belgian author has ever produced. Analyzes and discusses the qualities that make this novel representative of the achievement in both entertainment and literature of which Simenon is capable. Boucher supplies biographical details and a survey of Simenon's career.

Brophy, Brigid. "Simenon." In her *Don't Ever Forget: Collected Views and Reviews*. New York: Holt, Rinehart and Winston, 1966.
A review-essay of Simenon's *The Train* (1961) and *Maigret's Special Murder* (1948), translated in 1964. Brophy analyses Simenon's method in building up the two novels and compares the effects achieved in each category. Notes how much Maigret achieves his results as a detective in the manner of an author plotting a novel, and what the reader learns about the character in this novel that Simenon has not revealed before.

Cawelti, John G. "The Art of Simenon." In *Adventure, Mystery, and Romance: Formula Stories as Art and Popular Culture*. Chicago: University of Chicago Press, 1976.
Cawelti considers Simenon to be the greatest writer to work within the limits of the detective formula. Notes the differences of opinion on what Simenon has achieved, and proceeds to use *Maigret and the Reluctant Witnesses* (1959) as the basis for his demonstration. Defines the structure of detection and

mystification in Simenon and contrasts it with the more intricate one found in Agatha Christie and Dorothy L. Sayers.

Dubourg, Maurice. "Maigret and Co.: The Detectives of the Simenon Agency." *The Armchair Detective* 4 (January, 1971): 79-86.
A translation by Francis M. Nevins, Jr., of an article from the French *Mystère-Magazine*, December, 1964. Surveys Simenon's early detective stories and describes the facts of publication of the first Maigret stories. Dubourg discusses Simenon's other detective stories, published under pseudonyms, and the relationship of those detectives to the Maigret character.

Eames, Hugh. "Jules Maigret-Georges Simenon." In his *Sleuths, Inc.: Studies of Problem Solvers.* Philadelphia: J. B. Lippincott, 1978.
Describes the life and influence of François Eugène Vidocq as background to an understanding of the French police system in Simenon's novels. Discusses Maigret as the "enlightened man" in crime fiction and summarizes the plots of several novels. Describes the creation of Maigret, Simenon's 1934 involvement in the newspaper coverage of the Stavisky-Prince murders, and Simenon's decision to stop writing novels.

Gallant, Mavis. "Simenon in Spite of Himself." *The New York Times Book Review* 89 (July 1, 1984): 1, 29-30. Reprint. "Intimate Memoirs, Including Marie-Jo's Book." In *Paris Notebooks*, by Mavis Gallant. Toronto: Macmillan of Canada, 1986.
A review-essay of Simenon's autobiography that contrasts Maigret with his creator. Contrasts Simenon's books with the known facts of his life and notes how little of the real Simenon exists even in this 815-page book. Gallant considers the language of the original French edition of the book to be clumsy but the translation to be worse.

Gannett, Gary L. "All the Short Cases of Inspector Maigret." *The Armchair Detective* 10 (October, 1977): 347.
A checklist of the short fiction of detective and crime by Georges Simenon collected in five volumes and published in Paris between 1944 and 1951. Gannett gives the original French title, the English title, and the date of appearance in *Ellery Queen's Mystery Magazine*. Notes which stories belong to the Maigret series (twenty-seven) and which were not translated as of 1977.

Harris, Lis. "Maigret le Flaneur." *The New Yorker* 55 (April 2, 1979): 122-124.
Simenon has a gift for making the reader want to visit the places he writes about. He has preserved scenes that will be gone in the not-too-distant future. Harris discusses the recently translated *Maigret in Exile* (1942), *The Family Lie* (1978; a psychological novel), and *Maigret's Pipe* (1947; a collection of short stories). Considers Maigret more *flâneur* (a loafer) than detective.

Lambert, Gavin. "Night Vision." In his *The Dangerous Edge*. London: Barrie & Jenkins, 1975.

Lambert discusses Simenon's life in relationship to his writing. Takes up the Maigret series to indicate how they were planned and written and how they can be viewed as belonging to a changing cycle: from the relatively simple, uncomplicated early stories to a dark complex vision of the world in the later ones. Surveys some of Simenon's other novels and explains how they fit into the entire evolution of Simenon as man and writer.

Narcejac, Thomas. *The Art of Simenon*. London: Routledge & Kegan Paul, 1952.

Originally published in France in 1950, this is the first book-length study of Simenon in the English language. Narcejac describes Simenon's detective stories and how they differ from traditional detective stories. Discusses Simenon's themes, the autobiographical novel *Pedigree* (1948), the Maigret series (divided into periods of differing degrees of complication), the character of Maigret, and Simenon's use of atmosphere and psychology. Includes a bibliography from 1931 to 1952 with English translations noted.

Raymond, John. *Simenon in Court*. New York: Harcourt Brace & World, 1969.

The first book-length study of Simenon written by an English-language critic. Raymond discusses the Maigret series and Simenon's other novels with attention to plot, character, and style, and lists and comments on the works (excluding Maigret) he considers the best. A psychological approach relating Simenon's works to aspects of the author himself. Considers Maigret's role to be a "mender of destinies." (British edition, 1968, contains a bibliography of Simenon's books.)

Richardson, Maurice. "Simenon and Highsmith: Into the Criminal's Head." In *Crime Writers*, edited by H. R. F. Keating. London: British Broadcasting Corporation, 1978.

Discusses the works of Georges Simenon and Patricia Highsmith as examples of modern crime writers whose stories are entertaining yet serious contributions to literature. The biographical and critical commentary on Simenon and his detective stories accompanies some interesting comparisons with his mainstream novels. Discusses mood, style, the character of Maigret, and some of the unforgettable secondary characters in his books.

Rolo, Charles J. "Simenon and Spillane: The Metaphysics of Murder for the Millions." In *Mass Culture*, edited by Bernard Rosenberg and David Manning White. New York: Free Press, 1957.

An early consideration of the appeal of the murder mystery suggests that the answer lies in the accounting for human destiny that is part of each story. Rolo calls this a "metaphysical success story" and examines the work of

Mickey Spillane and Georges Simenon in an attempt to demonstrate how this works.

Schneiderman, Leo. "Simenon: To Understand Is to Forgive." *Clues: A Journal of Detection* 7 (Spring/Summer, 1986): 19-37.
Schneiderman considers the basis of Simenon's formula, both in his Maigret novels and his nonmystery novels, to be a story of sin and redemption. Summarizes Simenon's life to explain how this formula was developed and briefly discusses some of the novels, *Tropic Moon* (1933), *Tatala* (1937), *Pedigree* (1948), *Maigret in Vichy* (1968), *The Nightclub* (1933), and *Inspector Maigret and the Killers* (1952) to show how it has been employed.

Shaffer, Norman J. "A Bibliography and English Language Index to Georges Simenon's Maigret Novels." *The Armchair Detective* 3 (October, 1969): 31-37.
A list of seventy-one Maigret novels in alphabetical order by the original French titles, giving British and American titles, publisher, and date of first appearances in omnibuses and anthologies. Titles not translated by 1969 are also included. Index of British and American titles.

Symons, Julian. "Simenon and Maigret." In his *Bloody Murder: From the Detective Story to the Crime Novel, a History*. Rev. ed. New York: Viking Press, 1985.
Discusses Simenon's achievement in the detective story. Symons contrasts the realism of character and background to the improbabilities of Simenon's plots. Considers Simenon's art to be in making the implausible acceptable, with Maigret as his greatest achievement in this. Discusses *My Friend Maigret* (1949) as an example of his finest work in the genre and Maigret's own background and life within the series.

_____ . "A View of Simenon." In his *Critical Observations.* New York: Ticknor & Fields, 1981.
Symons suggests that no one can really understand Georges Simenon's work without taking into consideration his personality. Discusses his obsessive need for organization, his journals (*When I Was Old*, 1970), and his lack of interest in history and politics. Divides his work into "hard novels" and the Maigret series, which despite their excellence, he considers secondary. (Prefers the novellas to the short stories about Maigret.)

MAJ SJÖWALL and PER WAHLÖÖ

Biography

Bannon, Barbara A. "Authors and Editor." *Publishers Weekly* 200 (September 6, 1971): 13-15.
An interview with Maj Sjöwall and Per Wahlöö. Discusses the planning that went into the Martin Beck series, even before they wrote the first title *Roseanna* (1965), and their subsequent working methods. The two authors comment on the changes they have seen in Swedish society and the Swedish police force in the years since they began their collaboration. Discusses the worsening drug problem there.

"Copology." *The New Yorker* 47 (May 22, 1971): 28.
Maj Sjöwall and Per Wahlöö in New York to accept the Edgar Award from the Mystery Writers of America for their novel *The Laughing Policeman* (1968). They express themselves on police brutality and civil liberties in the United States and Sweden as well as the reason they chose Budapest as one of the cities for a forthcoming study of police forces. A lighthearted, brief interview.

Lundin, Bo. "Policemen." In *The Swedish Crime Story/Svenska Deckare*. Sundbyberg, Sweden: Tidskriften Jury, 1981.
Discusses the differences between the police procedural and the detective-puzzle story, explaining the features of the Martin Beck stories that are unique to Swedish crime fiction. Notes the influence of Sjöwall and Wahlöö on subsequent works. Includes the original Swedish-language text along with an English translation by Anna Lena Ringarp, Ralph A. Wilson, and Bo Lundin.

"Maj Sjoewall." In *Contemporary Authors*, edited by Jane A. Bowden, vols. 65-68. Detroit: Gale Research, 1977.
A brief list of the personal details of Sjöwall's life, along with a survey of her literary career and a checklist of the Martin Beck detective novels she wrote with her husband, Per Wahlöö. Gives original Swedish titles and titles of English translations. Contains a section of entry comments on the critical reception of the series with excerpts from some of the reviews. Selected list of biographical and critical sources in newspapers and magazines.

Commentary

Dove, George N. "Maj Sjöwall and Per Wahlöö." In his *The Police Procedural*. Bowling Green, Ohio: Bowling Green University Popular Press, 1982.

Dove notes that the Martin Beck stories may be remembered more for their social comment than for their mystery and detection. Surveys the series from its creation in 1965 to its end in 1975, noting three phases of influence from Georges Simenon, Ed McBain, and external politics. Discusses the narrative style and the social environment.

Duffy, Martha. "Martin Beck Passes." *Time* 106 (August 11, 1975): 58-59.
The death at forty-eight of Per Wahlöö, one of the authors of the Martin Beck police novels, means that the series will end with the tenth novel as his widow, Maj Sjöwall, does not intend to continue writing the books. Duffy briefly surveys the stories. Comments on the recurring characters and the social problems emphasized in the series.

Maxfield, James F. "The Collective Detective Hero: The Police Novels of Maj Sjöwall and Per Wahlöö." *Clues: A Journal of Detection* 3 (Spring/Summer, 1982): 70-79.
Maxfield considers references to Martin Beck as the hero of the novels of Maj Sjöwall and Per Wahlöö to be inaccurate, because the solution to each mystery is always the product of collective efforts. Surveys the series as representing the development of a Marxist critique of the ideological assumptions of a democratic society. A thematic approach rather than a book-by-book summary.

Mellerski, Nancy C., and Robert P. Winston. "Sjöwall and Wahlöö's Brave New Sweden." *Clues: A Journal of Detection* 7 (Spring/Summer, 1986): 1-17.
The authors survey the Martin Beck series in thematic terms, with an emphasis on its critique of society and its recurring images of pollution. Discusses much of the criticism that has been written about the books and provides a bibliography of the novels, indicating the translators and the original dates of publication in the United States.

Occhiogrosso, Frank. "The Police in Society: The Novels of Maj Sjöwall and Per Wahlöö." *The Armchair Detective* 12 (Spring, 1979): 174-177.
It is the ambivalent feeling about the role of the police in society that Occhiogrosso finds at the heart of the crime fiction of Sjöwall and Wahlöö. Surveys the themes that unite the ten Martin Beck books and comments on some of the sociological conclusions found there. (Some misplaced paragraphs in the text of this article make it confusing to read, but the article is complete.)

White, Jean M. "Wahlöö/Sjöwall and James McClure: Murder and Politics." *The New Republic* 175 (July 31, 1976): 27-29.
White considers the Martin Beck series by Sjöwall and Wahlöö to be an example of the police procedural's being used for political and social commen-

tary. Discusses the creation and planning of the ten-volume series and the character of Martin Beck. Provides a survey of some of the changes in Swedish society mirrored in the police novels.

Williams, Thomas E. "Martin Beck: The Swedish Version of Barney Miller Without the Canned Laughter." *Clues: A Journal of Detection* 1 (Spring, 1980): 123-128.
Outlines the disagreements between the purist or classic school of detective fiction and the liberal, realistic school that includes police procedurals. Williams surveys the Martin Beck series and briefly compares it to the television situation comedy *Barney Miller*. Much plot synopsis with liberal quotations from the novels.

MICKEY SPILLANE
(Frank Morrison Spillane)

Biography

Barson, Michael. "Just a Writer Working for a Buck." *The Armchair Detective* 12 (Fall, 1979): 292-299.

An interview with Mickey Spillane conducted in the spring of 1976 in his home at Murrell's Inlet. Barson notes that Spillane confronts the dark side of the American psyche in his books. Spillane discusses the writing of the early stories and why he finds revision unnecessary. Offers his opinions of the movies based on his books, on Raymond Chandler, and on the critics of his books.

Collins, Max Allan, and James L. Traylor. *One Lonely Knight: Mickey Spillane's Mike Hammer*. Bowling Green, Ohio: Bowling Green State University Popular Press, 1984.

The first full-length study of Mickey Spillane, who is presented as a serious contender for inclusion in the history of hard-boiled detective fiction next to Dashiell Hammett and Raymond Chandler. Collins and Traylor survey Spillane's work with as much biographical detail as necessary to understand the work in context, contributing greatly to the value of the book as a reference. Illustrated with photographs, primarily of book covers. Includes a bibliography of Spillane's novels and short fiction and a selected listing of magazine articles about Spillane. Lists of film and television adaptations.

Johnson, Richard W. "Death's Fair-Haired Boy." *Life* 32 (June 23, 1952): 79-80, 82-83, 86, 89-90, 92, 95.

Johnson's profile of Mickey Spillane begins by describing the phenomenon. Contrasts Spillane's sales figures with the lack of critical attention to his books. Describes his home, his family, and some of his friends, his early life, and the creation of Mike Hammer. Discusses his characters and the contradictions suggested by his membership in the Jehovah's Witnesses.

"Mickey Spillane." In *Current Biography Yearbook*. New York: H. W. Wilson, 1981.

A profile and biographical sketch with a survey of critical opinion about Mickey Spillane. Draws on previously published interviews and articles surveying the patterns of incident in Spillane's novels to identify the qualities that explain his popularity. Describes film and television adaptations and his own media appearances. Discusses his political sympathies as an evangelist against evil.

Commentary

Banks, R. Jeff. "Spillane and the Critics." *The Armchair Detective* 12 (Fall, 1979): 300-307.

Banks responds to the "uniformly superficial and unfair critical notices" of Spillane's work by surveying and commenting on some of the published criticism since 1969. Critics included: John Cawelti, George Grella, Judith Fetterley, John Reilly, and Kay Weibel. Extensive notes catalog errors of fact found in the criticism cited.

_____ . "Spillane's Anti-Establishmentarian Heroes." In *Dimensions of Detective Fiction*, edited by Larry N. Landrum, Pat Browne, and Ray B. Browne. Bowling Green, Ohio: Bowling Green University Popular Press, 1976.

Banks discusses the attitudes of Mickey Spillane's heroes toward authority and the establishment, especially in their relationships toward police and government figures. Surveys the Mike Hammer books of the 1950's, the title character of *The Deep* (1961), the revived Mike Hammer of the 1960's, the Tiger Mann stories, and the heroes of the nonseries books.

Cawelti, John G. "Mickey Spillane." In his *Adventure, Mystery, and Romance: Formula Stories as Art and Popular Culture*. Chicago: University of Chicago Press, 1976.

Simplistic generalizations do little to explain the popularity of Mickey Spillane. Cawelti contrasts Raymond Chandler's *Farewell, My Lovely* (1940) with Spillane's *I, the Jury* (1947) to indicate the differences in levels of complexity applied to the same basic formula. Discusses the basic themes and the structure of Spillane's novels, the use of patriotic hostility toward Communism, and an ambiguity toward society and women. Explains the appeal of the vivid directness of Spillane's formula and the appeal of Mike Hammer.

Collins, Max Allen. "Dats Mike Ham-muh?" *The Armchair Detective* 12 (Fall, 1979): 308-319.

Collins discusses the adaptations of Mike Hammer to movies, television, and other media. Discusses *I, the Jury* (1947), *My Gun Is Quick* (1950), *Kiss Me, Deadly* (1952), *The Girl Hunters* (1962) and the non-Hammer story *The Long Wait* (1951), the radio series *That Hammer Guy*, the Darren McGavin television series, and the record albums. Illustrated with scenes from *The Girl Hunters*, lobby cards from some of the other films, and a sequence from the newspaper comic strip *From the Files of Mike Hammer*.

_____ . Introduction to *Tomorrow I Die*, by Mickey Spillane. New York: Mysterious Press, 1984.

Discusses Spillane's public image and how it has helped the sales of his books.

Collins considers Spillane to be a literary artist and *One Lonely Night* (1951) to be his masterpiece. Briefly surveys Spillane's career and the short stories he wrote for *Cavalier*, *Manhunt*, and other publications, some of which appear in this collection.

La Farge, Christopher. "Mickey Spillane and His Bloody Hammer." In *Mass Culture*, edited by Bernard Rosenberg and David Manning White. New York: Free Press, 1957.
A discussion of three of Spillane's novels, *I, the Jury* (1947), *One Lonely Night* (1951), and *Kiss Me, Deadly* (1952), in which the theme, La Farge finds, is that the end justifies the means. Compares the vigilante tactics of Mike Hammer with those of Senator Joseph McCarthy, in an attempt to explain the reasons for the incredible popularity of Spillane. Speculates on the future if the attitudes they represent prevail.

Ruehlmann, William. "The Kid from Cyanide Gulch." In *Saint with a Gun: The Unlawful Private Eye*. New York: New York University Press, 1974.
A survey of Spillane's work as a member of the hard-boiled school of mystery fiction. Ruehlmann discusses Mike Hammer's role as avenger in *I, the Jury* (1947), *One Lonely Night* (1951), and *The Girl Hunters* (1962). Considers Spillane a craftsman with a sense of pace and a style that makes the reader turn the pages to learn what will happen next. Contrasts the goal of Spillane's hero with that of Dashiell Hammett and Raymond Chandler.

Sandels, Robert L. "The Battle of the Sexes." *The Armchair Detective* 20 (Fall, 1987): 350-358.
Surveys the critical response to Mickey Spillane's novels, examining the validity of the standard criticisms to determine where symbolic acts leave off and actual events in a Spillane novels begin. Sandels finds a discrepancy between the "sexual notoriety" of Spillane's heroes and their "sexual activity." Novels discussed: *I, the Jury* (1947), *The Long Wait* (1951), *One Lonely Night* (1951), *Kiss Me, Deadly* (1952), *The Death Dealers* (1965), *The Erection Set* (1972), and *The Last Cop Out* (1973).

_____ . "The Machinery of Government vs. People Who Cared: Rightism in Mickey Spillane's Tiger Mann Novels." *Clues: A Journal of Detection* 7 (Spring/Summer, 1986): 99-109.
The dominant theme of Mickey Spillane's four Tiger Mann spy novels is personal vengeance, not international intrigue. Sandels discusses the novels that he considers to be built around a "particular set of political beliefs," demonstrating how little Spillane's stories concern the realities of the external world.

Traylor, James L. "Characternyms in Mickey Spillane's Mike Hammer Novels." *The Armchair Detective* 16 (Summer, 1983): 293-295.
Contrary to general opinion, Mickey Spillane expresses a real sense of humor in his novels. Traylor surveys the Mike Hammer series to demonstrate how the names of characters are used to emphasize the characteristics Spillane has chosen for them. Considers the names given to major and minor characters.

Van Dover, J. Kenneth. "Mickey Spillane." In his *Murder in the Millions: Erle Stanley Gardner, Mickey Spillane, Ian Fleming*. New York: Frederick Ungar, 1984.
A brief biographical sketch of Spillane based on standard reference sources is followed by a detailed analysis of *I, the Jury* (1947) and a briefer consideration of *My Gun Is Quick* (1950), *Vengeance Is Mine!* (1950), *One Lonely Night* (1951), *The Big Kill* (1951), *Kiss Me, Deadly* (1952), *The Girl Hunters* (1962), *The Snake* (1964), *The Twisted Thing* (1966), *The Body Lovers* (1967), and *Survival . . . Zero!* (1970). Comments on the changes in the Mike Hammer formula between the 1950's and the 1960's titles. Discusses the books without Mike Hammer in a separate section.

Weibel, Kay. "Mickey Spillane as a Fifties Phenomenon." In *Dimensions of Detective Fiction*, edited by Larry N. Landrum, Pat Browne, and Ray B. Browne. Bowling Green, Ohio: Bowling Green University Popular Press, 1976.
Discusses the ways in which Mickey Spillane's seven novels published between 1947 and 1952 reflect the attitudes of readers in general and the opinions of men toward women at that time. Weibel profiles the decade of the 1950's in politics, literature, and the mass media to set Spillane in the context of his times.

Wylie, Philip. "The Crime of Mickey Spillane." *Good Housekeeping* 130 (February, 1955): 54-55, 207-209.
Wylie surveys Mickey Spillane's novels to determine what accounts for their great popular appeal. Discusses Mike Hammer, the structure of the books, and the amount of sex and violence they contain. Considers Spillane's "crime" to be that "he stands in contempt of humanity." Brief biographical account of Spillane with quotations from interviews to present his attitude toward life and literature.

REX STOUT

Biography

Baker, John F. "Rex Stout: No Man My Age Writes Books." *Publishers Weekly* 204 (October 29, 1973): 28-29.
   A photo-essay showing Rex Stout in his office at home, working on the typewriter he has used for thirty years, working with his plants, riding the electric chair-lift, and talking with Harold Salmon, who has worked for him for forty-two years. The occasion is his publication of *Please Pass the Guilt* (1973) and *The Nero Wolfe Cook Book* (1973) at the age of eighty-six.

Bester, Alfred. "Conversation with Rex Stout." *Holiday* 46 (November, 1969): 39, 65-67.
   An interview conducted at Rex Stout's home in Brewster, New York. Stout discusses his early writing, his interest in numbers and in baseball, his working methods, his boyhood reading (Nick Carter and Frank Merriwell), his views on detective fiction and on life and its meaning and his experiences in planning and building his own house and Frank Lloyd Wright's opinion of it.

Johnston, Alva. "Alias Nero Wolfe." Parts 1/2. *The New Yorker* 25 (July 19/23, 1949): 26-28, 33-38; 30-32, 34, 39, 43.
   A profile of Rex Stout and his detective, Nero Wolfe, that discusses the possible origins for the character in Stout's own personality. Johnston briefly surveys Stout's life, from his Kansas origins to his pulp-writing days before World War I to his designing and building of his own home, teaching himself all of the necessary skills from cement mixing to cabinetmaking.

McAleer, John. *Rex Stout: A Biography*. Boston: Little, Brown, 1977.
   The definitive biography of the creator of Nero Wolfe, written with the full cooperation of its subject. This may be one of the longest studies of a writer of popular fiction ever written. Eight sections: "Heritage," "A Prairie Boyhood," "The Nomadic Years," "A Liberal Awakening," "The Years of Choice," "Minister of Propaganda," "Citizen of the World," "A King's Ransom." Extensive notes and checklist of Rex Stout's publications. Illustrated with sixteen pages of photographs. Index.

Van Gelder, Robert. "An Interview with Rex Stout." In his *Writers and Writing*. New York: Charles Scribner's Sons, 1946.
   Rex Stout is interviewed on September 21, 1941, giving Van Gelder the impression of being more articulate than most writers. Discusses his reasons for writing serious fiction, his early years in Kansas, his goals, the creation of

Nero Wolfe, and why his other detective, Tecumseh Fox, was not a success. Talks about his concern that the United States enter the war against Adolf Hitler.

Whitman, Alden. "Rex Stout, the Creator of Nero Wolfe, Is Dead at 88." *The New York Times* October 28, 1955: 1, 36.

An obituary. A concise survey of Rex Stout's life and working methods in writing the Nero Wolfe mysteries. Some statistics on the number of copies sold and the number of languages into which the books have been translated. Stout is quoted on the origins of Nero Wolfe. Mentions the anecdote about Alexander Woollcott, who thought that he was the physical inspiration for the detective.

Commentary

Allen, L. David. "Rex Stout: *Black Orchids*." In his *Detective in Fiction*. Lincoln, Nebr.: Cliffs Notes, 1978.

Plot summaries of Rex Stout's *Black Orchids* and *Cordially Invited to Meet Death*, two novelettes published together in 1942. Allen follows this with a description of the major characters, Nero Wolfe, Archie Goodwin, and Inspector Cramer. Discusses the solutions to each case, how fair Stout plays, and how the Nero Wolfe stories relate to other detective fiction.

Anderson, David R. "Crime and Character: Notes on Rex Stout's Early Fiction." *The Armchair Detective* 13 (Spring, 1980): 169-171.

A review-essay. Discusses the dual themes of crime and character expressed in the fiction Rex Stout wrote before he created Nero Wolfe. Anderson surveys stories from the posthumous collection *Justice Ends at Home and Other Stories* (1977), originally published in magazines between 1914 and 1917. Traces the reappearance of these themes in the Nero Wolfe stories.

_____ . *Rex Stout*. New York: Frederick Ungar, 1984.

A critical study of Rex Stout's Nero Wolfe novels. Anderson begins with a chronology of events in Stout's life, then a biographical essay in chapter 1 and an overview of the Nero Wolfe series in chapter 2. Chapters 3, 4, and 5 survey a selection of the Nero Wolfe novels themselves; chapter 6 discusses Nero Wolfe the character; chapter 7 covers Archie Goodwin; and chapter 8, the other recurring characters. Chapter 9 presents an assessment of Stout's place in crime fiction. Includes notes, a selected bibliography, and an index.

Baring-Gould, William S. *Nero Wolfe of West Thirty-Fifth Street: The Life and Times of America's Largest Private Detective*. New York: Viking Press, 1969.

Rev. ed. New York: Penguin Books, 1982.

A close scrutiny of the Nero Wolfe series based on the premise that they are factual accounts. Baring-Gould discusses Wolfe's parentage and his relationship to the other characters in the series. Surveys the published record to the date of this survey. (Revised edition published after Baring-Gould's death adds information on the later novels and corrects errors of fact in the earlier edition.) Includes Nero Wolfe's philosophy and a chronology of cases. No index.

De Voto, Bernard. "The Easy Chair: Alias Nero Wolfe." *Harper's Magazine* 209 (July, 1954): 8-9, 12-15.

Based on a close reading of Rex Stout's detective stories and in response to a theory about Nero Wolfe's parentage, De Voto presents the known facts in the biography of the detective, suggesting that the reader will probably never learn Wolfe's true identity. Speculates on what Wolfe was doing between 1913 and 1916, his birth date, and the parentage of Archie Goodwin.

Jaffe, Arnold. "Murder with Dignity: Rex Stout." *The New Republic* 177 (July 30, 1977): 41-43.

Jaffe considers Nero Wolfe to represent the refuge readers of detective fiction seek in a world filled with confusion. Discusses the structure of Nero Wolfe's world and the rituals that make life and his chosen profession significant. Uses *Fer-de-Lance* (1934), *Too Many Cooks* (1938), *Prisoner's Base* (1952), *Some Buried Caesar* (1938), *The Red Box* (1937), and *And Be a Villain* (1948) to support his thesis.

Knight, Arden. "An Appreciation of Archie Goodwin." *The Armchair Detective* 12 (Fall, 1979): 328-329.

A character sketch of Archie Goodwin. Knight discusses Archie as the essential protagonist of Nero Wolfe's adventures, who reflects Rex Stout's wit and writing style, noting his speech patterns and his methods as a private detective. Compares Archie's role in the stories with that of Nick Carraway, the narrator of F. Scott Fitzgerald's *The Great Gatsby*.

McAleer, John. Introduction to *Death Times Three*, by Rex Stout. New York: Bantam Books, 1985.

McAleer gives an account of the discovery of three little-known Nero Wolfe novelettes collected in this volume for the first time. Examines the entries for these stories in Rex Stout's own writing record and the notes he made in his files for them. McAleer discusses the plots and characters of the stories and fits them into the sequence of internal events of the Nero Wolfe saga.

_____ . Introduction to *Justice Ends at Home and Other Stories*. New York: Viking Press, 1977.

Discusses Rex Stout's early writings in the context of his life and reading. McAleer surveys Stout's life story and gives an account of his publishing record from 1912 to 1929 when he published his first serious novel *How like a God* (1929). Discusses the characters and themes of his early work and Stout's own view of this part of his career.

Queen, Ellery. "The Great O-E Theory." In his *In the Queens' Parlor and Other Leaves from the Editor's Notebook*. New York: Simon & Schuster, 1957.
Rex Stout speculates on the evolution of the name Nero Wolfe and the possible subconscious patterning of it on the name of Sherlock Holmes. Ellery Queen expands this by discussing other linguistic similarities between the names of the two detectives and traces them back to the vowel combinations in Edgar Allan Poe's name.

Rauber, D. F. "Sherlock Holmes and Nero Wolfe: The Role of the 'Great Detective' in Intellectual History." In *Dimensions of Detective Fiction*, edited by Larry N. Landrum, Pat Browne, and Ray B. Browne. Bowling Green, Ohio: Bowling Green University Popular Press, 1976.
Rauber considers Sherlock Holmes and Nero Wolfe to be outstanding examples of the Great Detective in nineteenth and twentieth century literature. Compares the two characters and their methods of detection, and demonstrates how Rex Stout patterned his fictional world, in external matters, on that of Arthur Conan Doyle. Uses *A Right to Die* (1964) as his text in the discussion.

Townsend, Guy M., ed. *Rex Stout: An Annotated Primary and Secondary Bibliography*. New York: Garland Press, 1980.
Lists all English-language editions of Rex Stout's works published in the United States, Great Britain, and Canada with citations for the major book reviews. Includes articles, introductions to books by other writers, reviews, verse, radio broadcasts, interviews, and critical material on Stout's own work. Index.

Waugh, Thomas D. "The Missing Years of Nero Wolfe." *The Armchair Detective* 5 (October, 1971): 16-18.
According to the Baring-Gould chronology of events in the life of Nero Wolfe, there is a ten-year hiatus between 1918 and 1928. Waugh speculates on what might have taken place during that decade, using information found in the Sherlock Holmes stories and some of the detective stories of H. C. Bailey (the Reginald Fortune and Joshua Clunk series). Traces Wolfe's experiences that would be useful later when he had established his office in New York.

Weiner, Steve. "Sleuth Nero Wolfe, Minus His Author, Takes a New Case." *The Wall Street Journal* October 14, 1985: 1, 11.

Describes the appearance of the first pastiche of the Nero Wolfe stories, *Murder in E Minor* (1985), published with the full cooperation of Rex Stout's heirs. Discusses other attempts to revive successful series characters in popular fiction, including Sherlock Holmes and James Bond, and suggests that the basic reason for such revivals is a matter of economics.

JULIAN SYMONS

Biography

Bannon, Barbara A. *"PW* Interviews: Julian Symons." *Publishers Weekly* 222 (July 2, 1982): 12-13.

Symons not only writes intelligent crime novels; he writes intelligent criticism of crime fiction as well. Interviewed in New York on the occasion of being named Grand Master by the Mystery Writers of America, Symons discusses his school days, his verse writing, and his accidental entry in the crime-fiction field with a novel he had written almost as a joke. Comments on the place of serious crime fiction in the world of letters and his philosophy as a writer and reader.

Cooper-Clark, Diana. "Interview with Julian Symons." In her *Designs of Darkness: Interviews with Detective Novelists.* Bowling Green, Ohio: Bowling Green University Popular Press, 1983.

Symons discusses the role of crime novels in helping readers understand the reasons behind the crimes in society, the themes the English seem to use in crime fiction, why he sees no distinction between crime novels and mainstream novels, his views on detective fiction, the differences between British and American crime fiction, and the sources for the ideas behind some of his own novels.

Symons, Julian. "Introduction: Realism and the Crime Novel." In his *The Julian Symons Omnibus*. London: Collins, 1967.

Symons discusses his theories on crime fiction, which he considers "the adult fairy tales of the Western world" and realistic "in the sense that they are based on the real world around us." Explains the circumstances and ideas behind the writing of the three novels collected in this volume: *The Thirty-first of February* (1950), *The Progress of a Crime* (1960), and *The End of Solomon Grundy* (1964).

—————— . "Progress of a Crime Writer." In *Mystery and Detection Annual*, edited by Donald K. Adams. Beverly Hills, Calif.: Donald Adams, 1973.

Symons talks about his reading of crime fiction as a boy and the specific writers he enjoyed. His first crime story was written as a result of his friendship with poet Ruthven Todd, who also introduced him to *Black Mask* magazine. Discusses his reasons for writing crime fiction and his conscious use of acts of violence in his books to make a statement about society.

Commentary

Carter, Steven R. "Julian Symons and Civilization's Discontents." *The Armchair Detective* 12 (January, 1979): 57-62.

Surveys and discusses Symons' major crime novels to examine the ways he has increased the range of the genre. Novels discussed: *The Thirty-first of February* (1950), *The Narrowing Circle* (1954), *The Man Who Lost His Wife* (1970), *The Players and the Game* (1972), and *The Plot Against Roger Rider* (1973). Also discusses the short story "An Experiment in Personality." Carter cites statements by Symons about his own work from an essay ("Progress of a Crime Writer") and letters written in 1975 and 1976.

Grimes, Larry E. "Julian Symons." In *Twelve Englishmen of Mystery*, edited by Earl F. Bargainnier. Bowling Green, Ohio: Bowling Green University Popular Press, 1984.

A chronology of events in Symons' life is followed by a survey of his career as a writer. Grimes divides this into five sections: Social Critic and Man of Letters; From Detective Fiction to the Crime Novel; The Crime Novel and Social Criticism; Dreams, Games and Masks; and Concluding Observations. Discusses recurring themes in Symons' crime novels and surveys the novels against the background of his theories of fiction. Checklist of Symons' crime fiction from 1945 to 1979.

JOSEPHINE TEY
(Elizabeth Mackintosh)

Biography

Klein, Kathleen G. "Josephine Tey." In *Twentieth Century Crime and Mystery Writers*, edited by John M. Reilly. New York: St. Martin's Press, 1980.
A very brief list of recorded personal details of the life of Elizabeth Mackintosh, who wrote crime fiction as Josephine Tey, followed by a checklist of her work in that field and her plays in chronological order and arranged by category. Includes about one thousand words of commentary assessing her achievement as a writer of crime fiction.

Rollyson, Carl. "Josephine Tey." In *Critical Survey of Mystery and Detective Fiction*, edited by Frank N. Magill, vol. 4. Pasadena, Calif.: Salem Press, 1988.
Describes Tey's series characters Alan Grant and his assistant, Sergeant Williams, and discusses Tey's general contributions to the detective story in terms of her characterization. A brief biographical section describes the recorded facts of her life and career as a teacher and writer. A shy woman with few close friends, Tey never gave interviews and did not discuss her work. An extended analysis of her novels explains her contribution to the genre. Contains a list of the titles and dates of her books (but not a proper bibliography) and a selected bibliography of secondary sources.

Commentary

Aird, Catherine. "Josephine Tey." *The Armchair Detective* 2 (April, 1969): 156-157.
A survey of the career of Josephine Tey by mystery writer Catherine Aird (Kim Hamilton McIntosh). Aird includes comments about Tey's nonmystery novels and plays. No biographical information beyond her place of birth, education, and the time she spent caring for her widowed father. Includes a checklist of Tey's works from 1929 to 1953.

Bakerman, Jane S. "Advice Unheeded: Shakespeare in Some Modern Mystery Novels." *The Armchair Detective* 14 (Spring, 1981): 134-139.
Discusses the use of Shakespearean themes in four mystery novels: *The Daughter of Time* (1951), by Josephine Tey, *Bullets for Macbeth* (1976), by Marvin Kaye, *A Little Less than Kind* (1963), by Charlotte Armstrong, and *Hamlet, Revenge!* (1937) by Michael Innes. Bakerman comments on Innes' use of quotation as a unifying device, of the use of double-mystery (a novel-within-

a-novel), the characterizations, and the value to an appreciation of the novel of the reader's being familiar with the text of *Hamlet*.

Davis, Dorothy Salisbury. "On Josephine Tey." *The New Republic* 131 (September 20, 1954): 17-18.
A review-essay of the omnibus *Three by Tey* (1954) that contains *Miss Pym Disposes* (1946), *The Franchise Affair* (1948), and *Brat Farrar* (1949). Davis discusses Josephine Tey's work and its power to "evoke character, atmosphere, mores by conversation." Comments on the sources for the novels, her characters, and her ability to suggest violence without being explicit. Discusses her favorite Tey novel, *The Daughter of Time* (1951).

Mann, Jessica. "Josephine Tey." In her *Deadlier Than the Male: Why Are Respectable English Women So Good at Murder?* New York: Macmillan, 1981.
Mann gathers all the known biographical information about Josephine Tey and extrapolates others from her novels, especially settings or attitudes that may have been influenced by situations in her own life. Discusses her detective fiction and her interest in the theater. Considers *The Franchise Affair* (1948) to be her best novel. Draws some comparisons between her detective fiction and that of Ngaio Marsh.

Morris, Virginia B. "Josephine Tey." In *Dictionary of Literary Biography*, edited by Bernard Benstock and Thomas F. Staley, vol. 77. Detroit: Gale Research, 1989.
Since there is little that is known of Tey's private life, Morris concentrates on a survey and discussion of her eight detective novels. Notes characteristics her work shares with classic detective fiction and offers examples of unconventional aspects. Deals with characters, themes, and style, with indications of critical response to Tey's work. Includes a selected bibliography of Tey's work in all categories. Illustrated with covers from first American editions of her detective novels.

Roy, Sandra. *Josephine Tey*. Boston: Twayne, 1980.
The first full-length study of Elizabeth Mackintosh, who wrote novels, drama, and biography as Gordon Daviot and mystery fiction as Josephine Tey. Chapters 1 through 3 cover her life and works not in the mystery field; chapters 4 through 11 cover her eight detective novels, from *The Man in the Queue* (1929) to *The Singing Sands* (1952). Roy assesses Tey's achievement in chapter 12. Notes, references, and selected bibliography (Tey's publications in all categories. Secondary sources include reviews of her work). Index. The book was apparently completed before the famous controversy over *The Daughter of Time* (1951) in *The Armchair Detective*, 1977-1978.

Sandoe, James. Introduction to *Three by Tey*, by Josephine Tey. New York: Macmillan, 1954.

A brief survey and appreciation of the detective novels of Elizabeth Macintosh, who wrote as Josephine Tey. Sandoe considers her evocation of character to be among her leading achievements, with her detective Alan Grant a genteel and "satisfyingly human" figure. Discusses all eight novels (*Miss Pym Disposes*, 1946; *The Franchise Affair*, 1948; and *Brat Farrar*, 1949 are collected here), something of their origins, and their near-total lack of physical violence. Quotes John Gielgud's introduction to her collected plays published under the name Gordon Daviot.

Smith, M. J. "Controversy: Townsend, Tey, and Richard III." *The Armchair Detective* 10 (October, 1977): 317-319.
A response to Guy Townsend's critique of Josephine Tey's *The Daughter of Time* (1951), published in *The Armchair Detective*, July, 1977. Smith discusses the evidence in Townsend's article and concludes that the only proof on either side of the historical question is psychological, regarding the way people acted and reacted. Refers to outside sources but provides no bibliography. Other responses, from Edmund S, Meltzer, Guy Townsend, and Myrna J. Smith, appear in the letters columns in the next three issues of *The Armchair Detective* 11 (January/April/July, 1978).

Talburt, Nancy Ellen. "Josephine Tey." In *Ten Women of Mystery*, edited by Earl F. Bargainnier. Bowling Green, Ohio: Bowling Green University Popular Press, 1981.
Examines the main events in Tey's life and career and surveys the mystery novels to assess her achievement in the genre. Talburt analyzes the eight novels to indicate how Tey uses basic elements and conventions of the detective story, and how successful she is at including her own views and special interests in her fiction. Discusses the detectives under two headings: Inspector Alan Grant and the amateur detectives, and the rest of the books under four categories: the plots; the criminals and their crimes, the victims, and the suspects.

Townsend, Guy M. "Richard III and Josephine Tey: Partners in Crime." *The Armchair Detective* 10 (July, 1977): 211-224.
Townsend argues that *The Daughter of Time* (1951) is not a detective novel but a polemic about scholarly research in the guise of fiction. Summarizes the plot of Tey's novel, examines the version of events she presents in the life of Richard III, compares this with accounts in histories of the period and specialized studies, and concludes that enough evidence has been ignored in *The Daughter of Time* to cast doubts on Inspector Alan Grant's conclusions. Includes an annotated bibliography of historical sources. This article prompted a debate in the pages of *The Armchair Detective*.

ARTHUR W. UPFIELD

Biography

"Arthur W(illiam) Upfield." In *Current Biography, Who's News and Why, 1948*, edited by Anna Rothe and Constance Ellis. New York: H. W. Wilson, 1949.

A brief account of the personal details of Arthur Upfield's life and some facts about his career as a justice of the peace in Australia. Surveys the critical reception given his books, specifically mentioning *Murder Down Under* (1943), *Wings Above the Claypan* (1943), *The Mystery of Swordfish Reef* (1939), and seven other titles. For an obituary of Upfield, see *Current Biography Yearbook* for 1964.

Browne, Ray B. *The Spirit of Australia: The Crime Fiction of Arthur W. Upfield.* Bowling Green, Ohio: Bowling Green University Popular Press, 1988.

The first full-length study of Arthur W. Upfield. Begins with a chapter of biography followed by a survey of his crime fiction, book by book, in chronological sequence, and chapters on the themes, the characters, the role of women in the stories, the literary background of Upfield, his literary style, and other topics. Contains a glossary of Australian and aborigine terms and a bibliography. No index. Illustrated with photographs of Upfield and maps of the settings for his stories.

Donaldson, Betty. "Arthur W. Upfield." In *Twentieth Century Crime and Mystery Writers*, edited by John M. Reilly. New York: St. Martin's Press, 1980.

A brief list of the personal details of Arthur Upfield's life along with some facts of his literary career. Contains a checklist of his crime novels in chronological sequence with those about Napoleon Bonaparte noted. Includes about 750 words of commentary assessing Upfield's achievement as a writer.

_____ . "Arthur William Upfield: September 1, 1888–February 13, 1964." *The Armchair Detective* 8 (November, 1974): 1-11.

A biographical essay that notes some of the incidents from Arthur Upfield's life that he used in his detective novels. Discusses the origin of Bony (Inspector Napoleon Bonaparte), his methods and appearance, and the women characters who appear in the novels. Includes an annotated list of Upfield's detective novels and a map of Australia with story locations noted. Only the bibliography is reprinted in *The New Shoe* (1951), published by Publisher's Inc. in 1976.

Hawke, Jessica. *Follow My Dust! A Biography of Arthur Upfield.* London: Heinemann, 1957.

The first full-length biography of the creator of Inspector Napoleon Bonaparte covers Upfield's life to the beginning of his career as a writer. Identifies the original of Bony in a North Queensland man named Tracker Leon, with whom Upfield worked. Hawke tells much about Upfield's background but little about his detective fiction. Illustrated.

Matchie, Thomas. "Arthur W. Upfield." In *Critical Survey of Mystery and Detective Fiction*, edited by Frank N. Magill, vol. 4. Pasadena, Calif.: Salem Press, 1988.

Describes Upfield's work in four sections: his series character Detective Inspector Napoleon Bonaparte, his general contribution to detective fiction through this unique character, a short biographical essay, and an extended analysis of his detective fiction. Includes a list of titles and publication dates of his books and a selected bibliography of references on Upfield's life and work.

Commentary

Ball, John. Introduction to *The New Shoe*, by Arthur Upfield. Del Mar, Calif.: Publisher's Inc., 1976.

A biographical sketch of Upfield in which Ball draws some comparisons between the goals of the Australian writer and Arthur Sarsfield Ward, who became Sax Rohmer. Discusses the structure and characters in Upfield's mystery novels and fills in details about the setting of *The New Shoe* (1951) and where it fits in the series of novels about Bony. Provides a character sketch of Upfield's detective.

Browne, Ray B. "The Frontier Heroism of Arthur W. Upfield." In *Heroes and Humanities: Detective Fiction and Culture*, by Ray Browne. Bowling Green, Ohio: Bowling Green University Popular Press, 1986.

Discusses the differences between a natural hero and a social hero using the examples of Natty Bumppo in James Fenimore Cooper's Leatherstocking Tales and Ahab or Billy Budd in Herman Melville's fiction. Compares the frontiers confronted by those heroes with that encountered by Upfield's Detective-Inspector Napoleon Bonaparte. Surveys Upfield's detective novels to demonstrate his thesis.

Cawelti, John G. "Murder in the Outback: Arthur W. Upfield." *The New Republic* 177 (July 30, 1977): 39-41.

Discusses the way Upfield explores the tensions between cultures in his detective stories about the half-caste Inspector Napoleon Bonaparte. Cawelti finds that Upfield managed to turn the detective story into a kind of fable by using native legends from the outback and blending them with the description of the landscape and with themes of loyalty and justice.

Fox, Estelle. "Arthur William Upfield, 1888-1964." *The Armchair Detective* 3 (January, 1970): 89-91.

A brief survey of Upfield's detective stories in the context of his life story, with an account of how he created Inspector Napoleon Bonaparte. Fox presents a character sketch of Bony as a preface to her checklist of Upfield's books. Includes variant British and American titles, and publishers and dates. Titles are arranged in the original order of publication.

Sarjeant, William Anthony S. "The Great Australian Detective." *The Armchair Detective* 12 (Spring, 1979): 99-105.

Drawing on a close reading of Arthur Upfield's detective stories, Sarjeant constructs a biography of his half-caste aborigine detective Napoleon Bonaparte. Divides the account into seven sections: "His Early Life" "Bony in the Police Force" "His Appearance and Abilities," "His Family" "His Police Colleagues," "The Other Participants in his Cases," and "His Character." Includes a map of Australia with the locations of the cases and a checklist of the novels. "A Preliminary Chronology of the Documented Cases of Napoleon Bonaparte," intended to appear with this article, was printed two issues later in *The Armchair Detective*, Fall, 1979.

S. S. VAN DINE
(Willard Huntington Wright)

Biography

Beaman, Bruce R. "S. S. Van Dine: A Biographical Sketch." *The Armchair Detective* 8 (February, 1975): 133-135.

A concise biography of Willard Huntington Wright (1888-1939), noting his ambitions to excel in the arts, his positions as literary critic, drama critic, and editor of various publications, his creation of Philo Vance, and his fame as detective novelist S. S. Van Dine. Little more than a chronology of the essential events in Van Dine's life, Beaman's article includes a bibliography of works published under both Wright and Van Dine.

Braithwaite, William Stanley. "S. S. Van Dine—Willard Huntington Wright." In *Philo Vance Murder Cases*, by S. S. Van Dine. New York: Charles Scribner's Sons, 1936.

An appreciation of the personality, mind, and writings of Willard Huntington Wright before he became S. S. Van Dine. Braithwaite discusses Wright's novel *The Man of Promise* (1916) and its hero, Stanford West, as predecessors of the famous murder cases and their hero Philo Vance. Concludes with a discussion of Wright's work in aesthetics.

Loughery, John. "The Rise and Fall of Philo Vance." *The Armchair Detective* 20 (Winter, 1987): 64-68, 70-71.

Attempting to account for the extraordinary popularity of S. S. Van Dine's detective novels in the 1920's as well as their decline in popularity in later years, Loughery examines the life of the writer as well as the structure of the novels. Draws on information in the Willard Huntington Wright Scrapbooks and Scribner Archives at Princeton University and the Wright collection of family letters, University of Virginia. Some of his findings contradict Wright's own version of the story of the creation of Philo Vance.

Tuska, Jon. "The Philo Vance Murder Case." In his *Philo Vance: The Life and Times of S. S. Van Dine*. Bowling Green, Ohio: Bowling Green University Popular Press, 1971.

A survey of the life and detective novels of Willard Huntington Wright. Tuska tries to set Wright in the context of his times and assess his general contributions to the genre. Discusses the plots, characters, and style of the twelve Philo Vance novels and speculates on the reasons for Van Dine's decline in popularity. Illustrated with scenes from Philo Vance movies.

Van Dine, S. S. Introduction to *Philo Vance Murder Cases*, by S. S. Van Dine. New York: Charles Scribner's Sons, 1936.

Willard Huntington Wright in his persona as mystery writer S. S. Van Dine describes the events that lead to his nervous breakdown, his discovery of the detective story, and the creation of Philo Vance. Outlines his methods in writing the early novels and recounts the discovery of his true identity. This essay is a revised version of an article published in *The American Magazine*, September, 1928, under the title "I Used to Be a Highbrow, but Look at Me Now."

——————— . "Twenty Rules for Writing Detective Stories." In *Philo Vance Murder Cases*, by S. S. Van Dine. New York: Charles Scribner's Sons, 1936. Reprint. In *The Art of the Mystery Story*, edited by Howard Haycraft. New York: Simon & Schuster, 1947. Reprint. New York: Grosset & Dunlap, 1961.

Van Dine's rules for writing detective stories are often referred to or quoted in the secondary literature devoted to the genre. Fair play, a lack of love interest, the role of the detective and his deductive ability, the culprit, the method of murder, the style of writing, and the motivation form only a part of the list.

Commentary

Allen, L. David. "S. S. Van Dine, *The Benson Murder Case*." In *Detective in Fiction*. Lincoln, Nebr.: Cliffs Notes, 1978.

An overview of Philo Vance, S. S. Van Dine's detective, and his place in detective fiction is followed by four paragraphs summarizing the plot of this, the first of the Vance novels. Discusses Philo Vance as a character and his methods as a detective, his companion and biographer, S. S. Van Dine, District Attorney Markham, how Vance arrives at the solution, and whether the author played fair.

Dueren, Fred. "Philo Vance." *The Armchair Detective* 9 (November, 1975): 23-24.

Drawing on a close reading of S. S. Van Dine's twelve novels about Philo Vance, Dueren constructs a biographical sketch of the detective. Describes Vance's appearance, his character and personality, his associates, his methods of detection, and his sense of justice. Speculates on what happened to Vance after the events recorded in *The Winter Murder Case* (1939).

Garden, Y. B. "Philo Vance: An Impressionistic Biography." In *Philo Vance Murder Cases*, by S. S. Van Dine. New York: Charles Scribner's Sons, 1936.

Garden presents a who's who sketch of Philo Vance as the cold facts upon which he bases his account of the life of the amateur detective. Comments on his personality, his friends and acquaintances, and his habits. Provides an outline of his cases from *The Benson Murder Case* (1926) through *The Garden Murder Case* (1935). Suggests that there are still many cases with which he was connected that may be made public in the future.

Hagemann, E. R. "Philo Vance's Sunday Nights at the Old Stuyvesant Club." *Clues: A Journal of Detection* 1 (Fall/Winter, 1980): 35-41.
A survey of the eight true-crime narratives published in *Cosmopolitan* magazine between January, 1929, and January, 1930, written by S. S. Van Dine. Hagemann discusses the content, verifies them as based on actual cases, and assesses the role of Philo Vance in each of them. A lighthearted approach to biblio-criticism. List of the eight with full bibliographic citation.

Haycraft, Howard. "America: 1918-1930 (The Golden Age)." In *Murder for Pleasure: The Life and Times of the Detective Story.* New York: D. Appleton-Century, 1941.
Describes the events in the life of Willard Huntington Wright that led to his creating of Philo Vance and his becoming a writer of best-selling detective stories. Discusses the popular appeal of the Philo Vance books and the strengths and weaknesses of the series. Comments on the similarities between Vance and his creator.

Lowndes, R. A. W. "Dear Me, Mr. Van Dine." *The Armchair Detective* 7 (November, 1973): 30-31.
Lowndes attempts to apply the methods of the Sherlockian scholar to the Philo Vance novels of S. S. Van Dine and establish the true chronology of his cases. Compares the chapter datelines with calendar dates for the years prior to the publication dates of the novels to assign the proper years to each book. The cases of Philo Vance appear to have taken place between 1922 and 1925.

Maltin, Leonard. "Philo Vance at the Movies." In *Philo Vance: The Life and Times of S. S. Van Dine*, by Jon Tuska. Bowling Green, Ohio: Bowling Green University Popular Press, 1971.
A survey of the films based on S. S. Van Dine's Philo Vance detective novels. Maltin discusses cast and credits. Gives plot synopses from *The Canary Murder Case* (1929) to *Philo Vance's Secret Mission* (1947). Illustrated with scenes from selected films.

Rosenblatt, Roger. "The Back of the Book: S. S. Van Dine." *The New Republic* 173 (July 26, 1975): 32-34.
In trying to account for the popularity of the detective novels of S. S. Van Dine, Rosenblatt characterizes his detective, Philo Vance, and discusses the career of the creator. Notes that part of the appeal of Vance may have been that he was unlikable, stood alone, and was outside the law.

Symons, Julian. "The Golden Age: The Twenties." In *Bloody Murder: From the Detective Story to the Crime Novel, a History*. Rev. ed. New York: Viking Press, 1985.

A biographical sketch of S. S. Van Dine: how he created Philo Vance and adopted his pseudonym. Symons discusses the popularity of the Philo Vance stories and presents a character sketch of the detective. Contrasts Van Dine's erudition with that of Dorothy L. Sayers and lists the positive and negative features of the books, the best of which contained a "sort of grand imaginative folly."

Thomson, H. Douglas. "The American Detective Story." In his *Masters of Mystery: A Study of the Detective Story*. London: Collins, 1931. Reprint with notes. New York: Dover, 1978.

Describes the rise in popularity of S. S. Van Dine and the psychological methods of Philo Vance. Thomson discusses *The Benson Murder Case* (1926), *The Canary Murder Case* (1927), *The Greene Murder Case* (1928), *The Bishop Murder Case* (1929), and *The Scarab Murder Case* (1930), primarily concentrating on plot structure. Considers Philo Vance a humorous and delightful figure.

Tuska, Jon. *Philo Vance: The Life and Times of S. S. Van Dine*. Bowling Green, Ohio: Bowling Green University Popular Press, 1971.

The first monograph devoted to the study of S. S. Van Dine is composed of six sections: "the Philo Vance Murder Case," by Jon Tuska; "Philo Vance at the movies," by Leonard Maltin; S. S. Van Dine at Twentieth Century-Fox," by David R. Smith; "A Philo Vance Film Checklist;" "S. S. Van Dine Filmography," by Karl Thiede; and a bibliography. Illustrated with photographs of Van Dine and scenes from the Philo Vance films.

ROBERT H. VAN GULIK

Biography

Van de Wettering, Janwillem. *Robert van Gulik, His Life, His Work*. Miami Beach, Fla.: Dennis McMillan, 1987.
A brief yet thorough biography of Robert Hans van Gulik written by a fellow Dutch author of crime fiction, based on an analysis of van Gulik's work (both scholarly and popular) and interviews with his contemporaries. Includes van Gulik's own fictitious history of Judge Dee, with a bibliography of titles in the series. A bibliography of van Gulik's scholarly works appears separately. No index, but a section, "Bibliographical Notes," appears at the end of the book. Illustrated with photographs and drawings (some by van Gulik himself). The first edition of this book was limited to 350 copies, numbered and signed.

Commentary

Lach, Donald F. Introduction to *The Chinese Gold Murders*, by Robert Hans van Gulik. Chicago: University of Chicago Press, 1977.
Lach's introduction contains a short biography of van Gulik, followed by a discussion of popular Chinese fiction and culture, the Chinese detective story, the character of Judge Dee, how van Gulik transferred him to his novels, and how he has preserved the way of life in imperial China in this series. Includes a brief checklist of material on Chinese courtroom and detective stories. This same introduction appears in the University of Chicago Press editions of *The Chinese Maze Murders* (1956), *The Chinese Bell Murders* (1958), *The Chinese Lake Murders* (1960), and *The Chinese Nail Murders* (1961).

Lachman, Charles. "A Portrait of Judge Dee: Mystery and History in Seventh Century China." *Clues: A Journal of Detection* 8 (Spring/Summer, 1987): 1-10.
Discusses the preeminence of the Chinese tradition of crime literature, the figure of Judge Dee Jen-djieh, and the pastiches of events from his career. Lachman explains the historical background of another individual of the T'ang Dynasty, the artist, statesman, and scholar Yen Lee-ben, who appears in the *Dee goong an* (1949), and provides the portrait of the historical Judge Dee used as a frontispiece to that book.

Sarjeant, William Anthony S. "A Detective in Seventh-Century China: Robert van Gulik and the Cases of Judge Dee." *The Armchair Detective* 15 no. 4 (1982): 292-303.
A brief biographical essay on Robert van Gulik and his work in the Chinese

detective story precedes a biography of Judge Dee as he is presented in van Gulik's novels and stories. Sarjeant based his account on the chronology that appears in *Judge Dee at Work* (1967). Illustrated with van Gulik's drawings from the Judge Dee books. Includes a bibliography of the books and some secondary sources.

van Gulik, Robert. "Judge Dee Chronology." In *Judge Dee at Work*, edited by Robert van Gulik. New York: Charles Scribner's Sons, 1967.
A chronology of the Judge Dee stories (fifteen novels and eight short stories), giving time and place, Judge Dee's position in office, title of story; and information on Judge Dee, his family, his associates, and recurring characters. Concludes with a historical note on Judge Dee's successors. Omits *Celebrated Cases of Judge Dee (Dee goong an* 1949), van Gulik's first Judge Dee collection, from the chronology.

——————— . Translator's Postscript. In *Celebrated Cases of Judge Dee (Dee Goong An)*, by Robert H. van Gulik. New York: Dover, 1967.
Van Gulik describes the original Chinese-language text used to prepare his translation, giving his reasons for using only a portion of it. Discusses his translation and where and why it deviates from being a literal one. Provides an annotated bibliography of additional works on the Chinese detective story and six pages of notes expanding on or providing explanations for parts of his translation.

——————— . Translator's Preface to *Celebrated Cases of Judge Dee (Dee goong an)*, by Robert H. van Gulik. New York: Dover, 1967.
Van Gulik traces the history of the Chinese detective story with a catalog of the five main characteristics that distinguish it from the Western version. Van Gulik discusses the three cases that make up this novel, the role of the district magistrate who serves as its central figure and master detective, his lieutenants, and his methods of detection. Describes the administration of justice in ancient China.

EDGAR WALLACE

Biography

Curtis, Robert C. *Edgar Wallace—Each Way*. London: John Lane, 1932.

Anecdotes about Edgar Wallace written by his longtime secretary. Not a true biography; there are few dates or even an attempt at a chronological arrangement. Curtis tells a good story that conveys the personality of his employer and colleague, his public and private image, his opinions, and his working methods. Illustrated with seventeen photographs and drawings. No index.

Lane, Margaret. *Edgar Wallace: The Biography of a Phenomenon*. London: Heinemann, 1938, rev. ed., 1964.

A detailed literary biography of Edgar Wallace, his childhood in London, his years as a soldier, his career in journalism, and his career as a phenomenally prolific best-selling author. Lane analyzes the basic structure of the Wallace "thriller," but provides little critical comment on his works. Illustrated with eighteen photographs. Reproduces pages from Wallace's diary recounting his meeting Rudyard Kipling. Index.

Morland, Nigel. "The Edgar Wallace I Knew." *The Armchair Detective* 1 (April, 1968): 68-72.

A personal account of Edgar Wallace by mystery writer Nigel Morland, whose mother was an intimate friend of Wallace's family. Morland discusses the public figure and some of the advice Wallace gave to an aspiring writer. This article is accompanied by a ten-page checklist of Wallace's books (173 titles) giving contents of the short story collections compiled by Allen J. Hubin with assistance from Penelope Wallace, Lenore S. Gribbin, Norman Donaldson, and Herbert A. Smith.

Wallace, Edgar. *My Hollywood Diary: The Last Work of Edgar Wallace*. London: Hutchinson, 1932.

This comprises the diary dictated by Wallace between November 23, 1931 and February 7, 1932, on his trip to Hollywood, California, and mailed to his wife each week, in addition to his personal letters. Describes his experiences working on screenplays and his opinions of the United States. Illustrated with a colored frontispiece and eighteen photographs. Index.

——————. *People: A Short Autobiography*. London: Hodder & Stoughton, 1926. Reprint as *People: The Autobiography of a Mystery Writer*. Garden City, N.Y.: Doubleday, 1929.

Edgar Wallace's autobiography is lively and anecdotal but stops before he has become famous as a prolific writer of best-selling mysteries. Few dates of events in his life are mentioned. Tells of his meeting with Rudyard Kipling. Offers his opinions on politics, on publishing, on the publication of *The Four Just Men* (1905), on criminals, and on some of his best-known characters. No illustrations or index. (The subtitle of the American edition appears only on the spine, not on the title page of the book.)

Wallace, Ethel V. *Edgar Wallace by His Wife*. London: Hutchinson, 1932.
An anecdotal, rambling biography of Edgar Wallace by the former Ethel Violet King, who answered Wallace's advertisement for a typist during World War I and married him in 1921. Mrs. Wallace discusses their family life, Wallace's working methods, his travels, his delight in gadgets, and his public and private image. Includes the text of some of his letters. Illustrated with twenty-five photographs, many not found in other sources. Index.

Commentary

Adrian, Jack. Introduction to *The Death Room: Strange and Startling Stories*, by Edgar Wallace. London: William Kimber, 1986.
Compares Edgar Wallace's methods of composition and his prolific output to other writers of quantity: Max Brand, Charles Hamilton, Barbara Cartland, Walter Gibson, and John Creasey, among others. Adrian includes statistics on Wallace's short-story production, both in collected volumes and in magazines; surveys the periodical market in his day; and comments on the range of subjects represented in this collection.

_____ . Introduction to *The Road to London*, by Edgar Wallace. London: William Kimber, 1986.
Describes the plot of this novel and the discovery of a copy of the magazine serialization that turned out to be the original version of *The Northing Tramp* (1926). Adrian reconstructs the circumstances surrounding the writing, revising, and publication of the two stories and sheds much light on Edgar Wallace's working methods.

_____ . Introduction to *"The Sooper" and Others*, by Edgar Wallace. London: J. M. Dent & Sons, 1984.
Discusses Wallace's ability to make use of his own experiences in creating characters and situations in his books. His relationship with the shady tipster Patrick "Ringer" Barrie was put to good use in his Educated Evans stories and in his novel and play *The Ringer* (1926). Adrian includes comments on many of Wallace's series characters.

Cox, J. Randolph. "Edgar Wallace." In *Dictionary of Literary Biography*, edited by
Bernard Benstock and Thomas F. Staley, vol. 70. Detroit: Gale Research, 1988.
A survey of Edgar Wallace's mystery fiction against the background of his life
and personality. Cox discusses the Just Men series, the Mr. Commissioner
Sanders stories, selected thrillers, the basic characteristics of his work, and
Wallace's working methods. Illustrated with photographs and covers from
some of his works. Contains the competition rules for the correct solution to
The Four Just Men (1905). Includes a selected bibliography of his books
arranged in order of publication date.

Croydon, John. "A Gaggle of Wallaces: On the Set with Edgar Wallace." *The
Armchair Detective* 18 (Winter, 1985): 64-68.
Croydon tells about joining the staff at British Lion studios as location accoun-
tant in 1931, just as they were preparing to film Edgar Wallace's *The Ringer*
(1926), and his subsequent experiences working on films based on *The Case of
the Frightened Lady* (1931), *The Calendar* (1929), and *White Face* (1930).
Discusses the casts, some of the technical details of filming, and what his
experiences taught him. Illustrated with stills from the four films and a photograph of Edgar Wallace with director Walter Forde on location for *The Ringer*.

Greene, Graham. "Edgar Wallace." In *Collected Essays*, by Graham Greene. New
York: Viking Press, 1969.
Discusses the qualities that made Wallace memorable as a writer, including his
lively imagination. Greene describes a meeting between Wallace and best-
selling novelist Hugh Walpole and draws some comparisons and contrasts
between their goals in life and writing. Briefly comments on *The Four Just
Men* (1905), *The Man from Morocco* (1926), and *The Flying Squad* (1928).

Hogan, John A. "Exhumation of *The Tomb of Ts'in*." *The Armchair Detective* 6
(May, 1973): 167-171.
One of the rarest titles in Edgar Wallace's works is *The Tomb of Ts'in* (1916).
Hogan discusses the history of the book and gives a detailed synopsis of the
story, relating it to other works of Wallace written during the same period of
his life. Compares the text with that of another version of the same story and
provides a probable explanation for two publishers' issuing two versions of the
same basic plot during the same year.

―――――――― . "Stranger Than Fiction." *The Armchair Detective* 9 (February,
1976): 119-121.
Discusses the true-crime articles and books written by Edgar Wallace. Based
on Wallace's old files and Hogan's own large collection of Edgar Wallace's
works. Hogan divides these into four categories and provides examples of each
with information on variant titles and reprintings. Identifies Wallace's use of

the pseudonym Richard Cloud and gives an account of Wallace's agreement to serve as ghost writer for Evelyn Thaw's autobiography, *The Story of My Life* (1914).

Thomson, H. Douglas. "The Wallace Collection." In *Masters of Mystery: A Study of the Detective Story.* London: Collins, 1931. Reprint with notes. New York: Dover, 1978.
A survey of Edgar Wallace's works with comments on the quantity and popularity of his writing. Thomson touches briefly on his writing methods and provides a catalog of his virtues and vices as a writer. Classifies his novels into five groups and comments on Wallace's detective dramas.

DONALD E. WESTLAKE

Biography

Adams, Abby. "Living with a Mystery Writer." In *Murder Ink: The Mystery Reader's Companion*, edited by Dilys Winn. New York: Workman Publishing, 1977.

Donald E. Westlake's wife talks about the private person behind the professional writer, the characteristics he shares with the characters in his books, the different personas of his pseudonyms, and his working methods (including the brand of typewriter he prefers and the way the supplies on his desk are organized).

DeAndrea, William L. "The Many Faces of Donald E. Westlake." *The Armchair Detective* 21 (Fall, 1988): 340-344, 346, 348-350, 352-353, 356-360.

Westlake is interviewed February 19, 1988, in his home in Greenwich Village. Talks about being influenced by Dashiell Hammett, the writing of the first Parker novel and how it became a series, the writing of his first comic novels, his working methods, his experiences with editors and publishers, the ideas behind some of his specific books, and his opinions of the films based on his work.

Westlake, Donald E. "Hearing Voices in My Head." In *Murder Ink: The Mystery Reader's Companion*, edited by Dilys Winn. New York: Workman Publishing, 1977.

Westlake presents this article in the form of an interview with himself and the personas represented by his pseudonyms Tucker Coe, Richard Stark, and Timothy J. Culver. Discusses the outlook for the mystery story, the restrictions in the form for the writer, the first story he ever wrote, and his opinions of several other mystery writers.

Commentary

Bakerman, Jane S. "Patterns of Guilt and Isolation in Five Novels by Tucker Coe." *The Armchair Detective* 12 (Spring, 1979): 118-121.

Discusses the five novels about Mitchell Tobin written by Donald E. Westlake under the name Tucker Coe as a contrast in content and style with his comic novels published under his own name and as an exploration of two "traditional American themes—guilt and isolation—within the context of . . . the detective story." Bakerman finds that the character of Tobin unites the five novels and makes Westlake's purpose possible. Notes the critical response to the series.

Nevins, Francis M., Jr. "Walls of Guilt: Donald E. Westlake as Tucker Coe." *The Armchair Detective* 7 (May, 1974): 163-164.

Nevins surveys the Mitchell Tobin series of five novels written between 1966 and 1972 by Donald Westlake under the pseudonym Tucker Coe. Discusses the character and the continuing theme of guilt that unites the novels and the development of the series until Westlake decided to abandon the character and the series.

Westlake, Donald E. Introduction to *Levine*, by Donald E. Westlake. New York: Mysterious Press, 1984.

Westlake describes the circumstances behind the writing of the series of inter-connected novellas that make up this volume. Writing sequels to the first story about Abe Levine "The Best-Friend Murder" allowed him to explore different aspects of the character. The entire essay provides insight into Westlake's writing methods.

CORNELL WOOLRICH
(Cornell George Hopley-Woolrich)

Biography

Fisher, Steve. "Cornell Woolrich: '—I Had Nobody.' " *The Armchair Detective* 3 (April, 1970): 164-165.
A brief personal memoir of Cornell Woolrich by another writer for the pulps. Discusses his personality and style with some anecdotes about his literary agent and his last months. Fisher finds Woolrich's major fault as a storyteller to be his inability to end a story and tells how he found it difficult to write a screenplay based on Woolrich's "I Wouldn't Be in Your Shoes" with the original ending Woolrich had given it.

Malzberg, Barry N. "Woolrich: Afterword." In *The Fantastic Stories of Cornell Woolrich*, edited by Charles G. Waugh and Martin H. Greenberg. Carbondale: Southern Illinois University Press, 1981.
An impressionistic essay on the tragic aspects of Cornell Woolrich's life. Includes excerpts from letters written by Woolrich on his life and work. Malzberg discusses his characters, plots, themes, and the vision that tended toward the fantastic. Gives an account of Woolrich's last months and his death and funeral in 1968.

Nevins, Francis M., Jr. *Cornell Woolrich: First You Dream, Then You Die*. New York: Mysterious Press, 1988.
This is the definitive biography of Cornell Woolrich and the most extensive study of his work ever published. Based on years of research and reading of Woolrich's stories. Nevins devotes more space to discussing the writings than to the writer, since Woolrich never revealed the truth about himself to anyone. Documentation is internal where necessary, otherwise there are no footnotes or endnotes. Illustrated with sixteen pages of photographs. Includes a comprehensive checklist of Woolrich's work; film, radio and television adaptations of his work; and a selected secondary bibliography. Index.

Thailing, William. " 'Immortals Do Die' Cornell Woolrich (1903-1968): A Memoriam." *The Armchair Detective* 2 (April, 1969): 161-162.
On the occasion of the death of Cornell Woolrich, on September 25, 1968, Thailing recalls the first book of his he ever read (*The Black Angel*, 1943) and the impression it made on him. Describes his search for copies of Woolrich's stories and novels, his correspondence with Woolrich, and the opportunity to meet the man in 1958.

Commentary

Ellison, Harlan. Introduction to *Angels of Darkness*, by Cornell Woolrich. New York: Mysterious Press, 1978.

A tribute to Cornell Woolrich as an original and a great American writer. Ellison provides a very personal, impressionistic introduction to the man and his work with some biographical facts, and a description some of the impact reading Woolrich had upon him. Discusses the stories in this collection as intimations of how good the later Woolrich would become.

Lacassin, Francis. "Cornell Woolrich: Psychologist, Poet, Painter, Moralist." *Clues: A Journal of Detection* 8 (Fall/Winter, 1987): 41-78.

Originally published in Paris in 1974, Lacassin's essay appears here in English for the first time. Discusses Woolrich's writing to demonstrate how he can be called the "impressionist of the detective novel." Some biographical information. The essay is divided into two sections: "Tragedies in Black" and "Tragedies in Blue." Includes translator's notes and a selected bibliography.

Nevins, Francis M., Jr. Afterword to *Angels of Darkness*, by Cornell Woolrich. New York: Mysterious Press, 1978.

Discusses the eight stories in this collection, each of which is narrated by or told from the viewpoint of a woman. Nevins provides a brief summary of each story, along with the facts of its publication, identification of reprints, and adaptations to radio.

——————— . "Brief Loves: The Early Short Stories of Cornell Woolrich." *The Armchair Detective* 14 (Spring, 1981): 168-172.

Before he began to write suspense stories, Cornell Woolrich produced short fiction for magazines such as *College Humor*, *McClure's*, *College Life*, and *Illustrated Love*. Nevins surveys eighteen stories, published between 1926 and 1934, to indicate the presence of themes that recur in Woolrich's more serious work in later years. Cites titles of stories and magazines, and dates of appearance.

——————— . "Cornell Woolrich." Parts 1-3. *The Armchair Detective* 2 (October, 1968-April, 1969): 25-28, 99-102, 180-182.

This is the earliest extensive survey of the works of Cornell Woolrich. Nevins concentrates on the suspense fiction from 1935 to the end of Woolrich's career, discussing recurring themes and motifs and noting the variety of types of crime stories Woolrich mastered. Part 1 deals primarily with the short fiction, Part 2 with the novels, and part 3 with the emotion in his work and his use of suspense. (Rewritten as the introduction to *Nightwebs*, 1971; by Cornell Woolrich.)

————————— . "Cornell Woolrich: The Years Before Suspense." *The Armchair Detective* 12 (Spring, 1979): 106-110.
A biographical and critical survey of the life and work of Cornell Woolrich, the Edgar Allan Poe of the twentieth century. Nevins discusses Woolrich's early novels *Cover Charge* (1926), *Children of the Ritz* (1927), *A Young Man's Heart* (1930), and *Manhattan Love Song* (1932), noting where he established the themes of tragedy that figured in his later suspense stories. Indicates films based on this early work.

————————— . "Cornell Woolrich on the Small Screen." *The Armchair Detective* 17 (Spring, 1984): 174-185.
Surveys the television films between 1949 and 1982 adapted from Cornell Woolrich's stories. Nevins discusses the quality of the scripts and performances and provides a checklist in chronological order with complete credits for forty-one titles adapted for television. Considers the best film to have been "Four O'Clock" on the National Broadcasting Company's *Suspicion*, September 30, 1957.

————————— . "Fade to Black: Cornell Woolrich on the Silver Screen." Parts 1/2. *The Armchair Detective* 20 (Winter/Spring, 1987): 39-51, 160-175.
Surveys Cornell Woolrich's relationship with Hollywood both in his writing of screenplays and in his work's being adapted for the screen. Part 1 covers his brief stay in Hollywood before 1931 and discusses the following films: *Street of Chance* (1942), *The Leopard Man* (1943), *Phantom Lady* (1942), and *Deadline at Dawn* (1946); Part 2 includes detailed discussions of *Rear Window* (1954) and *The Bride Wore Black* (1968). Illustrated with scenes from several films.

————————— . Introduction to *The Black Path of Fear*, by Cornell Woolrich. New York: Ballantine, 1982.
A biographical sketch with a survey of Woolrich's work, particularly the novels in the so-called Black series and the books he published under the name William Irish. Discusses stories adapted to radio and film and the motifs and devices that appear in his fiction. This introduction also appears in the Ballantine editions of *The Bride Wore Black* (1940), *Black Alibi* (1942), *The Black Curtain* (1941), *Phantom Lady* (1942), *The Black Angel* (1943), *Deadline at Dawn* (1944), *Night Has a Thousand Eyes* (1945), *Waltz into Darkness* (1947), *I Married a Dead Man* (1948), and *Rendezvous in Black* (1948).

————————— . Introduction to *Darkness at Dawn: Early Suspense Classics*, by Cornell Woolrich. Edited by Francis M. Nevins, Jr., and Martin H. Greenberg. Carbondale: Southern Illinois University Press, 1985.
Describes the creation of the phrase *film noir* to refer to a particular genre of films based on a particular genre of fiction; discusses the part Cornell Wool-

rich's work played in this. Nevins provides a biographical sketch of Woolrich and a discussion of the prominent characteristics of his fiction. Cites original publication data for the stories collected here, with plot resumes.

——————— . Introduction to *Nightwebs: A Collection of Stories*, by Cornell Woolrich. New York: Harper & Row, 1971.
A biographical and critical survey of Cornell Woolrich and his work. This essay is an extensively revised and rewritten version of the three-part series published in *The Armchair Detective* in 1968 and 1969. At different times, it has been reworked to serve as the introduction to other collections of Woolrich's short fiction edited by Nevins. This collection also includes "Cornell Woolrich: A Checklist" by Harold Knott, Francis M. Nevins, Jr., and William Thailing originally published in *The Armchair Detective* in 1969.

——————— . "The Poet of the Shadows: Cornell Woolrich." In *The Fantastic Stories of Cornell Woolrich*, edited by Charles G. Waugh and Martin H. Greenberg. Carbondale: Southern Illinois University Press, 1981.
A biographical sketch of Cornell George Hopley-Woolrich, who wrote under the names Cornell Woolrich and William Irish. Also contains a concise survey of his best work and a consideration of the man behind the bleak visions and the world that he "transmuted into dark poetry." The information and critique of Woolrich in this essay appears in different form in introductions Nevins has contributed to other collections of Woolrich's stories.

Soitos, Stephen. "Some Psychological Themes in One of Cornell Woolrich's Novels." *Clues: A Journal of Detection* 7 (Spring/Summer, 1986): 75-87.
Discusses *The Black Curtain* (1941), identifying themes related to psychology contained in the novel. Concerns personality trauma, mental derangement, notions of consciousness and unconsciousness, the question of identity, schizophrenia, and psychological terror. Cites passages from studies in psychology as well as passages in the Woolrich novel to support his thesis.

MASTERS OF MYSTERY AND DETECTIVE FICTION

INDEX

INDEX